P9-BYH-764

Stand ye in Holy Places

Harold B. Lee

Stand ye in Holy Places

Selected sermons and writings of President Harold B. Lee

Wherefore, stand ye in holy places, and be not moved, until the day of the Lord come; for behold, it cometh quickly, saith the Lord. —D&C 87:8

Published by
Deseret Book Company,
Salt Lake City, Utah
1976

ISBN 0-87747-526-1
Library of Congress Catalog No. 74-77591

Lithographed by

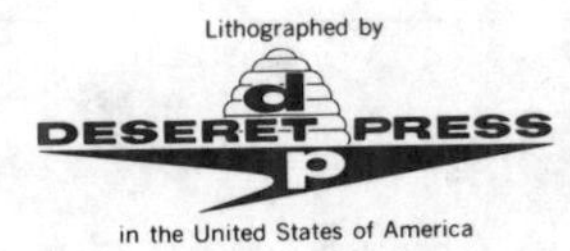

in the United States of America

FOREWORD

"Wherefore, stand ye in holy places, and be not moved, until the day of the Lord come; for behold, it cometh quickly, saith the Lord." (D&C 87:8.)

Those of us who knew and loved President Harold B. Lee over the years have heard him so many times refer to the above quotation, a phrase of which becomes the title for this book.

To read this book is to learn more of our beloved friend and brother, President Harold B. Lee. As we ponder the sermons found herein, we come to know even better this great man through his writings, which are but a reflection of the way he lived his own life.

The incidents and philosophies portrayed within these pages are not the result of merely repeating what others have said, or relating their life experiences, but they are a simple recital of that which he personally lived and experienced and enjoyed and suffered throughout his own lifetime.

As he deals with a matter, immediately there comes to mind the realization that here is a man who knows his antecedents and knows the meaning and purpose of life.

When he speaks of making the Lord your friend, he is asking you to do what he has done, and to find the Lord in the same way that he found Him. Perhaps the Lord was thinking of him and those like him when He said, "Henceforth I call you not servants . . . but I have called you friends." When he speaks of those who come in the name of the Lord, you feel his reverence, his love for the Master and his subservience and determination to subscribe to all the requirements of the gospel laid down by our dear Lord.

When he speaks of the trumpet giving a certain sound, he is calling men to action, to worthiness, to cleanliness.

His counsel is firm, yet loving, and given with forthrightness to help men gain an eternal perspective and to live their lives as taught by the Lord, who set the pattern for all mankind.

When he speaks of and says "eye hath not seen," he is penetrating into the depths of the spiritual life and giving to us a deeper understanding of the things of God which can be understood only by the Spirit of God.

Within the covers of this book are personal experiences with Divinity, as told by one who communed with his Heavenly Father.

Whenever President Lee announced a text for a sermon, for illustrations he immediately drew upon personal experiences and the scriptures with which he had such an intimate personal acquaintance.

As he speaks within these pages, President Lee urges the reader to stand in holy places, as he himself did during his lifetime; and this is the very essence of the life of Harold B. Lee as he would have all men live it.

To all who would learn more of President Harold B. Lee and thus come to love him the more, I commend this volume.

Spencer W. Kimball

President Spencer W. Kimball

CONTENTS

Foreword v

SECTION ONE: LEARNING TO KNOW GOD, CHRIST, AND THE HOLY GHOST

1 "Who Am I?" 3
2 Make Our Lord and Master Your Friend 17
3 "Lord, What Wilt Thou Have Me Do?" 26
4 Are You Truly a Christian? 35
5 "Blessed Is He That Cometh in the Name of the Lord" 39
6 Born of the Spirit 47

SECTION TWO: OUR SEARCH FOR TRUTH

7 Our Search for Truth 69
8 Watch Always, That Ye May Be Ready 79
9 When Your Heart Tells You Things Your Mind Does Not Know 90
10 The Abundant Life 96
11 A Sure Sound of the Trumpet 104
12 "Eye Hath Not Seen" 112

SECTION THREE: REVELATION

13 The Rock of Revelation 125
14 Revelation and You 132

SECTION FOUR: THE PROPHET, SEER, AND REVELATOR

15 The Place of the Living Prophet, Seer, and Revelator 149
16 "May the Kingdom of God Go Forth" 165
17 David O. McKay: "He Lighted the Lamps of Faith" 173

Section Five: Basic Principles and Ordinances of the Gospel

18 "Stand Ye in Holy Places" 183
19 Testimony Is a Divine Witness 192
20 "Search Diligently, Pray Always, and Be Believing" 197
21 "What Lack I Yet?" 206
22 Successful Sinners? 217
23 True Brotherhood 223
24 Time to Prepare to Meet God 230
25 How to Receive a Blessing from God 241

Section Six: The Priesthood and the Church

26 Magnify Your Priesthood 251
27 Priesthood: The Strength of the Church 258
28 "And This Is My Gospel . . ." 268
29 The Lord's Plan for Times of Difficulty 277
30 "By Their Fruits Ye Shall Know Them" 286
31 Meeting the Needs of a Growing Church 294
32 Signs of the True Church 311
33 The Sixth Article of Faith 320

Section Seven: Put on the Whole Armor of God

34 Your Coat of Armor 327
35 The Constitution for a Perfect Life 340
36 The Iron Rod 349
37 "After All We Can Do" 360
38 As a Man Thinketh 369
39 Concept of the Christlike Life 372
40 Follow the Counsel of the Brethren 379

Appendix 387
Index 391

Section One

LEARNING TO KNOW GOD, CHRIST, AND THE HOLY GHOST

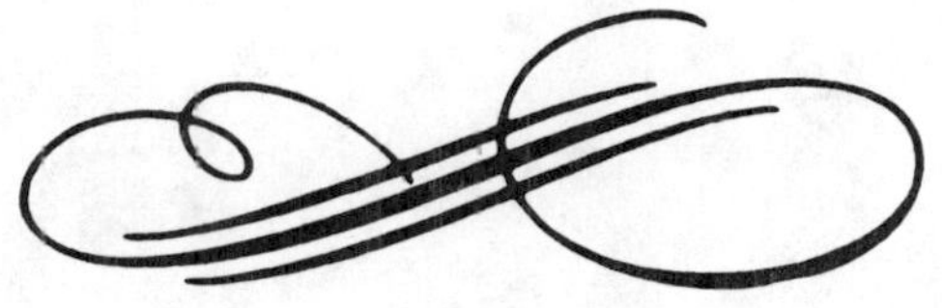

1

"Who Am I?"

MAY I make some comments about a condition which is of great concern to all of us today. I speak of the shocking lack of self-respect by so many individuals, as is evidenced by their dress, their manner, and engulfing waves of permissiveness which seem to be moving over the world like an avalanche.

We see among us so many who seem to be forsaking standards of decency or an understanding of the meaning of time-honored words which, since the beginning of time, have had real meaning to our forebears; words that have made for strength of character and righteousness and harmony and unity and peace in the world.

There are eternal words which, if understood and taught and practiced, would bring salvation to every man, woman, boy and girl who does now live or has lived or will yet live in the world.

To some it may seem old-fashioned to speak of virtue and chastity, honesty, morality, faith, character, but these are the qualities which have built great men and women and point the way by which one may find happiness in the living of today and eternal joy in the world to come. These are the qualities which are the anchors to our lives, in spite of the trials, the tragedies, the pestilences, and the cruelties of war which bring in their wake appalling destruction, hunger, and bloodshed.

Those who fail to heed the warnings of those who are striving to teach these principles and choose to go in the opposite course will eventually find themselves in the pitiable state which you are witnessing so often among us. The prophet Isaiah described the tragic result most dramatically when he repeated the words of God which came to him as he sought to fortify his people against the wickedness of the world:

> . . . Peace, peace to him that is far off, and to him that is near, saith the Lord; and I will heal him. But the wicked are like the troubled sea, when it cannot rest, whose waters cast up mire and dirt. There is no peace, saith my God, to the wicked. (Isaiah 57:19-21.)

Other prophets have declared likewise, so forcibly as to not be misunderstood, that "wickedness never was happiness." (Alma 41:10.)

As I have prayerfully thought of the reasons why one chooses this course which is dramatically described by the prophet Isaiah—when one who has departed from the path which would have given him peace is like the troubled sea, casting up mire and dirt—it seems to me that it all results from the failure of the individual to have self-respect. Listen to these words of wisdom from those whose lives have been worthy of emulation and who have experienced the realities of the periods of time from which they speak.

"Self-respect—that corner-stone of all virtue."—Sir John Frederick William Herschel.

"Self-respect is the noblest garment with which a m can clothe himself, the most elevating feeling with whi the mind can be inspired."—Samuel Smiles.

"Every man stamps his value on himself. The price challenge for ourselves is given us by others.—Man made great or little by his own will."—Johann von Schille

A lovely mother in a nearby community wrote this me. "I love America, I love my husband, I love my childre I love my God, and why is this possible? Because I tru love myself."

Such are the fruits of self-respect. Conversely, whe one does not have that love for himself of which this sis ter speaks, other consequences can be expected to follow He ceases to love life. Or if he marries, he has lost his lov for his wife and children—no love of home or respect fo the country in which he lives—and eventually he has los his love of God. Rebellion in the land, disorder and the lack of love in the family, children disobedient to parents loss of contact with God, all because that person has lost all respect for himself.

I recall an invitation I had to speak to men who, for the most part, had not been advanced in the Church because of their lack of desire or their lack of understanding of the importance of conforming to certain standards required for advancement. The subject on which I was to speak was "Who Am I?" As I pondered this subject and searched the word of God to prepare for this assignment, I immediately sensed that I was to talk about a subject that is of first importance to each of us as it was to those men among whom, no doubt, there were some who had not found themselves and who lacked the basis of a solid foundation upon which to build their lives.

The rowdiness of children, the incorrigibility of adolescents are more often than not a bid for a kind of at-

rity that physical and mental endow-
ite. So the blase girl and the unkempt
t a reflection of an individual who is
rficial adornment or by abnormal con-
e way), to supply that indefinable quality
is charm—a clumsy attempt to draw at-
uct which certainly reflects that inward
ise of the lack of understanding of their
a human being.

"Who am I?" Those lacking in that impor-
ling, and, consequently, in some degree
hold themselves in the high esteem which
ve if they did understand, are lacking self-

gin to answer that question by posing two
n scriptural texts which should be impressed
ul.

nist wrote:

> an, that thou art mindful of him? and the son of man,
> t him? For thou hast made him a little lower that the
> crowned him with glory and honour. (Psalm 8:4-5.)

next is the question the Lord posed to Job:

> ast thou when I laid the foundations of the earth? declare,
> nderstanding . . . [of] when the morning stars sang to-
> the sons of God shouted for joy?" (Job 38:4-7.)

d to more simple language than the words of
ions from the scriptures, the prophets in these
are simply asking each of us, "Where did you
? Why are you here?"

eat psychologist, MacDougall, once said: "The
to be done to help a man to moral regeneration
ore if possible his self-respect." Also I recall the
the old English weaver, "O God, help me to hold

a high opinion of myself." That should be the prayer of every soul; not an abnormally developed self-esteem that becomes haughtiness, conceit, or arrogance, but a righteous self-respect that might be defined as "belief in one's own worth, worth to God, and worth to man."

Now, consider these answers to the searching questions which must be burned into the consciousness of all those who have strayed away or who have not arrived at a true evaluation of themselves in this world of chaos.

The Apostle Paul wrote:

> Furthermore we have had fathers of our flesh which corrected us, and we gave them reverence: shall we not much rather be in subjection unto the Father of spirits, and live? (Hebrews 12:9.)

This suggests that all who live upon the earth, who have their fathers on earth, likewise have a father of their spirits. So did Moses and Aaron, as they fell upon their faces, cry out: "O God, the God of the spirits of all flesh, shall one man sin, and wilt thou be wroth with all the congregation?" (Numbers 16:22.)

Note how they addressed the Lord, ". . . the God [Father] of the spirits of all flesh [mankind]. . . ."

From the revelations through Abraham, we get a glimpse of who and what the spirit is:

> Now the Lord had shown unto me, Abraham, the intelligences that were organized before the world was, and among all these there were many of the noble and great ones;
>
> And God saw these souls that they were good, and he stood in the midst of them, and he said: These I will make my rulers; for he stood among those that were spirits, and he saw that they were good: and he said unto me: Abraham, thou art one of them; thou wast chosen before thou wast born. (Abraham 3:22-23.)

There we are told that the Lord promised that those who were faithful in that premortal world would be added upon, by having a physical body in the second estate of this earth's existence and, furthermore, if they would keep the commandments as God taught by the revelations, they would have "glory added upon their heads for ever and ever." (Abraham 3:26.)

Now, there are several precious truths in that scripture. First, we have a definition of what a spirit is, as it relates to our physical body. What did it look like in that premortal world (if we could see it apart from our mortal body)? A modern latter-day prophet gives us an inspired answer:

> . . . that which is spiritual being in the likeness of that which is temporal; and that which is temporal in the likeness of that which is spiritual; the spirit of man in the likeness of his person, as also the spirit of the beast, and every other creature which God has created. (D&C 77:2.)

The next truth we learn from this scripture is that you and I, having been spirits and now having bodies, were among those who passed that first test and were given the privilege of coming to earth as mortal individuals. If we hadn't passed that test, we wouldn't be here with mortal bodies, but would have been denied this privilege and would have followed Satan or Lucifer, as he came to be known, as did one-third of the spirits created in that premortal existence who were deprived of the privilege of having mortal bodies. These are now among us, but only in their spiritual form, to make a further attempt to thwart the plan of salvation by which all who would obey would have the great glory of returning to God our Father who gave us life.

So the Old Testament prophets declared with respect to death: "Then shall the dust [meaning our mortal bodies] return to the earth as it was: and the spirit shall return unto God who gave it." (Ecclesiastes 12:7.)

Obviously we could not return to a place where we had never been, so we are talking about death as a process as miraculous as birth, by which we return to "our Father who art in heaven," as the Master taught His disciples to pray.

A further truth is clearly set forth in that scripture (Abraham 3:22-23), that many were chosen, as was Abraham, before they were born, as the Lord told Moses and also Jeremiah. This was made still more meaningful by the latter-day prophet, Joseph Smith, who declared: "I believe that every person who is called to do an important work in the kingdom of God, was called to that work and foreordained to that work before the world was." Then he added this, "I believe that I was foreordained to the work that I am called to do." (*Documentary History of the Church*, 6:364.)

But now there is a warning: Despite that calling which is spoken of in the scriptures as "foreordination," we have another inspired declaration: "Behold, there are many called, but few are chosen. . . ." (D&C 121:34.)

This suggests that even though we have our free agency here, there are many who were foreordained before the world was, to a greater state than they have prepared themselves for here. Even though they might have been among the noble and great, from among whom the Father declared he would make his chosen leaders, they may fail of that calling here in mortality. Then the Lord poses this question: ". . . and why are they not chosen?" (D&C 121:34.)

Two answers were given: First, "Because their hearts are set so much upon the things of this world. . . ." And second, they ". . . aspire to the honors of men." (D&C 121:35.)

Now then, to summarize, may I ask each of you again the question, "Who are you?" You are all the sons and daughters of God. Your spirits were created and lived as organized intelligences before the world was. You have been blessed to have a physical body because of your obedience to certain commandments in that premortal state. You are now born into a family to which you have come, into the nations through which you have come, as a reward for the kind of lives you lived before you came here and at a time in the world's history, as the Apostle Paul taught the men of Athens and as the Lord revealed to Moses, determined by the faithfulness of each of those who lived before this world was created.

Hear now the significant words of that powerful sermon to "The Unknown God" preached by the Apostle Paul to those who were ignorantly worshiping images of stone and brass and wood:

> God that made the world and all things therein, seeing that he is Lord of heaven and earth, dwelleth not in temples made with hands;
>
> And hath made of one blood all nations of men for to dwell on all the face of the earth [now mark you this], and hath determined the times before appointed, and the bounds of their habitation;
>
> That they should seek the Lord, if haply they might feel after him, and find him, though he be not far from every one of us. (Acts 17:24, 26-27.)

Here, then, again we have the Lord making a further enlightening declaration to Moses as recorded in the book of Deuteronomy:

> When the most High divided to the nations their inheritance, when he separated the sons of Adam, he set the bounds of the people according to the number of the children of Israel. (Deuteronomy 32:8.)

Now, mind you, this was said to the children of Israel before they had arrived in the Promised Land, which was to be the land of their inheritance.

Then note this next verse: "For the Lord's portion is his people; Jacob is the lot of his inheritance." (Deuteronomy 32:9.)

It would seem very clear, then, that those born to the lineage of Jacob, who was later to be called Israel, and his posterity, who were known as the children of Israel, were born into the most illustrious lineage of any of those who came upon the earth as mortal beings.

All these rewards were seemingly promised, or foreordained, before the world was. Surely these matters must have been determined by the kind of lives we had lived in that premortal spirit world. Some may question these assumptions, but at the same time they will accept without any question the belief that each one of us will be judged when we leave this earth according to his or her deeds during our lives here in mortality. Isn't it just as reasonable to believe that what we have received here in this earth life was given to each of us according to the merits of our conduct before we came here?

Now there is another important understanding that we have from the scriptures. We are all free agents, which means to some people who manifest a spirit of rebellion that they are free to do anything they please, but that is not the correct meaning of free agency as the prophets have declared in the scriptures where free agency has been defined:

> Wherefore, men are free according to the flesh; and all things are given them which are expedient unto man. And they are free to choose liberty and eternal life, through the great mediation of all men, or to choose captivity and death, according to the captivity and power of the devil; for he seeketh that all men might be miserable like unto himself. (2 Nephi 2:27.)

The Apostle Paul impressed the sacredness of our individual bodies in this statement:

> Know ye not that ye are the temple of God, and that the Spirit of God dwelleth in you? If any man defile the temple of God, him shall God destroy; for the temple of God is holy, which temple ye are. (1 Corinthians 3:16-17.)

And, again, he said further to those who had been baptized members of the church that they had received the gift of a special endowment known as the Holy Ghost. This was his teaching:

> What? know ye not that your body is the temple of the Holy Ghost which is in you, which ye have of God, and ye are not your own? . . . therefore glorify God in your body, and in your spirit, which are God's. (1 Corinthians 6:19-20.)

If we can get a person to think what those words mean, then we can begin to understand the significance of the word of the renounced psychologist, MacDougall, from whom I have previously quoted, "The first thing to be done to help a man to moral regeneration is to restore, if possible, his self-respect." How better may that self-respect be restored than to help him so fully understand the answer to that question, "Who am I?"

When we see one devoid of respect for himself, as indicated by his conduct, his outward appearance, his speech, and his utter disregard of the basic measures of decency, then certainly we are witnessing the frightening aspect of one over whom Satan has achieved a victory, as the Lord declared he would try to do "to deceive and to blind men, and to lead them captive at his will . . . to destroy the agency of man." (Moses 4:14.) This is the fate of "even as many as would not hearken unto my voice" (Moses 4:4), so declared the Lord to Moses.

Some years ago I read a report from a survey made by ministers who had studied a number of cases of students who had committed suicide. This was their firm conclusion after an exhaustive study: "The philosophy of the students who took their lives was so lacking that when a severe crisis came in their lives, they had nothing to hold fast to, and so they took the coward's way out."

Such could be the awful state of those described by the Master in a parable with which He concluded the Sermon on the Mount:

> And every one that heareth these sayings of mine, and doeth them not, shall be likened unto a foolish man, which built his house upon the sand:
>
> And the rain descended, and the floods came, and the winds blew, and beat upon that house; and it fell: and great was the fall of it. (Matthew 7:26-27.)

The Lord's eternal purpose with respect to His plan of salvation was declared to Moses: "For behold, this is my work and my glory—to bring to pass the immortality and eternal life of man." (Moses 1:39.)

The first goal in that eternal plan was for each of us to come to earth and gain a physical body, and then, after death and the resurrection which would follow, the spirit and the resurrected body would not thereafter be subject to death. All of this was a free gift to every living soul, as Paul declared: "For as in Adam all die, even so in Christ shall all be made alive." (1 Corinthians 15:22.)

What this means to one dying with a malignant malady or to a mother bereft of a child may be illustrated by the expressions of a young mother whom I visited in the hospital some years ago. She said to me, "I have thought all this through. It doesn't make any difference whether I go now or whether I live to seventy, eighty, or ninety. The sooner I can get to a place where I can be active and doing things that will bring me eternal joy, the better for all concerned." She was comforted by the thought that she had lived such a life as to be worthy to enter into the presence of God, which is to enjoy eternal life.

The importance of taking advantage of every hour of precious time allotted to each of us here was impressed forcibly upon me by an incident in my own family. A young mother came with her beautiful flaxen-haired six-year-old daughter to her grandparents. The mother asked if we would like to hear a beautiful new children's song the daughter had just learned in her Primary class. While the little mother accompanied her, she sang:

I am a child of God,
And He has sent me here,
Has given me an earthly home
With parents kind and dear.

I am a child of God,
And so my needs are great;
Help me to understand His words
Before it grows too late.

I am a child of God,
Rich blessings are in store;
If I but learn to do His will
I'll live with Him once more.

(Chorus)
Lead me, guide me, walk beside me,
Help me find the way.
Teach me all that I must do
To live with Him some day.

—*Sing with Me*, no. B-76

Her grandparents were in tears. Little did they know then that hardly before that little girl would have had the full opportunity for her mother to teach her all that she should know in order to return to her heavenly home, the little mother would be suddenly taken away in death, leaving to others the responsibility of finding the answer to the pleadings of that childhood prayer, to teach and train and to lead her through the uncertainties of life.

What a difference it would make if we really sensed our divine relationship to God, our Heavenly Father, our relationship to Jesus Christ, our Savior and our Elder Brother, and our relationship to each other.

Contrasted with the sublime peace to one such as

that wonderful sister I visited in the hospital is that terrifying state of those who do not, as they approach death, have that great comfort, for as the Lord has told us plainly: "And they that die not in me, woe unto them, for their death is bitter." (D&C 42:47.)

It was George Bernard Shaw who said, "If we all realized that we were the children of one father, we would stop shouting at each other as much as we do."

Now, I trust that I might have given to you, and to others who have not yet listened to such counsel, something to stimulate some sober thinking as to who you are and whence you came; and, in so doing, that I may have stirred up within your soul the determination to begin now to show an increased self-respect and reverence for the temple of God, your human body, wherein dwells a heavenly spirit. I would charge you to say again and again to yourselves, as the Primary organization has taught the children to sing, "I am a [son or a daughter] of God," and by so doing, begin today to live closer to those ideals which will make your life happier and more fruitful because of an awakened realization of who you are.

God grant that each of us here today may so live that all among us, and with us, may see not us, but that which is divine and comes from God. With that vision of what those who have lost their way may become, my prayer is that they may receive strength and resolution to climb higher and higher and upward and onward to that great goal of eternal life and also that I may do my part in seeking to show by example, as well as by precept, that which will be the best of which I am capable of doing.

I again bear my solemn witness to the great truth of the Master's profound words to the sobbing Martha: "I am the resurrection, and the life: he that believeth in me, though he were dead, yet shall he live." (John 11:25.)

I thank God that I too can say, with the same spirit as did Martha, who bore her testimony as the Spirit witnessed to her from the depths of her soul: "Yea, Lord: I [too know] that thou art the Christ, the Son of God, which [came] into the world." (John 11:27.)

2

Make Our Lord and Master Your Friend

DURING a mission tour, I listened to a brilliant young man bear his testimony wherein he quoted a recorded incident in which the Master referred to His disciples as His "friends." Then the young man impressively expressed his most fervent hope that he too could so conduct his life that one day the Master would find him worthy to be called by the Lord His "friend."

Possibly he had read what the apostle James said about Father Abraham: "Abraham believed God, and it was imputed unto him for righteousness: and he was called the Friend of God." (James 2:23.)

He remembered what the Master had said as He defined the bond of brotherhood existing between Him and His disciples:

> Greater love hath no man than this, that a man lay down his life for his friends.
>
> Ye are my friends, if ye do whatsoever I command you.

> Henceforth I call you not servants; for the servant knoweth not what his lord doeth: but I have called you friends; for all things that I have heard of my Father I have made known unto you. (John 15:13-15.)

The apostle James elsewhere declared: ". . . a friend of the world is the enemy of God." (James 4:4.)

The use of the word *world* in this sense is defined in the scriptures when they speak of the "end of the world" as the destruction of the wickedness that is in the world. (See Joseph Smith 1:4.)

The world to which the apostles James and John and the Master make reference is that moral and spiritual system which is hostile to God and which seeks to delude us into thinking that we and mankind generally do not need God. It is a society that in every age has operated and is operating on wrong principles, from selfish desires, from improper motives, unworthy standards, and false values. Those who do not accept God's revelation through His prophets have devised numerous philosophies from their limited human reasoning and seemingly think that they can find happiness and the satisfaction of their souls by ignoring God's plan of salvation.

One of the greatest threats to the work of the Lord today comes from false educational ideas. There is a growing tendency of teachers within and without the Church to make academic interpretations of gospel teachings—to read, as a prophet-leader has said, "by the lamp of their own conceit." Unfortunately, much in the sciences, the arts, politics, and the entertainment field, as has been well said by an eminent scholar, is "all dominated by this humanistic approach which ignores God and His word as revealed through the prophets." This kind of worldly system apparently hopes to draw men away from God by making man the "measure of all things," as some worldly philosophers have said.

That this danger would be among us today was foreshadowed by the ancient prophets, who gave us a sure measure by which we might know that which is of God and that which emanates from evil sources.

Here is a prophet speaking:

> . . . for every thing which inviteth to do good, and to persuade to believe in Christ, is sent forth by the power and gift of Christ, wherefore ye may know with a perfect knowledge it is of God.
>
> But whatsoever thing persuadeth men to do evil, and believe not in Christ, and deny him, and serve not God, then ye may know with a perfect knowledge it is of the devil; for after this manner doth the devil work, for he persuadeth no man to do good, no, not one; neither do they who subject themselves unto him. (Moroni 7:16-17.)

You will note that this statement makes no distinction as to whether it be labeled as religion, philosophy, science, or politics, or ugly dress patterns of today, or the world of so-called entertainment.

True Christians who know the word of God understand that invisible forces are waging war against God and His people who are striving to do His will.

The Apostle Paul understood this and clearly depicted the nature of this eternal struggle. He wrote to the Ephesians: "For we wrestle not against flesh and blood, but against principalities, against powers, against the rulers of the darkness of this world, against spiritual wickedness in high places." (Ephesians 6:12.)

The Master referred to Satan as the "prince of this world" when He warned: "Hereafter I will not talk much with you: for the prince of this world cometh, and hath nothing in me." (John 14:30.)

"Then Jesus said unto them, Yet a little while is the light with you. Walk while ye have the light, . . . for he that walketh in darkness knoweth not whither he goeth." (John 12:35.)

If we would be free from the pitfalls of these evil forces, we must understand the Master's words. Satan and his hordes are ever present in the midst of us. We must make certain that when he comes, as the Master warned, he will have nothing on us and will go away and leave us alone. As long as we walk in the light of the revealed truths of the gospel of Jesus Christ, we need never walk in darkness but may always be sure of our course and know "whither [we] goeth."

One of our pioneer leaders, Heber C. Kimball, foresaw this battle with invisible forces that would come to us in the supposedly sheltered valleys of the Rocky Mountains. It was as though this prophet-leader saw the very conditions existing today in which some would be relaxing in fancied security, thinking that they were well isolated from the outside world. While his words are directed to those in the valleys of the mountains, they could just as well be applied to the Church members as well as Christian peoples everywhere. In this prophetic statement he said:

> . . . we think we are secure here in the chambers of the everlasting hills, where we can close those few doors of the canyons against . . . the wicked and the vile, . . . but I want to say to you, my brethren, the time is coming when we will be mixed up in these now peaceful valleys in that extent that it will be difficult to tell the face of a Saint from the face of an enemy to the people of God. . . . (Orson F. Whitney, *Life of Heber C. Kimball*, p. 446.)

Need I say more to this people, in light of present threats to the influence of the kingdom of God? Now is the time for the Saints and righteous people in this and other lands to again revive that old rallying song of our fathers:

> Who's on the Lord's side? Who?
> Now is the time to show;
> We ask it fearlessly;
> Who's on the Lord's side? Who?
> —*Hymns,* no. 175

It seems curious that in all dispensations, our worst enemies have been those within, those who have betrayed the works of the Lord. There were the sons of Mosiah and the younger Alma before their miraculous conversions. It was so in the days of the Master, who said of His betrayer, Judas, "Have not I chosen you twelve, and one of you is a devil?" (John 6:70.) Likewise did Joseph Smith have his betrayers.

We may well expect to find our Judases among those professing membership in the Church, but, unfortunately for them, they are laboring under some kind of evil influences or have devious motives.

A great thinker and scientist has described most aptly the troubled state of the world today. Said he:

> Rarely before has mankind had such an urgent need for the guidance and healing qualities of spiritual insight, because rarely before has man been so confused and frightened.
>
> The tomorrows ahead of us will be crowded with great challenges and opportunities. But they will be crowded, too, with great dangers.
>
> Already the human race has at its disposal the power to destroy in a moment what it would take many years to rebuild. And the precious lives that would be extinguished could never be rebuilt. (David Sarnoff, *Wisdom*, April 1958.)

Over one hundred years ago the Lord spoke to the people of our day as though we were then present. He said:

> . . . in that day shall be heard of wars and rumors of wars, and the whole earth shall be in commotion, and men's hearts shall say that Christ delayeth his coming until the end of the earth.
>
> And there shall be earthquakes also in divers places, and many desolations; yet men will harden their hearts against me, and they will take up the sword, one against another, and they shall kill one another. (D&C 45:26, 33.)

In these days of our generation, many are asking: Where is safety?

The word of the Lord is not silent. He has admonished us:

> But my disciples shall stand in holy places, and shall not be moved; but among the wicked, men shall lift up their voices and curse God and die. (D&C 45:32.)

The Lord has told us where these "holy places" are:

> And it shall come to pass among the wicked, that every man that will not take his sword against his neighbor must needs flee unto Zion for safety. (D&C 45:68.)

Where is Zion?

During the various periods of time or dispensations, and for specific reasons, the Lord's prophets, His "mouthpieces," as it were, have designated gathering places where the Saints were to gather. After designating certain such places in our dispensation, the Lord then declared:

> Until the day cometh when there is found no more room for them; and then I have other places which I will appoint unto them, and they shall be called stakes, for the curtains or the strength of Zion. (D&C 101:21.)

Thus, the Lord has clearly placed the responsibility of directing the work of gathering in the hands of His divinely appointed leaders. I fervently pray that all Saints and truth seekers everywhere will attune their listening ears to these prophet-leaders instead of to some demagogue who seeks to make capital of social discontent and gain political influence.

There are several meanings of the word *Zion.*

It may have reference to the hill named Mount or, by extension, the land of Jerusalem. It has some been used, as by the prophet Micah, to refer to the location of "the mountain of the house of the Lord" (Micah 4:1) as some place apart from Jerusalem.

Zion was so called by Enoch in referring to the "City

of Holiness" (Moses 7:19) or the "City of Enoch." The land of Zion has been used to refer, in some connotations, to the Western Hemisphere.

But there is another most significant use of the term by which the Church of God is called Zion: It comprises, according to the Lord's own definition, "the pure in heart." (D&C 97:21.)

As one studies the Lord's commandments and the attending promises for compliance therewith, one gets some definite ideas as to how we might "stand in holy places," as the Lord commands—how we will be preserved with protection in accordance with His holy purposes, in order that we might be numbered among the "pure in heart" who constitute Zion.

Listen to some of the Lord's beacon lights pointing the way to safety.

If you would have the windows of heaven opened and have blessings poured out "that there should not be room enough to receive" them, then "bring ye all the tithes into the storehouse, that there may be meat in mine house," as the Lord commanded through His prophet Malachi. (Malachi 3:10.)

If you would keep yourself and your own "unspotted from the world," the Lord said you should "go to the house of prayer and offer up thy sacraments upon my holy day." (D&C 59:9.)

In other words, keep the Sabbath day holy!

If you would qualify so that in times of trouble you could call and the Lord would answer, that you could cry and the Lord would say, "Here I am," the Lord gave the way through His prophet Isaiah: You must observe the fast day of the Lord, and deal out "thy bread to the hungry

. . . that thou hide not thyself from thine own flesh." (Isaiah 58:9, 7.)

If you would escape from the devastations when God's judgments descend upon the wicked, as in the days of the children of Israel, you must remember and do what the Lord commands: ". . . all saints who remember to keep and do these sayings"—meaning keep His great law of health, known as the Word of Wisdom—and in addition thereto walk "in obedience to the commandments," which would include honesty, moral purity, together with all the laws of the celestial kingdom, then "the destroying angel shall pass by them, as the children of Israel, and not slay them." (D&C 89:18, 21.)

May I conclude with words familiar to many of us, in a song that we often sing:

> Hear, O men, the proclamation:
> Cease from vanity and strife;
> Hasten to receive the gospel
> And obey the words of life.
> Soon the earth will hear the warning.
> Then the judgments will descend!
> Oh, before the days of sorrow
> Make the Lord of hosts your friend!
>
> Then when dangers are around you,
> And the wicked are distressed,
> You, with all the Saints of Zion,
> Shall enjoy eternal rest.
>
> —*Hymns*, no. 342

As one studies the commandments of God, it seems crystal clear that the all-important thing is not where we live, but whether or not our hearts are pure.

God grant that it may be so for all those whose minds are distressed and who are worried and frightened during these disturbing times. "My disciples shall stand in holy places, and . . . not be moved." (D&C 45:32.) ". . . watch, therefore, for you know not at what hour your Lord doth come." (Joseph Smith 1:46.) The Lord's promises are sure, and His word will not fail.

3

"Lord, What Wilt Thou Have Me Do?"

SOME time ago I heard a leader in a high Church position explain his method of endeavoring to arrive at just and equitable decisions in his council meetings. He explained that as problems would be presented, he would frequently ask himself, "As measured by the record of the Master's teaching, just what would He do in this given situation, or just how would He answer this question or solve this problem?" That remark reminded me of the story of a young prince of the nobility of India who was found by his friend teaching little outcast children on his veranda, although it involved the risk of breaking caste rules, and he was asked by his friend why he did it. His reply was simple: "I thought it was the kind of thing Jesus Christ would do."

Perhaps even more important than trying to speculate as to what Jesus would do in a given situation is to endeavor to determine what Jesus would have us do. Of course, in order to give intelligent answers to such questions, one must have intimate acquaintance with the life of the Master and the account of His ministry and an understanding of the applications He made to the lessons he taught. History, either religious or secular, is valuable to us, for by learning how others adjusted in the past to given situations, we ourselves form patterns of conduct that will guide us to act similarly under similar circumstances.

We may read of pioneer persecutions with measurable interest, but when we learn that our own ancestors were among the persecuted, we then view the monument to their memory, depicting a pioneer father and mother at the grave of the infant child who had just died, as a monument to our own, and the father and mother in the sculptured model as our grandparents who lost their own loved child. The sculptured figures of the monument might well have been our own loved ones, and we are therefore drawn closer to it in our understanding of those represented.

Before we can feel kinship to our Savior and be influenced by His teachings in all our thoughts and deeds, we must be impressed by the reality of His existence and the divinity of His mission.

To have due reverence for God, our Heavenly Father, in our devotions requires an understanding of His personality and His existence. Indeed, the expressed purpose of some of the most important revelations of the Lord through the prophets is "that you may understand and know how to worship, and know what you worship, that you may come unto the Father in my name, and in due time receive of his fulness." (D&C 93:19.)

A prophet of this dispensation taught us:

> . . . if any of us could see the God we are striving to serve, if we could see our Father who dwells in the heavens, we should learn that we are as well acquainted with him as we are with our earthly father; and he would be as familiar to us in the expression of his countenance and we should be ready to embrace him, if we had the privilege. We know

much about God, if we but realized it, and there is no other item that will so much astound you, when your eyes are opened in eternity, as to think that you were so stupid in the body. (Brigham Young.)

Yes, we are all well acquainted with Him, for we lived in His house in the spirit world. We are seeking to become acquainted with Him when the fact is that we have merely forgotten what we previously knew.

The Prophet Joseph Smith confirms this teaching of the reality of God our Father as a person. He says:

God himself was once as we are now, and is an exalted man and sits enthroned in yonder heavens! . . . if you were to see him today, you would see him like a man in form—like yourselves in all the person, image, and very form as a man; for Adam was created in the very fashion, image and likeness of God, and received instruction from, and walked, talked and conversed with him, as one man talks and communes with another. (*Teachings of the Prophet Joseph Smith*, Joseph Fielding Smith, comp., 1938, p. 345.)

And finally, in latter-day scriptures we read:

When the Savior shall appear we shall see him as he is. We shall see that he is a man like ourselves. . . . the idea that the Father and the Son dwell in a man's heart is an old sectarian notion, and is false. (D&C 130:1-3.)

. . . the Holy Ghost has not a body of flesh and bones, but is a personage of Spirit. . . . (D&C 130:22.)

One of the most beautiful pictures of the Master has come down to us in the writings of John the Beloved, who was speaking both from his memories of Jesus and from a vision given him wherein the Lord appeared:

His head and his hairs were white like wool, as white as snow; and his eyes were as a flame of fire;

And his feet like unto fine brass, as if they burned in a furnace; and his voice as the sound of many waters.

. . . and his countenance was as the sun shineth in his strength.

And when I saw him I fell at his feet as dead. And he laid his right hand upon me, saying, Fear not; . . .

I am he that liveth, and was dead. . . . (Revelation 1:14-18.)

Suppose we were to put ourself in the place of one who had received such a visitation from a holy personage. Hardly had the sting of mourning been soothed after the death of Jesus when Mary, fearing that someone had stolen the Master's body from the tomb, was searching for Him in the garden. She heard Him speak her name and heard Him say, "I ascend unto my Father, and to your Father; to my God, and your God." (John 20:17.) Then she went and told Peter and the disciples as they mourned and wept, "And they, when they had heard that he was alive, and had been seen of her, believed not." (Mark 16:11.)

After that, He appeared to two of them near Emmaus in a form that they failed to recognize at first, as they walked in the country. He accepted their invitation to "abide with them" when it was eventide and the day was far spent. He sat at meat with them and gave a blessing on the bread, and they ate, and their eyes were opened so that they knew Him. (Luke 24:29-31.) When they told their experience to the disciples, their story was treated as had been the story of Mary Magdalene.

Jesus thereafter appeared to the disciples without Thomas being present, and again He quieted their fears with His blessing, "Peace be unto you." (Luke 24:36.) Here it was that He "upbraided them with their unbelief and hardness of heart, because they believed not them which had seen him after he was risen." (Mark 16:14.) He invited them to see the prints of the nails in His hands and feet and the wound in His side and to handle Him to make them sure of His reality as a tangible resurrected being. (Luke 24:37-41.) He dined on broiled fish and honeycomb with seven of His disciples on the shores of the Sea of Tiberias.

After forty days He gathered them together on Mount

Olivet near Jerusalem to witness His ascension. (Acts 1:9.) But there remained with them the abiding memory of His last words to them,". . . lo, I am with you alway even unto the end of the world." (Matthew 28:20.) They knew that He meant what He said.

Perhaps if we, too, were to have such a visitation, we would ask, as did Saul of Tarsus when the Lord appeared to him on the way to Damascus, "Lord, what wilt thou have me to do?" (Acts 9:6.) His appearance to his disciples after His resurrection convinced them of His continuing existence. Though they could not have Him continually in sight after His ascension, there certainly was no confusion in their minds as to the reality of His existence. Never again would they leave their ministry to go fishing without hearing His accusing question, ". . . lovest thou me more than these?" (John 21:15.) Peter, who shrank from the consequences of revealing his identity at the time of the crucifixion, now went unafraid to his ordained responsibilities of leadership and later to a martyr's death without fear, for he had seen in the Master the rewards of a just life through a glorious resurrection.

Would not the partaking of a sacrament in remembrance of Him take on new significance now? How could the two at Emmaus thereafter ask a blessing upon their food and give thanks to God for it without remembering that the resurrected Lord had sat across the table from them and that now, though invisible, He might be very near? No longer could Peter walk alone on the shores of Galilee without a feeling that he was not alone, nor when imprisoned at Antioch by Herod was he greatly surprised when he heard the voice of the angel commanding him to arise quickly, although he was securely bound to two sleeping guards. He never doubted because he knew the power of the risen Lord.

As the Apostle Paul stood before King Agrippa, he

retold the story of his conversion and of the appearance of the Lord, and he declared with boldness that now in his ministry he could not be "disobedient unto the heavenly vision." (Acts 26:19.) With zeal unbounded, and unmindful of personal safety, he labored unceasingly to carry the gospel to the gentile nations.

And so it was with the Prophet Joseph Smith in our own day, as he declared in his own story to the world:

> I had actually seen a light, and in the midst of that light I saw two Personages, and they did in reality speak to me; and though I was hated and persecuted for saying that I had seen a vision, yet it was true; and while they were persecuting me, reviling me, and speaking all manner of evil against me falsely for so saying, I was led to say in my heart: Why persecute me for telling the truth? I have actually seen a vision; and who am I that I can withstand God, or why does the world think to make me deny what I have actually seen? For I had seen a vision; I knew it, and I knew that God knew it, and I could not deny it, neither dared I do it; at least I knew that by so doing I would offend God, and come under condemnation. (Joseph Smith 2:25.)

After the vision left him, do you think for one moment although he no longer continued to see the Father and the Son, he was not constantly assured, amidst his persecutions and imprisonment, that his Heavenly Father was mindful of his every act? With that sublime knowledge, it was only natural that as new problems presented themselves to him in carrying out instructions in the translation of the gold plates and in the setting up of the kingdom of God on the earth as he was commanded to do, he turned to the Lord in mighty prayer; and, like the brother of Jared spoken of in the Book of Mormon, "having this perfect knowledge of God, he could not be kept from within the veil; therefore he saw Jesus; and he did minister unto him." (Ether 3:20.)

One who has such perfect knowledge would, as did the Prophet Joseph or Peter or Paul, walk daily in the company of angels and have conversation with them and receive from them such instructions and authority as are necessary to establish the great work he might be called to do.

Not many have seen the Savior face to face here in mortality, but there is no one of us who has been blessed to receive the gift of the Holy Ghost after baptism but that may have a perfect assurance of His existence as though we had seen. Indeed, if we have faith in the reality of His existence even though we have not seen, as the Master implied in his statement to Thomas, even greater is the blessing to those who "have not seen, and yet have believed" (John 20:29), for "we walk by faith, not sight" (2 Corinthians 5:7). Although not seeing, yet believing, we rejoice with joy unspeakable in receiving the end of our faith, even the salvation of our souls. (1 Peter 1:8-9.)

The testimony of Jesus is the spirit of prophecy (Revelation 19:10) and comes only by the power of the Holy Ghost, for "no man can say that Jesus is the Lord, but by the Holy Ghost" (1 Corinthians 12:3). If we have lived worthy of such a testimony, we may have "a more sure word of prophecy" (2 Peter 1:19) by asking God, "nothing doubting," and "by the power of the Holy Ghost, [we] may know the truth of all things" (Moroni 10:5).

With such a testimony, the youth of this day go not alone. They "shall abide under the shadow of the Almighty." (Psalm 91:1.) If they are beckoned into dens of vice where danger lurks, if they are faced with temptations where wrong decisions mean disaster, if they are confronted with great problems to solve or obstacles to surmount, they will always ask, as did Paul, in the depths of their humility, "Lord, what wilt thou have me to do?" I fancy I can hear the Master's answer to this question: "Be thou humble; and the Lord thy God shall lead thee by the hand, and give thee answer to thy prayers." (D&C 112:10.) "If any of you lack wisdom, let him ask of God, that giveth to all men liberally, and upbraideth not; and it shall be given him. But let him ask in faith, nothing wavering. For he that wavereth is like a wave of the sea driven with the wind and tossed." (James 1:5-6.)

If we have the assurance of the existence of things divine, we will be at peace even in the face of impending doom; and though we walk through the valley of the shadow of death, we will fear no evil, but will feel the nearness of God's presence. "Surely goodness and mercy shall follow [us] all the days of [our] life: and [we] will dwell in the house of the Lord for ever." (Psalm 23:6.)

If we are called into positions of great responsibility, such a testimony would make us answerable to our Divine Maker for the acts of our high office and would humble us with the realization that "he that is greatest among you shall be [the] servant." (Matthew 23:11.)

If we are shrouded in deep mourning for Him who was and is no more, by faith we will hear again that glorious promise, "In my Father's house are many mansions: if it were not so I would have told you. I go to prepare a place for you.

"And if I go and prepare a place for you, I will come again, and receive you unto myself; that where I am, there ye may be also.

"And whither I go ye know, and the way ye know." (John 14:2-4.)

Youth must strive with all their hearts, with all their souls, with all their minds to gain an abiding testimony that God lives and that He is the Father of the spirits of all that are born into mortality, and that Jesus Christ, His Only Begotten in the flesh, still lives and says today to all who have ears to hear: "Behold, I stand at the door, and knock; if any man hear my voice, and open the door, I will come in to him, and will sup with him, and he with me." (Revelation 3:20.)

When they become parents, with their little ones at their knees, they must realize that theirs is the golden opportunity to plant in their children's hearts the first seeds of a beautiful testimony that "heaven lies about us in our infancy."

The Church must realize its responsibility to provide youth the opportunities to strengthen that testimony by study and service in the Church, that through the perils of life they might be kept as if in the hollow of God's hand. Because there are those today who have forsaken their sins and have come unto the Lord, who have called on His name, obeyed His voice, and kept His commandments (see D&C 93:1), some have seen His face, and all such know that He is. They know that in hours of great extremity they may reach out with the yearnings of a faithful son or daughter to their Heavenly Father and find in Him the wisdom to answer every question and the strength to meet every problem. As one of the least among you, I humbly bear my testimony that I know that God is the Father of our spirits and that through His Son, Jesus Christ, He exercises His "power over his saints, and shall reign in their midst" (D&C 1:36) while His judgments descend upon the world because of their wickedness.

May our youth be blessed and guided always by the power of an abiding testimony of the tangible reality of our Heavenly Father and His Son, our Savior.

4

Are You Truly a Christian?

SUPPOSE that a Pharisee or a Sadducee in the meridian of time had written a biography of Jesus. What sort of a book would it have been? We should have had, undoubtedly, in such a writing, what He was not rather than what He was. The miracle of the immaculate conception of the Holy Infant by the Jewish handmaiden Mary would have been branded as a subterfuge; the signs that accompanied His birth would have been called a hoax; over its pages again and again would have appeared such words as "false prophet," "blasphemer," "destroyer of the law," "winebibber," and "prince of Beelzebub." The writers would have accompanied their scurrilous denunciations with "facts" and "evidences" that to their prejudiced minds, steeped with traditions and philosophies of their own creation, and to their puny souls, dwarfed by an egotistical self-importance, would have seemed sufficient proof.

Those in that day who professed a form of godliness

but who denied the power thereof (2 Timothy 3:5) were not known as "Christians." The Master's title for them was "hypocrites" because, as He described them, they were "teaching for doctrines the commandments of men," and they "draweth nigh unto me with their mouth, and honoureth me with their lips; but their heart is far from me." (Matthew 15:9, 8.)

The title "Christians," as we are told in the New Testament, was first applied to the disciples in Antioch. (Acts 11:26.) Fortunately for the world, the story of Jesus as written by these faithful disciples was vastly different than a pharisaic recital would have been. To these faithful Christian followers, Jesus was "the Christ, the Son of God, which should come into the world." (John 11:27.)

When the Master pointed out the cost of true discipleship to those who had followed Him out of curiosity or for ulterior motives, "many," we are told, ". . . went back, and walked no more with him." (John 6:66.) By contrast, the true Christian disciples declared, with heaven-sent conviction, ". . . thou hast the words of eternal life. And we believe and are sure that thou art that Christ, the Son of the living God." (John 6:68-69.) To them, He was the "stone . . . which is become the head of the corner. Neither is there salvation in any other: for there is none other name under heaven given among men, whereby we must be saved." (Acts 4:11-12.) The true measure of service by which one was to gain right to the title as a follower of Christ was laid down by the Master in one terse injunction: ". . . the works that I do shall he do also. . . ." (John 14:12.)

As we contrast the convictions and the devotion of these true Christian followers of Jesus' day with those who were merely professors or pretenders of the truth, we are brought upstanding by the modern definition that the dictionary gives of a Christian. It reads: "One who believes or professes or is assumed to believed in Jesus Christ and the truth as taught by him." Here is clearly an implied recognition that among us today are those who claim to be, but are, in fact, only pretenders. In all sincerity I ask all of you who profess to be Christians if you do the works of the Master. Do you accept Him as Jesus the Christ, the Son of the living God? Do you believe that He alone has the words of eternal life and that there is none other name under heaven given among men whereby we must be saved?

In the year 1805 was born in an obscure country village in Vermont the boy christened by his parents Joseph Smith, who later, by divine revelation and command, became the organizer of the church which bears the sacred name of the Savior of the world. We subscribe fully to the declaration of our prophet-founder with reference to the mission of the Lord Jesus Christ. Said he:

> The fundamental principles of our religion are the testimony of the Apostles and Prophets, concerning Jesus Christ, that He died, was buried, and rose again the third day, and ascended into heaven; and all other things which pertain to our religion are but appendages to it. (*History of the Church* [*DHC*] 3:30.)

To that conviction, as to the fundamental principles on which the true Christian religion must be founded, I bear solemn witness.

Early in the rise of the Church there was impressed, by the Lord, a great soul-searching thought as to the prime requisite for membership in God's eternal kingdom: "For if you will that I give unto you a place in the celestial world, you must prepare yourselves by doing the things which I have commanded and required of you." (D&C 78:7.) In other words, ours must be a "faith in action" if we would be saved.

In these days when threatening clouds of impending doom gather in thick darkness about us, may we hear again with deeper understanding the Master's farewell to His faithful followers: ". . . in me ye might have peace. In the world ye shall have tribulation: but be of good cheer; I have overcome the world." (John 16:33.)

It has been well said that "happiness is the object and design of our existence; and will be the end thereof, if we pursue the path that leads to it; and this path is virtue, uprightness, faithfulness, holiness, and keeping all the commandments of God." (*DHC* 5:134-35.)

5

"Blessed Is He That Cometh in the Name of the Lord"

MY text is taken from the "Hosanna shout" which sounded from the multitude who jubilantly acclaimed Jesus, the lowly Nazarene, as He rode triumphantly into Jerusalem from Bethany on a colt that had been borrowed for that occasion. As the animal upon which He rode had been designated in their literature as the ancient symbol of Jewish royalty (Zechariah 9:9) and their acquaintanceship with the might of His messianic power impressed the appropriateness of His kingly right to such an entry, they cast their garments before Him and cast palm branches and other foliage in His path as though carpeting the way of a king. What might at first have been but the humble testimony of a faithful few increased into a mighty chorus of voices as the multitude shouted in harmony: "Blessed be the King that cometh in the name of the Lord." (Luke 19:38.) "Hosanna to the Son of David." (Matthew 21:9.)

And then perhaps, as they remembered the angels' announcement to the shepherds on the night of His birth, they reverently repeated the theme of the angels' song: ". . . peace in heaven, and glory in the highest." (Luke 19:38.) And again, probably remembering the charge He had given His disciples to carry on after He would be taken from them, and as a supplication for their Master and those who would carry on after His ascension, as well as in the remembrance of the ancient prophets whom they revered, came the expressions of adulation from the multitude: "Blessed is he that cometh in the name of the Lord." (Matthew 21:9.)

At the commencement of His ministry, He seemingly had seldom, and then only guardedly, declared that He was the Christ who would take away the sins of the world, but now His earthly ministry was reaching a consummation and His fearful agony on the cross was near. It seemed altogether appropriate that He should now demonstrate His kingly place as the King of kings and the Prince of Peace. Thus demonstrated, His devoted disciples could thereafter likewise bear witness to the divinity of His mission as the Savior of mankind and the "rock" upon which His church was to be founded in the meridian of time.

There was an occasion during His ministry when His chief apostle, Peter, had fervently declared his faith and testimony of the divinity of the mission of the Master: "Thou art the Christ, the Son of the Living God." The Lord had replied to Peter by declaring," . . . flesh and blood hath not revealed it unto thee, but my Father which is in heaven" and that upon "this rock"—or in other words, the revealed testimony of the Holy Ghost, the revelation that Jesus is the Christ—His church is founded, and "the gates of hell shall not prevail against it." (Matthew 16:16-18.)

It was of this same foundation upon which the church was laid that the Apostle Paul referred when he wrote to the Ephesian saints:

Now, therefore, ye are no more strangers and foreigners but fellow citizens with the saints and of the household of God; And are built upon the foundation of the apostles and prophets, Jesus Christ himself being the chief corner stone. (Ephesians 2:19-20.)

I would like to make some explanation as to just how "blessed is he that cometh in the name of the Lord," from that day even to the present time.

At the commencement of His ministry, the Master chose twelve men whom He separated from the rest by the name *apostles.* These were to be special witnesses of the sanctity of His life and of His divine mission, and to be responsible for transmitting to the latest posterity a genuine account of His doctrines, principles, and ordinances essential to the salvation of the human soul. History records that these men, as judged by worldly standards, were "illiterate, poor, and of mean extraction." It would seem that He avoided using in this ministry persons endowed with the advantages of fortune or birth or enriched with the treasures of eloquence or learning, lest "the fruits of their embassy, and the progress of the gospel should be attributed to human and natural causes." (Mosheim, *Ecclesiastical History.)*

True servants in the kingdom of God, when properly authorized, received an endowment of holy power except for which their ministry would be as "sounding brass, or a tinkling cymbal." (1 Corinthians 13:1.) This heavenly endowment of His chosen twelve came as a result of three sacred experiences. First, they were baptized of water, maybe by John the Baptist, or possibly as the only ones the Master Himself did baptize, for John records that He and his disciples were in Judea, "and there he tarried with them, and baptized." (John 3:22.) And He "breathed on them, and saith unto them, Receive ye the Holy Ghost" (John 20:22), which in all likelihood was the confirmation and the commission to receive the Holy Ghost, or the baptism of the Spirit, by the laying on of hands, for that was the procedure followed thereafter by His disciples.

The meaning of this baptism of water and of the Holy Ghost by one who comes in the name of the Lord is best understood by the words of a prophet on the western continent. Addressing a group of baptized converts, he said this:

> There is no other name given whereby salvation cometh; therefore, I would that ye should take upon you the name of Christ, all you that have entered into the covenant with God that ye should be obedient unto the end of your lives. (Mosiah 5:8.)

The third of the remarkable spiritual experiences to which the disciples were privileged is thus described by the Master Himself: "Ye have not chosen me, but I have chosen you, and ordained you, . . . that whatsoever ye should ask the Father in my name, he may give it you." (John 15:16.) Try to imagine, if you can, being "called" by the Master and "ordained" under His hands. That these ordinations resulted in an endowment of power from on high as well as giving authority to act officially as the Lord's representatives is well attested by the miraculous events that followed, which made of them "men different" because of that divine commission.

Not alone were these special apostolic witness to receive and enjoy these heavenly gifts. They were commissioned to transmit them by ordinations to others who had received the witness of the divine mission of the risen Lord. Acting by authority of their priestly office, it was as though the Lord were saying, as He did through a prophet in recent times, "And I will lay my hand upon you by the hand of my servant . . . and you shall receive . . . the Holy Ghost. . . ." (D&C 36:2.)

Historians have given us a summary and a thrilling description of how men so chosen and so ordained were blessed with heavenly gifts because they "came in the name of the Lord."

After the departure of Jesus from the disciples, He gave them the first proof of that majesty and power by which He was exalted; by the radiant gift of the Holy Ghost upon them on the day of Pentecost, according to His promise. Dr. Mosheim in his *Ecclesiastical History* writes that "no sooner had the apostles received this special gift, this celestial guide, than their ignorance was turned into light, their doubts into certainty, their fears into firm and invincible fortitude, and their former backwardness into an ardent and inextinguishable zeal. . . ."

The growth of the Church among the gentile nations during this period was phenomenal. How was it possible that a handful of apostles, who were fishermen and publicans, could engage the learned and the mighty as well as the simple and those of low degree to forsake their religion and embrace a new religion? There can be but one answer to that question. There were undoubted marks of a celestial power perpetually attending their ministry. There was in their very language an "incredible energy or amazing power of sending light into the understanding and conviction of the heart." (Mosheim, *Ecclesiastical History* 1:56-68.)

Then the historians enumerate the miracles, the gift of prophecy, the power of discernment, a contempt for riches, and a serene tranquillity in the face of death, and all the while the apostles maintained their lives above reproach; and the historians conclude with this declaration: "Thus were the messengers of the divine Savior, the heralds of his spiritual and immortal kingdom, furnished for their glorious work as the voice of ancient history so loudly testifies." (Ibid.)

As we review again the matchless and unselfish devotion of these early prophets and martyrs to the gospel of

Christ, may we bow in reverence and repeat with a greater appreciation and comprehension, as with the multitude in Jerusalem on the occasion of the triumphal entry, the words: "Blessed is he that cometh in the name of the Lord."

The place of these heaven-endowed messengers who represent the Lord in every dispensation of the gospel upon the earth may be illustrated by an incident related by a traveler in northern Europe. Our traveler was leaving by boat from Stockholm, Sweden, traveling out into the Baltic Sea. To do so, the boat had to pass through a thousand or more islands. Standing on the foreward deck, the traveler found himself becoming impatient because of what seemed to him to be a careless course. Why not a course near this island or another, a more interesting one than the one the pilot had chosen? Almost in exasperation he was saying to himself, "What's wrong with the old pilot? Has he lost his sense of direction?" Suddenly he was aware of markers along the charted course, which appeared as mere broom handles sticking up in the water. Someone had carefully explored these channels and had charted the safest course for ships to take. So it is in life's course on the way to immortality and eternal life. "God's engineers," by following a blueprint made in heaven, have charted the course for safest and happiest passage and have forewarned us to the danger areas.

How dreary and frustrated is the human soul who not only does not come "in the name of the Lord," but who disregards the guideposts marked out by "God's engineers"! Of this the Apostle Paul wrote: "If in this life only we have hope in Christ, we are of all men most miserable." (1 Corinthians 15:19.) That misery certainly can only be matched in him who in this life has no faith or hope in Christ. Without such faith, man is, as someone has said, "but a creature of circumstance." Truly, as the Master instructed His faithful Peter, His church, the true religion in which the Master Himself was the "chief cornerstone," was to be built upon a "rock," the rock of revelation. All others are tossed about by storm on the waves of time.

But what strength and fortitude comes to him who puts his trust in the Lord! I once heard a missionary for the Church tell of an incident that occurred in an atheist-dominated country. A young student with a fervent belief in God and in the mission of the Savior of the world was ridiculed and abused by her teacher, who scorned the idea of a God. As a punishment, the teacher required that the student write twenty times "There is no God." The young student refused. In a rage the teacher demanded that she write her denial of God fifty times, and she added, as a veiled threat, "If you don't, something terrible will happen."

That night mother and daughter fasted and prayed far into the night to that God whom they could not and dared not deny. When school time came the next morning, mother and daughter went to see the teacher. The school convened and the teacher had not yet arrived. As they waited, the principal of the school came to inform them that the teacher had died suddenly in the night of a heart attack. Something terrible had happened but not to this young girl, who came without fear "in the name of the Lord."

The triumphal entry of Jesus into Jerusalem was in truth but a prelude to the greater day of triumph only a few days distant. Before His crucifixion, He spoke of His personal triumph over worldly things when He said: ". . . in me ye might have peace. In the world ye have tribulation; but be of good cheer; I have overcome the world." (John 16:33.) But there was yet that greater day of victory when He triumphed over death and opened the way to a universal resurrection. The Apostle Paul in exultation wrote to the Corinthians:

> Death is swallowed up in victory. O death, where is thy sting? O grave, where is thy victory? . . . Thanks be to God, which giveth us the victory through our Lord Jesus Christ. (1 Corinthians 15:54, 56-57.)

Today, as did the followers of Christ in past dispensations, we declare boldly that—

> . . . the fundamental principles of our religion are the testimony of the Apostles and Prophets, concerning Jesus Christ, that He died, was buried, and rose again the third day, and ascended into heaven; and all other things which pertain to our religion are only appendages to it. (*Teachings of the Prophet Joseph Smith,* p. 121.)

O that the inhabitants of an unrepentant world would humble themselves and with faith in the Redeemer of mankind join in the chorus of the multitude who welcomed the Master into the Holy City: "Blessed be the King that cometh in the name of the Lord." "Hosanna to the Son of David." "Peace in heaven and glory in the highest." "Blessed is he that cometh in the name of the Lord."

6

Born of the Spirit

IN the book of John, we read how a Pharisee named Nicodemus, a ruler of the Jews, came to Jesus by night and said:

Rabbi, we know that thou art a teacher come from God: for no man can do these miracles that thou doest, except God be with him.

Jesus answered and said unto him, Verily, verily, I say unto thee, Except a man be born again, he cannot see the kingdom of God.

Nicodemus saith unto him, How can a man be born when he is old? Can he enter the second time into his mother's womb, and be born?

Jesus answered, Verily, verily, I say unto thee, Except a man be born of water and of the Spirit, he cannot enter into the kingdom of God.

That which is born of the flesh is flesh; and that which is born of the Spirit is spirit.

Marvel not that I said unto thee, Ye must be born again.

Then He added this final significant statement:

The wind bloweth where it listeth, and thou hearest the sound thereof, but canst not tell whence it cometh, and whither it goeth: so is every one that is born of the Spirit. (John 3:3-8.)

Many deductions might be taken from that statement, but there are three that I want to call to your attention. In order even to *see* the kingdom of God, one must be born again. This suggests that to become converted, one has to have some spiritual change in order to know the gospel or to see the Church. There must be some kind of spiritual experience. And to enter into the kingdom of God—that is, to become members of The Church of Jesus Christ of Latter-day Saints—there has to be a new birth. The final deduction, knowing how this birth takes place, is as impossible to explain as to explain where the wind comes from or where it goes. In other words, one who is born of the Spirit is like the wind when it comes or when it goes. Now hold those three deductions in your mind as I call your attention to some other scriptures.

Before the Church was organized, two revelations were given to which I would like to direct your attention. These revelations indicate that there was a manifestation of the Spirit even to see what was necessary to "see," even before those first leaders were baptized. To the three witnesses, whose mission was being spelled out (this was given in March 1829), the Lord said: "And behold, whosoever believeth on my words, them will I visit with a manifestation of my Spirit."

Now you see, the Lord is talking to some who had not yet (for a year or more) been baptized. "And they shall be born of me, even of water and of the Spirit." (D&C 5:16.)

To my thinking, first there seems to be, by some kind of an inward conviction, a manifestation of the Spirit that leads one, if he follows thereafter, to the baptism of water and then to the reception of the Holy Ghost.

To Oliver Cowdery in April 1829 (this was, of course, before he had been baptized or ordained), the Lord said:

> Oliver Cowdery, verily, verily, I say unto you, that assuredly as the Lord liveth, who is your God and Redeemer, even so surely shall you receive a knowledge of whatsoever things you shall ask in faith with an honest heart, believing that you shall receive a knowledge concerning the engravings of old records, which are ancient, which contain those parts of my scripture of which has been spoken by the manifestation of my Spirit.

You see, you will receive them "by a manifestation of my Spirit" (which preceded Oliver Cowdery's baptism):

> Yea, behold, I will tell you in your mind and in your heart, by the Holy Ghost, which shall come upon you and which shall dwell in your heart.
>
> Now, behold, this is the spirit of revelation; behold, this is the spirit by which Moses brought the children of Israel through the Red Sea on dry ground (D&C 8:1-3.)

If you will have that in mind, remember what Moroni wrote to those who were obviously investigators of the gospel:

> And when ye shall receive these things, I would exhort you that ye would ask God, the Eternal Father, in the name of Christ, if these things are not true; and if ye shall ask with a sincere heart, with real intent, having faith in Christ, he will manifest the truth of it unto you, by the power of the Holy Ghost. (Moroni 10:4.)

Or, in other words, by a manifestation of the Spirit you shall begin to glimpse the kingdom of God on earth.

Now that brings us to that classical explanation that the Prophet Joseph Smith made of the incident of Cornelius, who was one of the first of the gentiles to be baptized. The Prophet explained:

> There is a difference between the Holy Ghost and the gift of the Holy Ghost. Cornelius received the Holy Ghost before he was baptized, which was the convincing power of God unto him of the truth of the Gospel—

Could that be, in the language of those other generations, a manifestation of the Spirit to Cornelius by the Holy Ghost? Then the Prophet added:

—but he could not receive the gift of the Holy Ghost until after he was baptized. Had he not taken this sign or ordinance upon him, the Holy Ghost which convinced him of the truth of God, would have left him. (*DHC* 4:555.)

Until he obeyed these ordinances and received the gift of the Holy Ghost by the laying on of hands, according to the order of God, he could not have the Spirit in him, for the spirits might say unto him, as the evil spirit said to the sons of Sceva, "Jesus I know, and Paul I know; but who are ye?" (Acts 19:15.)

Now the plan of salvation, as it was first given to man, is a pretty good index, and I shall take you back to the earliest scriptures we have had by revelation in order to understand how that first man received these things of which we speak and which were to be the pattern of all the sons of Adam and Eve.

Note three essentials of conversion that the Lord explained when the question was asked as to what Adam must do. He had been driven out of the Garden of Eden; he had been told to offer a sacrifice; and then the Lord said unto him:

> If thou wilt turn unto me, and hearken unto my voice and believe [that's the first], and repent [the second] of all thy transgressions, and be baptized [the third] even in water, in the name of my Only Begotten Son, who is full of grace and truth, which is Jesus Christ, the only name which shall be given under heaven, whereby salvation shall come unto the children of men, ye shall receive the gift of the Holy Ghost, asking all things in his name, and whatsoever ye shall ask, it shall be given you. (Moses 6:52.)

This is in complete agreement with a revelation found in the thirty-ninth section of the Doctrine and Covenants and is an answer to some of our critics who say, "How can you say the Book of Mormon contains a *fulness* of the gospel of Jesus Christ?" The definition of the "fulness of the gospel" might be in this one sentence, which is in agreement with what I've said. The Lord says:

> And this is my gospel—repentance and baptism by water, and then cometh the baptism of fire and the Holy Ghost, even the Comforter, which showeth all things, and teacheth the peaceable things of the kingdom. (D&C 39:6.)

When a man has the gift of the Holy Ghost, he has that which is necessary to reveal to him every principle and ordinance of salvation that pertains unto man here on the earth. The question was asked by one of Adam's sons when that first instruction was given to Adam, "Why be baptized of water?"

In the following verses of scripture you find one of the most excellent summations and explanations of the initiatory ordinances of the gospel. The Lord said:

> Therefore I give unto you a commandment, to teach these things freely unto your children, saying: by reason of transgression cometh the fall, which fall bringeth death, and inasmuch as ye were born into the world by water, and blood, and the spirit, which I have made, and so become of dust a living soul, even so ye must be born again into the kingdom of heaven, of water, and of the Spirit, and be cleansed by blood, even the blood of mine Only Begotten: that ye might be sanctified from all sin, and enjoy the words of eternal life in this world, and eternal life in the world to come, even immortal glory. For by the water ye keep the commandment; by the Spirit ye are justified, and by the blood ye are sanctified. (Moses 6:58-60.)

I want to comment about this one statement: "by the Spirit ye are justified." Now I've struggled with that statement, and I have found a definition that seems to indicate to me what I'm sure the Lord intended to convey. The definition that I think is significant says: "Justify means to pronounce free from guilt or blame, or to absolve." Now if the Spirit, the Holy Ghost, is to pronounce one free from guilt or blame, or to absolve, then we begin to see something of the office of the Holy Ghost that relates to the subject about which we are talking: what it means to be born of the Spirit.

I shall inject here another phrase that is oft discussed (and I think is misunderstood) and to which we try to attach some mysteries. This phrase, where the Lord directs that all of these things are to be eternal, is: "must be sealed by the Holy Spirit of promise." Let me refer first to the 76th section of the Doctrine and Covenants. Speaking of those who are candidates for celestial glory, the Lord says:

> They are they who received the testimony of Jesus, and believed on his name and were baptized after the manner of his burial . . . That by keeping the commandments they might be washed and cleansed from all their sins, and receive the Holy Spirit by the laying on of the hands . . . And who overcome by faith, and are sealed by the Holy Spirit of Promise, which the Father sheds forth upon all those who are just and true. (D&C 76:51-53.)

In other words, baptism is only efficacious, and the initiary ordinance is applicable, when it is sealed by the Holy Spirit of Promise. We have that same phrase repeated in section 132, verse 19, for the Lord is speaking now of celestial marriage.

> . . . if a man marry a wife by my word . . . and it is sealed unto them by the Holy Spirit of Promise, . . . they shall pass by the angels, and the gods, which are set there, to their exaltation and glory in all things. . . .

And with reference to the priesthood, when the Lord discusses in the 84th section the oath and covenant, exactly the same principle is implied. By the laying on of hands we get the promise of power and authority, but it will not be ours—worlds without end—unless we keep our part of the covenant.

In the following verse, in explaining still further the mission of the Holy Ghost, the Lord said:

Therefore it is given to abide in you; the record of heaven; the Comforter; the peaceable things of immortal glory; the truth of all things; that which quickeneth all things, which maketh alive all things; that which knoweth all things; and hath power according to wisdom, mercy, truth, justice, and judgment. (Moses 6:61.)

Now with that in mind, let me refer to two other scriptures. In the twentieth chapter of Revelation, John said:

And I saw the dead, small and great, stand before God; and the books were opened: and another book was opened, which was the book of life: and the dead were judged out of those things which were written in the books, according to their works [done in the flesh]. (Revelation 20:12.)

And in the 128th section of the Doctrine and Covenants: ". . . and the book which was the book of life is the record which is kept in heaven. . . ." (D&C 128:7.)

Now, who is the keeper of that record kept in heaven? I ask you to think about that.

Here is an explanation one of the brethren made about this phrase "sealed by the Holy Spirit of Promise." Elder Melvin J. Ballard, in his *Three Degrees of Glory* pamphlet, said:

We may deceive men, but we cannot deceive the Holy Ghost, and our blessings will not be eternal until they are also sealed by the holy spirit of promise, the Holy Ghost, one who reads the thoughts and hearts of men and gives his sealing approval to the blessings pronounced upon their heads. Then it is binding, and of full force, (*Sermons and Missionary Service of Melvin J. Ballard*, Deseret Book Co., 1949, p. 237.)

Now note carefully the following verse:

And now, behold, I say unto you: This is the plan of salvation unto all men, through the blood of mine Only Begotten, who shall come in the meridian of time. (Moses 6:62.)

Then Adam was baptized. The Spirit caught him away and took him down under the water "and thus he was baptized, and the Spirit of God descended upon him, and he was born of the Spirit, and became quickened in the inner man." (Moses 6:65.)

Now there is a definition of what it means to be born again. It means to be quickened in the inner man. That's another way of saying it.

> And he heard a voice out of heaven, saying: Thou art baptized with fire, and with the Holy Ghost. This is the record of the Father and the Son, from henceforth and forever. (Moses 6:66.)

And the meaning of that, I feel certain, is what Paul wrote to the Corinthians:

> . . . no man speaking by the Spirit of God calleth Jesus accursed: and no man can say [the Prophet Joseph Smith said that should have been, "no man can know"] that Jesus is the Lord, but by the Holy Ghost. (1 Corinthians 12:3.)

And that is the record of the Father and the Son from henceforth forever and forever. Without it man cannot know the Father and the Son. Finally, we have this concluding statement, at the end of that marvelous exposition of the plan of salvation as it began to apply to the lives of human beings. The Lord said: "Behold, thou art one in me, a son of God: and thus all become my sons." (Moses 6:68.)

That means that by the same procedure, we can experience the same things Adam experienced. It means exactly the same to us as it did to Adam. "Thus all become my sons."

As taught to the Nephites, you remember the Master's statement:

> And no unclean thing can enter unto his kingdom; therefore nothing entereth into his rest save it be those who have washed their garments in my blood, because of their faith, and their repentance of all of their sins, and their faithfulness unto the end.

> Now this is the commandment: Repent, all ye ends of the earth, and come unto me and be baptized in my name, that ye may be sanctified by the reception of the Holy Ghost, that ye may stand spotless before me in the last day. (3 Nephi 27:19-20.)

King Benjamin also explains this same experience. Talking to some who have just come into the church, he says:

> And now, because of the covenant which ye have made ye shall be called the children of Christ, his sons, and his daughters; for behold, this day he hath spiritually begotten you; for ye say that your hearts are changed through faith on his name; therefore, ye are born of him and have become his sons and his daughters. (Mosiah 5:7.)

There's another explanation: when our hearts are changed through faith on his name, we are born again.

The covenant of baptism, which Alma explained, contains a similar thought. You will remember that when he was preparing those who were standing at the water's edge to understand the nature of the covenant that baptism implied, he asked them if they were prepared to—

> stand as witnesses of God at all times and in all things, and in all places that ye may be in, even until death, that ye may be redeemed of God, and be numbered with those of the first resurrection, that ye may have eternal life—
>
> Now I say unto you, if this be the desire of your hearts, what have you against being baptized in the name of the Lord, as a witness before him that you have entered into a covenant with him, that ye will serve him and keep his commandments, that he may pour out his Spirit more abundantly upon you? (Mosiah 18:9-10.)

That is the part of the covenant that *He* gives when we keep our part of the covenant.

Then followed the baptism of Helam:

> And when he had said these words, the Spirit of the Lord was upon him, and he said: Helam, I baptize thee, having authority from the Almighty God, as a testimony that ye have entered into a covenant to serve him until you are dead as to the mortal body; and may the Spirit of the Lord be poured out upon you. . . . (Mosiah 18:13.)

Now, to me, that's exactly parallel to our saying "receive ye the Holy Ghost" when we confirm someone. It's a command, a prayer form to that individual who has been baptized, and who now has had hands laid upon his head, to so live that he will be worthy to receive the baptism of the Spirit:

> . . . and may the Spirit of the Lord be poured out upon you; and may he grant unto you eternal life, through the redemption of Christ, whom he has prepared from the foundation of the world. (Mosiah 18:13.)

Now then, when may it be said that one is born of the Spirit? The Prophet Joseph Smith said: "No man can receive the Holy Ghost without receiving revelations. The Holy Ghost is a revelator. " (*Teachings of the Prophet Joseph Smith,* p. 328.)

I think we would be just as correct if we were to say that revelations from God cannot come to man except by the Holy Ghost. But the Prophet said something else: "Salvation cannot come without revelation." (*Teachings,* p. 160.) That's the understanding thing: without revelation, there's no salvation.

> . . . it is in vain for anyone to minister without it. No man is a minister of Jesus Christ without being a Prophet. No man can be a minister of Jesus Christ except he has a testimony of Jesus; and this is the spirit of prophecy. (*Teachings*, p. 160.)

Whenever salvation has been administered, it has been testimony. "Men of the present time testify of heaven and hell and have never seen either, and I say that no man knows these things without revelation."

What do we mean when we say the *gift* of the Holy Ghost? I think that perhaps one of the most lucid explanations is made by President Joseph F. Smith. He said:

> Therefore, the presentation or "gift" of the Holy Ghost simply confers upon a man the right to receive at any time, when he is worthy of it and desires it, the power and light of truth of the Holy Ghost,

although he may often be left to his own spirit and judgment. (*Gospel Doctrine*, eleventh edition, 1959, pp. 60-61.)

The bestowal of the gift is actually, then, a command to so live that when we need and desire it, we may have the accompaniment of the power of the Holy Ghost. Cyprian, the great defender of the faith after the apostolic period, put in a very lovely sentence when he said, speaking of his own conversion and baptism of the Spirit:

> Into my heart, purified of all sin, there entered a light which came from on high and then suddenly, and in a marvelous manner, I saw certainty succeed doubt.

I don't think you'll find anywhere a more beautiful explanation from a man who received the birth of the Spirit.

Let me refer again from President Joseph F. Smith:

> Every elder of the Church who has received the Holy Ghost by the laying on of hands, by one having authority, has power to confer that gift upon another; it does not follow that a man who has received the presentation or gift of the Holy Ghost shall always receive the recognition and witness and presence of the Holy Ghost himself, or he may receive all these, and yet the Holy Ghost not tarry with him, but visit him from time to time; . . . and neither does it follow that a man must have the Holy Ghost present with him when he confers the Holy Ghost upon another, but he possesses the gift of the Holy Ghost, and it will depend upon the worthiness of him unto whom the gift is bestowed, whether he will receive the Holy Ghost or not. (*Gospel Doctrine*, p. 61.)

It's like all other gifts. If I have something to give you and you won't receive it, then I haven't given you a gift, have I? It's only a gift when you receive it.

There are different effects of the Holy Ghost upon different individuals. Recall again what the Prophet Joseph Smith said: "This first Comforter or Holy Ghost has no other effect than pure intelligence." Now I want you to get that. Some people think otherwise. Some people think that there was to be outward demonstration.

It is more powerful in expanding the mind, enlightening the understanding, and storing the intellect with present knowledge, of a man who is of the literal seed of Abraham, than one that is a Gentile, though it may not have half as much visual effect upon his body; for as the Holy Ghost falls upon one of the literal seed of Abraham, it is calm and serene; and his whole soul and body are only exercised by the pure spirit of intelligence; while the effect of the Holy Ghost upon a Gentile, is to purge out the old blood, and make him actually of the seed of Abraham. That man that has none of the blood of Abraham (naturally) must have new creation by the Holy Ghost. (*Teachings*, pp. 149-50.)

There is another way in which it manifests itself. The Prophet explains this. It applies in our daily lives, in our teachings, in our performance in our families, and so on:

The spirit of revelation is in connection with these blessings. A person may profit by noticing the first intimation of the spirit of revelation; for instance, when you feel pure intelligence flowing into you, it may give you sudden strokes of ideas, so that by noticing it, you may find it fulfilled that very day or soon: (i.e.) those things that were presented in your mind by the Spirit of God, will come to pass; and thus, by learning the Spirit of God and understanding it, you may grow into the principle of revelation, until you become perfect in Christ Jesus. (*DHC* 3:381.)

The question, then, that sometimes we wrestle with is: Must there always be a visible, spiritual manifestation before one might be said to be born of the Spirit? We have some very dramatic incidents in which this is illustrated, including the Apostle Paul's theophany, when he heard and he saw, in his conversion. And perhaps that experience is only matched by the great conversion of younger Alma. Alma, in reciting his experience, says:

For, said he, I have repented of my sins, and have been redeemed of the Lord; behold I am born of the Spirit.

And the Lord said unto me: Marvel not that all mankind, yea, men and women, all nations, kindreds, tongues and people, must be born again; yea, born of God, changed from their carnal and fallen state, to a state of righteousness, being redeemed of God, becoming his sons and daughters;

And thus they become new creatures; and unless they do this, they can in nowise inherit the kingdom of God. (Mosiah 27:24-26.)

Then he describes a little more intimately his experience:

. . . I ask you, my brethren of the church, have ye spiritually been born of God? Have ye received his image in your countenances? Have ye experienced this mighty change in your hearts?

I say unto you, ye will know at that day that ye cannot be saved, for there can no man be saved except his garments are washed white; yea, his garments must be purified until they are cleansed from all stain, through the blood of him of whom it has been spoken by our fathers, who should come to redeem his people from their sins. (Alma 5:14, 21.)

And then, again, he summarizes and ecstatically tells us about how he felt:

And oh, what joy, and what marvelous light I did behold; yea, my soul was filed with joy as exceeding as was my pain!

Yea, I say unto you, my son, that there could be nothing so exquisite and so bitter as were my pains. Yea, and again I say unto you, my son, that on the other hand, there can be nothing so exquisite and sweet as was my joy.

Yea, methought I saw, even as our father Lehi saw, God sitting upon his throne, surrounded with numberless concourses of angels, in the attitude of singing and praising their God; yea, and my soul did long to be there.

But behold, my limbs did receive their strength again, and I stood upon my feet, and did manifest unto the people that I had been born of God.

Yea, and now from that time even until now, I have labored without ceasing, that I might bring souls unto repentance; that I might bring them to taste of the exceeding joy of which I did taste; that they might also be born of God, and be filled with the Holy Ghost. (Alma 36:20-24.)

There are some of us who think that that same kind

of experience has to be experienced by everybody, or he can't be saved. I once ran into a very serious situation where one of our teachers had inflamed some women, in a class he was teaching, until they almost had the kind of feeling that they had to have some kind of demonstration or else they hadn't been born of the Spirit.

Another story that some people who support that idea recite is the conversion of Lorenzo Snow. President Snow had been a young college student; when he finally had an intellectual conviction of the truth, he sought for a deep-seated testimony, which he had not had at his baptism. And so, he reported, he went out one night to pray. This is how he describes the experience:

> It was a complete baptism, a tangible immersion in the heavenly principle or element, the Holy Ghost, and even more real and physical in its effect upon my system, than the immersion of water. Dispelling forever, as long as reason and memory last, all possibility of doubt and fear in relation to the fact, handed down to us historically, that the babe of Bethlehem is truly the Son of God; also communicating knowledge, the same as in apostolic times.

Now, I repeat, because of some of these dramatic experiences, some of our teachers jump to the conclusion that one isn't born of the Spirit until he has had some such dramatic experience.

Let me point out something from the Prophet Joseph Smith. This was an editorial in the *Times and Seasons*:

> Various and conflicting are the opinions of man with regard to the gift of the Holy Ghost. Some people have been in the habit of calling every supernatural manifestation the effects of the spirit of God, whilst there are others that think [there] is no manifestation connected with it at all; and that it is *nothing* but a mere impulse of the mind, or an inward feeling, impression, or secret testimony or evidence which men possess, and that there is no such thing as an outward manifestation.

Then the Prophet said:

Then the Prophet said:

> It is not to be wondered at that men should be ignorant, in a great measure, of the principles of salvation, and more especially of the nature, office, power, influence, gifts and blessings of the Gift of the Holy Ghost; when we consider that the human family have been enveloped in gross darkness and ignorance for many centuries past without revelation or any just criterion to arrive at a knowledge of the things of God which can only be known by the spirit of God. Hence it not infrequently occurs that when the elders of this church preach to the inhabitants of the world, that if they obey the gospel they shall receive the gift of the Holy Ghost, that people expect to see some wonderful manifestation; some great display of power, or some extraordinary miracle performed; and it is often the case that young members in this church, for want of better information, carry along with them their old notions of things and sometimes fall into egregious errors.

Then the Prophet follows with this statement:

> We believe that the Holy Ghost is imparted by the laying on of hands of those in authority, and that the gift of tongues, and also the gift of prophecy, are gifts of the spirit, and are obtained through that medium; but then to say that men always prophesied and spoke in tongues when they had the imposition of hands, would be to state that which is untrue, contrary to the practice of the apostles, and at variance to holy writ. For Paul says: "For to one is given the gift of healing, and again do all prophesy, do all speak with tongues, do all interpret? . . ." (*Times and Seasons* 1:823.)

Evidently not all possess these several gifts, but one receives one gift and another receives another gift. All do not prophesy, all do not speak in tongues, all do not work miracles, but all *do* receive the gift of the Holy Ghost. Sometimes in the days of the apostles some spoke in tongues and prophesied, and sometimes they did not. The same is the case with us today. Frequently there are no manifestations at all—that is, manifestations visible to the surrounding multitude. This will appear plain when we consult the writing of the apostles and note their proceedings in these matters.

Some assurances that are less dramatic are also

recited. King Benjamin said, to some who had now been convicted of their sins:

> And it came to pass that after they had spoken these words the Spirit of the Lord came upon them, and they were filled with joy, having received a remission of their sins, and having a peace of conscience, because of the exceeding faith which they had in Jesus Christ who should come, according to the words which King Benjamin had spoken unto them. (Mosiah 4:2.)

The converts of Alma said:

> . . . he hath granted unto us that we might repent of these things, and also that he hath forgiven us of those our many sins and murders which we have committed, and taken away the guilt from our hearts, through the merits of his Son.
>
> And now behold, my brethren, since it has been all that we could do, (as we were the most lost of all mankind) to repent of all our sins and the many murders which we have committed, and to get God to take them away from our hearts, for it was all we could do to repent sufficiently before God that he would take away our stain. (Alma 24:10-11.)

Then came that peace of conscience—not dramatic. No outward show. But within, the individual knew.

Recall Enos's experience. His soul hungered and he went out to pray. All day and all night he prayed. And then there came a voice that said unto him:

> Enos, thy sins are forgiven thee, and thou shalt be blessed. And I, Enos, knew that God could not lie; wherefore my guilt was swept away. (Enos 5-6.)

The key to the retention of the Holy Ghost is contained in the next thing that Enos said:

> And while I was thus struggling in the spirit, behold, the voice of the Lord came into my mind again, saying: I will visit thy brethren according to their diligence in keeping my commandments. . . . (Enos 10.)

Now as to the error that we fall into. I remember President Heber J. Grant startled me one time when he said, "You know, whenever I hear one of my brethren who has borne testimony that he has seen so many who have had such an experience, who have become puffed up and thought that they were more favored than those who didn't have the personal manifestation, their pride has led them away from the Church." He said: "I'm always anxious about a man who has had a personal visitation from the Lord."

One of the members of the Council of the Twelve, whom my brethren say had one of the greatest gifts of prophecy that they had ever seen, said in his last recorded sermon: "That person is not truly converted until he sees the power of God resting upon the leaders of this church, and it goes down into his heart like fire." That is the very thing that cost the man his standing in the Church, and ultimately his membership in the Church.

Oh, if only we could always be humble when we have these marvelous experiences; to say, as did Moses: "Now, for this cause I know that man is nothing, which thing I never had supposed." (Moses 1:10.) That was the beginning of learning and wisdom in Moses.

How may one of men obtain this new birth? Nephi said:

> For we labor diligently to write, to persuade our children, and also our brethren, to believe in Christ, and to be reconciled to God; for we know that it is by grace that we are saved after all that we do. (2 Nephi 25:23.)

To gain this is a matter of being born of the Spirit, and a witness that can only come when one is born of the Spirit. The Lord has said it in the first verse of the 93rd section:

> Verily, thus saith the Lord: It shall come to pass that every soul who forsaketh his sins and cometh unto me, and calleth on my name, and obeyeth my voice, and keepeth my commandments, shall see my face and know that I am.

But remember this, as the Lord told us: there is a possibility that man may fall from grace and depart from the living God. I call your attention to Peter's dramatic testimony when he said, "Thou art the Christ, the Son of the living God," which the Master told him was a revelation. Only a year or two later the Master chastised him for some reason and said to him:

> Satan hath desired to have you, that he may sift you as wheat: But I have prayed for thee, that thy faith fail not: and when thou are converted, strengthen thy brethren. (Luke 22:31-33.)

It is a possibility that one may be born of the Spirit and then, because of his sinfulness or slothfulness, he may lose the Spirit and fall from grace. The Spirit will not dwell in unholy tabernacles.

I shall conclude with this one final thought. In the Doctrine and Covenants the Lord said:

> . . . that which doth not edify is not of God and is darkness.
>
> That which is of God is light; and he that receiveth light, and continueth in God, receiveth more light; and that light groweth brighter and brighter until the perfect day. (D&C 50:23-24.)

May I bear my own testimony. Some years ago two missionaries came to me with what seemed to them to be a very difficult question. A young Methodist minister had laughed at them when they had said that apostles were necessary today in order for the true church to be upon the earth. They said that the minister said, "Do you realize that when the apostles met to choose one to fill the vacancy caused by the death of Judas, they said it had to be one who companied with them and had been a witness of all things pertaining to the mission and resurrection of the Lord? How can you say you have apostles, if that be the measure of an apostle?"

And so these young men said, "What shall we answer?"

I said to them, "Go back and ask your minister friend two questions. First, how did the Apostle Paul gain what was necessary to be called an apostle? He didn't know the Lord, had no personal acquaintance. He hadn't accompanied the apostles. He hadn't been a witness of the ministry nor of the resurrection of the Lord. How did he gain his testimony sufficient to be an apostle? And the second question you ask him is, How does he know that all who are today apostles have not likewise received that witness?"

I bear witness to you that those who hold the apostolic calling may, and do, know of the reality of the mission of the Lord. To know is to be born and quickened in the inner man.

Section Two

OUR SEARCH FOR TRUTH

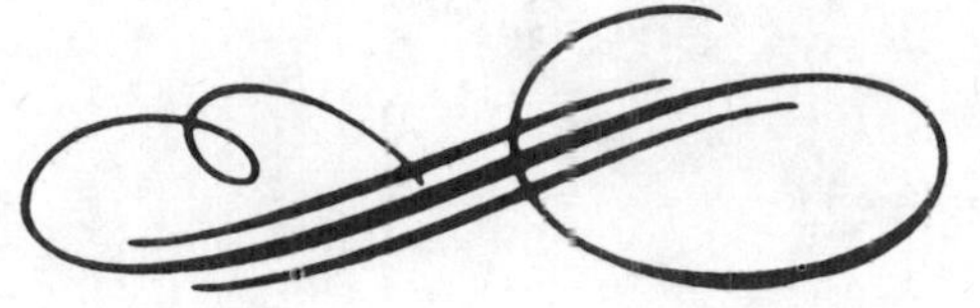

7

Our Search for Truth

JESUS was being tried before Pilate on the charge of blasphemy.

> Pilate therefore said unto him, Art thou a king then? Jesus answered, Thou sayest that I am a king. To this end was I born, and for this cause came I into the world, that I should bear witness unto the truth. Every one that is of the truth heareth my voice. Pilate said unto him, What is truth? (John 18:37-38.)

To Adam and Eve, our first parents on this earth, God gave the commandment, "Be fruitful, and multiply, and replenish the earth, and subdue it: and have dominion. . . ." (Genesis 1:28.) Truth is the scepter of power which, if man possesses it, will give him "dominion" and the ability to "subdue all things." It has been well said that—

> If you have truth on your side, you can pass through the dark valley of slander, misrepresentation and abuse, undaunted as though you wore a magic suit of mail that no bullet could enter, no arrow could pierce. You can hold your head high, toss it fearlessly and defiantly, look every man calmly and unflinchingly in the eye, as though you rode, a victorious king, returning at the head of your legions with banners

waving and lances glistening, and bugles filling the air with music. (William George Jordan.)

Is there any one of us who would not desire with all our heart to be thus equipped to meet the problems of life! Ours then should be a daily quest for truth, but in order that our search be fruitful, we must first know the answer to the question Pilate put to the Master, "What is truth?"

In a revelation given to the Church on May 6, 1833, the Lord gave us this definition of truth: "And truth is knowledge of things as they are, and as they were, and as they are to come." (D&C 93:24.) In the next verse the Lord gives us also a definition of untruth: "And whatsoever is more or less than this," meaning more or less than the knowledge of things present, past, and future, "is the spirit of that wicked one who was a liar from the beginning." (Verse 25.) It was Jesus who declared to the believing Jews that "ye shall know the truth, and the truth shall make you free. . . . Whosoever committeth sin is the servant of sin." (John 8:32, 34.)

To us in this day the Lord has said: "He that keepeth his [God's] commandments receiveth truth and light, until he is glorified in truth and knoweth all things." (D&C 93:28.) And again we are told, "The glory of God is intelligence, or, in other words, light and truth." (D&C 93:36.) Furthermore, the Master has impressed the vital necessity of a fulness of knowledge if we would gain eternal life, and likewise the supreme or the ultimate object of our quest for truth and indeed what it is that constitutes a fulness of truth. Ponder seriously these words: "And this is life eternal, that they might know thee the only true God, and Jesus Christ, whom thou hast sent." (John 17:3.)

It is no small wonder that with the spread of truth thus so vital to the triumph of God's plan for the redemption and exaltation of the human soul, Satan, the master of lies, should seek to overthrow truth to the end that he might "lead captive at his will, even as many as would not hearken" unto the voice of the Lord by which a true knowledge of "things as they are, as they were, and as they are to come" would be revealed.

In order that the young, vigorous, and inquiring minds of youth in all ages might have a standard and an unfailing guide by which to measure all learning and thus be able to sift the golden kernels of truth from the chaff of delusion and untruth, we have had the scriptures from the beginning that were given—

> . . . by inspiration of God, and [are] profitable for doctrine, for reproof, for correction, for instruction in righteousness: That the man of God may be perfect, throughly furnished unto all good works. (2 Timothy 3:16-17.)

So the Master counseled us to search the scriptures, for in them we would find the way to eternal life, for they testify of the way men must travel to gain eternal life with Him and with "the Father which hath sent [Him]." (John 5:30.) This is the evident meaning of the Lord's statement to Pilate to which I made reference at the beginning of this discussion: "For this cause came I into the world, that I should bear witness unto the truth." So has it been the purpose of every prophet and teacher of righteousness to preserve the truth and to combat error, for the salvation of every soul whose purity of life has made of him a fit vessel to receive truth when it should be made known to him.

You and I have been privileged to be born in a dispensation known in the scriptures as the fulness of times, which is to precede the second coming of Jesus Christ, when there would be a "restitution of all things, which God hath spoken by the mouth of all his holy prophets since the world began." (Acts 3:21.) This is the day the prophet Ezekiel foresaw when the "stick" or record of Judah, which is the Bible, and the "stick" or record of Joseph and Ephraim and his brethren, which is contained in the Book of Mormon, were to be joined together and were to become one in the hands of a man whom He would raise up. All of this has been done for a purpose explained by the Lord in revelation to us:

> Behold, . . . these commandments [contained in the fulness of the gospel] are of me, and were given . . . that [his children] might come to understanding.
>
> And inasmuch as they erred, it might be made known;
>
> And inasmuch as they sought wisdom they might be instructed;
>
> And inasmuch as they sinned they might be chastened, that they might repent;
>
> And inasmuch as they were humble they might be made strong, and blessed from on high, and receive knowledge from time to time. (D&C 1:24-28.)

The place of the Church in preserving truth in these "the latter times" is thus pointed out when—

> . . . some shall depart from the faith, giving heed to seducing spirits, and doctrines of devils; Speaking lies in hypocrisy; having their conscience seared with a hot iron; Forbidding to marry, and commanding to abstain from meats. . . . (1 Timothy 4:1-3.)

This, our day, was prophesied of as a day when "there shall be false teachers among you, who privily shall bring in damnable heresies, even denying the Lord that brought them, and . . . many shall follow their pernicious ways; by reason of whom the way of truth shall be evil spoken of." (2 Peter 2:1-2.) So the Church of Jesus Christ declares with a boldness that is always characteristic of truth. "We believe that He will yet reveal many great and important things pertaining to the Kingdom of God." (Article of Faith 9.) And again, ". . . We believe all things, we hope all things. . . . If there is anything virtuous, lovely, or of good report or praiseworthy, we seek after these things." (Article of Faith 13.) Indeed, the Church of Jesus Christ does not ask us to give up any truth that we may learn from science or philosophy, law or medicine. Rather, the Church has commanded—

> . . . that you may be instructed more perfectly in theory, in principle, in doctrine, in the law of the gospel, in all things that pertain unto the kingdom of God, that are expedient for you to understand; Of things both in heaven and in the earth, and under the earth; things which have been, things which are, things which must shortly come to pass, things which are at home, things which are abroad; the wars and the perplexities of the nations, and the judgments which are on the land; and a knowledge also of countries and of kingdoms. (D&C 88: 78-79.)

If we will carefully analyze that commandment of the Lord, we will find broadly enumerated many of the studies outlined in scholastic courses: astronomy, the physical sciences, mineralogy, history, current events, political science, law, medicine, world history, and so on through the entire school curriculum. What the Church does ask of us in all our worldly studies are these two things:

First, that we measure every teaching to be found in the world of book learning by the teachings of revealed truth, as contained in the gospel of Jesus Christ. If we find in school texts claims that contradict the word of the Lord as pertaining to the creation of the world, the origin of man, or the determination of what is right or wrong in the conduct of human souls, we may be certain that such teachings are but the theories of men; and as men improve their learning and experimentation, the nearer will their theories coincide with the truths that God has given to His church. And second, that there are, beyond the things we can discern by the physical senses of "the natural man," things of a spiritual nature:

> . . . the things of God knoweth no man, but the Spirit of God.
>
> . . . the natural man receiveth not the things of the Spirit of God: for they are foolishness unto him: neither can he know them, because they are spiritually discerned. (1 Corinthians 2:11-14.)

Within the limits of the natural man, methods of experimentation are pretty well established. With mortar and pestle, test tubes and Bunsen burners, with acids and materials to be analyzed, we can proceed to our discovery of the component parts of water or to learn the various properties of phosphorus, for example. A student of science soon comes to realize the limitations of his scientific research. When one climbs Pikes Peak he discovers that even from his vantage point the surrounding country is but a territory with receding horizons and yet other mountains to climb. So the naturalist stands in reverent awe as he contemplates how the delicate coloring, the fragrant odors and delicious tastes of nature's products are made by processes far beyond his grasp. The great surgeon, by dissection and with scalpel and microscope, has learned much about the human body and how it works, but he knows full well that beyond his reach is the soul or intelligence in man that defies analysis with the tools at his command. Every astronomer knows likewise that all he has been able to discern with the powerful telescope now provided for his use but leads him to realize that there are worlds without number beyond his present scientific sight.

It was the great scientist, Sir Isaac Newton, in recognition of man's limitation, who declared:

> I do not know what I may appear to the world, but to myself I seem to have been only like a boy playing on the seashore and diverting myself in now and then finding a smoother pebble or a prettier shell than ordinary, whilst the great ocean of truth lay all undiscovered before me.

My association with men of great learning in science and philosophy or in religion leads me to conclude that one's faith in spiritual matters is disturbed by his scientific or philosophical studies only because his knowledge in either or both science and religion is deficient.

In things of the spiritual world that can only be spiritually discerned, the methods of finding truth are no less clearly defined than in the physical laboratory. It was the

Master who, in reply to the question as to how His hearers were to know whether His teachings were of God or whether He spoke of himself, suggested a simple method for perceiving spiritual truth: "If any man will do [God's] will, he shall know. . . ." (John 7:17.) In numerous revelations His will and the steps that must be taken by him who would learn spiritual truths are made clear:

> . . . if ye shall ask with a sincere heart, with real intent, having faith in Christ, he will manifest the truth of it unto you, by the power of the Holy Ghost. And by the power of the Holy Ghost ye may know the truth of all things. (Moroni 10:4-5.)

There must be, first, desire, then study, then prayer, and finally practice. "Prove me now herewith and see," the Lord constantly enjoins him who would know divine truth. We make a grave mistake that leads only to confusion when we presume to discover spiritual truths by the methods of the physical laboratory.

I was greatly impressed when I heard one of the greatest scientists and scholars of our day, Dr. Robert A. Millikan, at a convention of scientists at Fresno, California, in 1937, counsel his listeners to be as scientific in proving religious teachings as they were in their studies in science. He declared that nothing spiritual should be discarded until it had been submitted to the most careful experimentation and testing to prove or disprove the whole matter.

It has been said by some who speak loosely that "he who never doubted, never thought." Youth must understand that faith, not doubt, is the beginning of all learning, whether in science or religion. It is faith in the wisdom of ages past that leads one to further study, experimentation, and new discovery. It is faith that leads us to seek for spiritual knowledge and power by studying out in our own mind the matter in question, by applying all possible human wisdom to the solution of the problem, and then asking God if the conclusion is right. If it is right, our bosom shall burn within us and we shall "feel" that it is right, but if our conclusion is not right, we shall have a stupor of thought that shall cause us to forget the thing that is wrong. (See D&C 9:8-9.)

The expert in the scientific field is one who by his experimentation has come to know that an announced theory is true. An "expert," so-called, in the spiritual world is in the making when he, by humility and faith, knows that God hears and answers prayer. Such a one has "arrived" when he has an unshakable testimony that God is our Father and that through His Son, Jesus Christ, all mankind may be saved by obedience to the laws and ordinances of the gospel. The Lord has given the inspired truth that "it is impossible for a man to be saved in ignorance." (D&C 131:6.) Does this mean that one must be a college graduate or a man of letters to be saved? Not at all. Man cannot be saved in ignorance of those saving principles of the gospel of Jesus Christ even if he were to have all the book learning in the world. We have been plainly taught by the leaders of this dispensation that "the principle of knowledge is the principle of salvation . . . [and that] the principle of salvation is given us through the knowledge of Jesus Christ." (*Teachings of the Prophet Joseph Smith,* p. 297.)

> Reading the experiences of others, or the revelation given to *them,* can never give *us* a comprehensive view of our condition and true relation to God. Knowledge of these things can only be obtained by experience through ordinances of God set forth for that purpose. (Ibid., p. 324.)

But the Lord has encouraged us to strive diligently for knowledge and intelligence from every source. Here are the Prophet's inspired words of counsel:

> Whatever principle of intelligence we attain unto in this life, it will rise with us in the resurrection.
>
> And if a person gains more knowledge and intelligence in this life

> through his diligence and obedience than another, he will have so much the advantage in the world to come. (D&C 130:18-19.)

One who violates the fundamental human virtues cannot have the greatest truths of the spiritual world unfolded to him.

In a university publication I once read an article by a student entitled "Up from Heaven," suggesting that belief in the supernatural was childish and must eventually be overcome by advancement in intellectual studies.

Each of us has no doubt known many like this young student, who, because of their "little learning," think they have outgrown the Church and religion. As a matter of fact, when we consider seriously the fact that the Church of Jesus Christ requires sacrifice of one's time and talents and means in order to qualify as a worthy citizen of the kingdom, and that "pure religion and undefiled before God and the Father is this, To visit the fatherless and widows in their affliction, and to keep [ourself] unspotted from the world" (James 1:27), we are led to this sure conclusion: that person who thinks he has outgrown his church and his religion has in reality proved himself too small to bear the responsibilities his membership entails and has shut himself up in his small intellectual world, and the vast treasures in the unseen world of spiritual truths are closed to his understanding.

> And if your eye be single to [God's] glory, your whole bodies shall be filled with light, and there shall be no darkness in you; and that body which is filled with light comprehendeth all things. (D&C 88:67.)

Many of our youth have completed their high school or university education, some of them have been graduated to still higher schools of education, and some of them have taken jobs or have become married and have settled down to the serious problem of everyday living. They must not be among those who are blinded to the wealth of learning beyond the understanding of the "natural man." They are standing on the threshold of the most profound of all schools of learning, the "University of Spirituality," if they will only keep God's commandments.

May each of us seek out of the best books "all that has been revealed" and be guided in our search for the truth and seek just as earnestly to know "all that may yet be revealed" and thus make our lives balanced and complete.

8

Watch Always, That Ye May Be Ready

SOME time ago I was visited by a journalist from a large intermountain newspaper who came to inquire about the missionary activities of the Church. After we had explained our worldwide activities in missions being expanded into such areas as the Fiji Islands, Korea, Hong Kong, Indonesia, Thailand, Spain, Italy, and heretofore remote areas of Latin America, and among the Indian tribes, she asked, as she contemplated the magnitude of the worldwide missionary activities, "Are you people out to convert the whole world?"

I replied by quoting the Master's commission to His early disciples:

> And he said unto them: Go ye into all the world, and preach the gospel to every creature.
>
> He that believeth and is baptized shall be saved; but he that believeth not shall be damned.

The Master then spoke of the signs which would evidence the divinity of their callings: "So then after the Lord had spoken unto them, he was received up unto heaven. . . ."

Then, as the gospel writers have recorded: "And they went forth, and preached everywhere, the Lord working with them, and confirming the word with signs following." (Mark 16:15-16, 19-20.)

I then recalled for her the words of a revelation to the Lord's disciples in early years of this dispensation, that through their administration,

> the word may go forth unto the ends of the earth, unto the Gentiles first, and then, behold, and lo, they shall turn unto the Jews.
>
> For it shall come to pass in that day, that every man shall hear the fulness of the gospel in his own tongue, and in his own language, through those who are ordained unto this power. . . . (D&C 90:9, 11.)

We are witnessing a great expansion of the work of the Church throughout the world. It would seem that the early revelations of the Lord to the Church pointed us to a preparation for this day, when He promised:

> Behold, and lo, I will take care of your flocks [meaning, of course, the congregations of Church members], and will raise up elders and send unto them.
>
> Behold, I will hasten my work in its time. (D&C 88:72-73.)

Never, it seems, has there ever been more unmistakable evidence of a need for spiritual guidance than today, as we see people seeking for answers to problems that confront them on every side. We sense that everywhere there is much dissatisfaction with the churches to which they have belonged. The real reason for this decline seems to stem from the fact, as one columnist has summarized it, that "organized religion isn't being attacked. It's busily committing suicide trying to keep up" with the type of philosophy that would "tune out that corny old Bible, split out of that moldy church and turn on with relevance!" (Dr. Max Rafferty, "Church Should Examine Own Action in Decline of Religion," *Salt Lake Tribune,* September 19, 1971, p. A-13.)

They want a true definition of what constitutes divine authority. They are clamoring for security or a salvation, not just in the world to come, but for a temporal salvation, here and now, that they don't have to die to get. There is a need for their churches to have concern about the personal welfare of the individual, so that each one could be aided to help himself through a unified church effort and a brotherhood in the church that concerns itself with temporal and social, as well as spiritual, needs.

They are looking for a church where there is not only unity to be found within their local congregations, but which reaches out to a unification of effort in meeting the challenging problems confronting mankind; where a church congregation in one nation links hands with those of a common faith that spans the continents and the oceans and proclaims a universal brotherhood to which they may look with confidence in matters of health and education, strengthening of home ties, and in evolving and promoting constructive church activities; where youth are taught correct principles so that they can learn to become effective leaders themselves; where wholesome activities are in such abundance that there is less time to engage in the evils that beckon on every side.

In short, the demand everywhere is for a church that is holding fast to the basic ideals of Christianity, as the apostle James has defined it: "Pure religion and undefiled before God and the Father is this, To visit the fatherless and widows in their affliction, and to keep himself unspotted from the world." (James 1:27.)

We have in our church a strong central authority that inspires a confidence that shows the way ahead—where the strong are marshaled to give liberally of their leadership, of their means, of their talents; where the weak are urged to maximum effort in providing for themselves; where emergency needs can be met in a way that fosters brotherhood, instead of a deadening process that is described, scripturally, as to "grind the faces of the poor." (Isaiah 3:15.)

Never has there been a greater need in the Church for training in leadership and in effective teaching to offset the clever and diabolical methods of evil power that "pacify, and lull them away into carnal security," stirring them up to anger, saying that all is well and with flattery telling them there is no hell nor is there a devil, for this is the way, as the ancient prophets have warned, that "the devil cheateth their souls, and leadeth them away carefully down to hell." (See 2 Nephi 28:20-22.)

It is frightening to observe that in places where there is the greater prosperity, there is the unmistakable evidence that, like the peoples of other dispensations, when the people prosper they forget God. They are seemingly rich in things that money can buy, but they are devoid of most of the precious things money cannot buy.

The prophets have issued a clear signal of warning to those who are lifted up in the pride of their hearts because of their ease and their exceeding great prosperity:

> Yea, and we may see at the very time when he doth prosper his people . . . yea, then is the time that they do harden their hearts, and do forget the Lord their God, and do trample under their feet the Holy One—yea, and this because of their ease, and their exceedingly great prosperity. (Helaman 12:2.)

And so do we, as we witness these things, lament with those who have gone before us:

> Yea, how quick to be lifted up in pride; yea, how quick to boast, and to all manner of that which is iniquity; and how slow are they to remember the Lord their God, and to give ear unto his counsels, yea, how slow to walk in wisdom's paths! (Helaman 12:5.)

There comes back to us more clearly than ever before the application of the words of the Master as He closed His

Sermon on the Mount: that only that person or that church (meaning a congregation of individuals, of course) which will stand through these testing years will be that which is founded upon the rock, as the Master declared, by hearing and obeying the fundamental and never-changing principles upon which the true church is founded, when the winds of delusion blow, or when the floods of filth and wickedness engulf us, or when the rains of criticism or derision are rained down upon those who are holding fast to the truth.

Constantly there come among us men and women of great renown, and their observations, as they learn of the Church and its far-reaching activities, are, in a sense, but confirmation of what the Apostle Paul declared long ago to the Romans:

> For I am not ashamed of the gospel of Christ: for it is the power of God unto salvation to every one that believeth. . . .
>
> For therein is the righteousness of God revealed. . . .
>
> For the wrath of God is revealed from heaven against all ungodliness and unrighteousness of men, who hold the truth in unrighteousness. (Romans 1:16-18.)

One renowned lecturer at a service club, Mr. George Rony, remarked to me after I had taken him, at his request, to see some of our Church welfare activities, "Your welfare plan should engulf the world, and I have no doubt after seeing it in operation that one day it will be the master plan for Christian living."

Frequently, prominent visitors inquire about the educational system of the Church, by which, outside of our church and school institutions, and within our seminaries and institutes, the Church is reaching out to every home with home Primaries on week days for small children, and with home-study courses on week days for the youth, for the teaching of vital principles essential to Christian living.

These visitors invariably seek for the secret as to how

our school campuses have been able to maintain law and order. This question, of course, prompts an explanation of the family home evening programs in the homes from which most of our youth have come. Attention is called to the student organizations among our college youth where students themselves are organized into church units and are schooled in how they can communicate responsibly in the way the Lord's plan provides.

These observations, and many others, similarly, are sobering, and they challenge us to strive the more diligently to carry out the perfect plan that has been given us, by which the world may be saved, if all men would be constrained to "search diligently, pray always, and be believing, and all things shall work together for [their] good" (D&C 90:24) and His name's glory.

At the historic area general conference of the members of the Church in the British Isles, at Manchester, England, were assembled over twelve thousand members. The intensity of the interest there manifest bore eloquent witness to the growing awareness that the kingdom of God, meaning The Church of Jesus Christ of Latter-day Saints, is worldwide, and that the people of Great Britain have a firm resolution to establish the Church more firmly in their native land. This was dramatically demonstrated when they concluded the three-day conference with an original song composed by one of their local leaders, entitled "This Is Our Place." This song concluded with this impressive declaration:

> God's work is ours: we must not fail
> To labour with our heart and strength,
> With him beside us, we'll not fear,
> Here we will live, here we will serve.
>
> —Ernest Hewett
> President, Leicester Stake

As we have visited the various countries, whether in the Far East, in Europe, in the Latin American nations, or in other parts of the world, we have noted unmistakable signs of a strong desire on the part of our church members to see the Church grow in their own countries. They are looking for a day when their membership and a developed leadership will be able to assume positions of responsibility to preside over districts and missions and temples, if and when their strength will be so manifest that they can govern themselves after they have been taught correct principles.

It is a standing marvel to see how susceptible these leaders are to training in the Church, when they have been taught by someone to show the way. As Church members catch the spirit of the work, they have an intense desire to go to a holy temple where they can receive the promised blessings of the priesthood, which, through their faithfulness, will gain them heaven's highest privileges in the world to come.

Everywhere we go and here at home people are asking about our efforts in behalf of the so-called underprivileged peoples. This give us the opportunity to explain how, from the finding of new converts, there proceeds, step by step, the introduction of the family home evening program, where parents are helped with family problems, small units of organization, of Sunday Schools, branches and districts, culminating into stakes—all for the purpose, as the Lord revealed, to provide "for a defense, and for a refuge from the storm, and from wrath when it shall be poured out without mixture upon the whole earth." (D&C 115:6.)

When I recall the words of a heavenly messenger to the young prophet in the early days of this dispensation, that the purpose of the restored church was to prepare a people ready to receive the coming of the Lord, I remember that when the disciples gathered around the Master before He left them, they asked Him as to the signs of His second coming and the end of the world, or the destruction of the wicked, which was the end of the world. He gave them certain signs that would foretell that this second coming was near, even at their very doors. He spoke of great tribulations, of wars, famines, and earthquakes.

One of the most significant among the signs of which the Master spoke, and about which I had often wondered, was that prior to His coming there would be false Christs and false prophets who would show great signs and wonders in order to deceive the faithful who are looking forward to that glorious day when the Master will return again to the earth. We are actually seeing this present among us today, where individuals are coming forward with claims of deity for their leaders. These arch-deceivers are among us, and some have come in person claiming to be God; and we may well expect others to rise up to do likewise in fulfillment of the Master's declaration that false Christs and false prophets would come forth.

The Master gave a sure way for the saints to herald the coming of the Lord again to the earth, as He promised. This is how the Savior said He would appear:

> Wherefore if they [meaning the false Christs] shall say unto you, behold, he is in the desert; go not forth: behold, he is in the secret chambers; believe it not.
>
> For as the lightning cometh out of the east, and shineth even unto the west; so shall also the coming of the Son of man be. (Matthew 24:26-27; see also Joseph Smith 1:25-26.)

If we could remember that and put to flight all the foolish ideas about how the Savior will appear, we would be ready when He comes.

In preparation for that marvelous event the Master counseled:

> Watch therefore: for ye know not what hour your Lord doth come.

Therefore be ye also ready: for in such an hour as ye think not the Son of man cometh.

Then there was this promise to his servants who had been living faithfully:

"Blessed is that servant, whom his Lord when he cometh shall find so doing." (Matthew 24:42, 44, 46; see also Joseph Smith 1:46, 48, 50.)

A faith-promoting report came to us from a young mission president and his wife who had presided over a mission in Peru, where there was experienced one of the worst calamities in the history of the world, in which an estimated seventy thousand persons were buried when an earthquake moved an entire mountain over two cities, which were completely destroyed. Four missionaries were laboring there, two in each city. When the earthquake came, they were at the Lord's business; two of them were teaching a gospel lesson on the outskirts of the town and the other two were in a preparation meeting in another city.

After the three terrifying days of semidarkness from the choking dust, they philosophized that this might be like the time when the Savior was crucified, when there were three days of darkness, and when He would come again, when two should be grinding at the mill, and one would be taken and the other left; two would be working in the field, and one would be taken and the other one left. (See Matthew 24:40-41.)

When an earthquake strikes, every person might be taken as he is then living—if at a movie, or a tavern, or in a drunken stupor, or whatever. But the true servants of God, those who are doing their duty, will be protected and preserved if they will do as the Lord has counseled: "stand ye in holy places, and be not moved," when these days should come. (D&C 87:8.)

So we are saying to our Church members in every land, everywhere, stand in your places and say, as the British Saints have sung:

> God's work is ours: we must not fail
> To labour with our heart and strength;
> With Him beside us, we'll not fear,
> Here we will live, here we will serve.

To our faithful Saints everywhere and to all our friends who are the honest in heart, we say: have your family prayers, keep your home ties strong, and let love abound therein.

You who are the priesthood watchmen, don't fail in the sacred charge to "watch over the church . . . and be with and strengthen them." (D&C 20:53.)

You leaders, put into full gear the total programs that are heaven-sent in these days to stem the tide of wickedness that is rolling over the earth as an avalanche.

Lighten your individual burdens, you leaders, by increasing the activities of others, that all may be benefitted thereby.

Above all, teach the gospel of Jesus Christ with power and authority and continue to bear witness of the divine mission of our Lord and Master, Jesus Christ.

And to all who are honest in heart and who are sincere seekers after truth, we bear our solemn witness that "through the Atonement of Christ, all mankind may be saved, by obedience to the laws and ordinances of the Gospel" (Article of Faith 3), as administered by authorized servants who hold the keys of salvation for both the living and the dead.

I would that all would be comforted, in this dispensation, as those in other troublous times have been comforted and shielded from the pitfalls of the adversary. Hear the Master's words as He referred to His people as His children:

> Fear not, little children, for you are mine, and I have overcome the world, and you are of them that my Father hath given me;
>
> And none of them that my Father hath given me shall be lost.
>
> Wherefore, I am in your midst, and I am the good shepherd, and the stone of Israel. He that buildeth upon this rock shall never fall.
>
> And the day cometh that you shall hear my voice and see me, and know that I am.

And then he said: "Watch, therefore, that ye may be ready." (D&C 50:41-42, 44-46.)

I believe with all my soul that that promise is for you and me today, as we qualify ourselves to be worthy to be called His children.

9

When Your Heart Tells You Things Your Mind Does Not Know

THE most important responsibility that we, as members of the Church of Jesus Christ, have is to see that we are converted to the truthfulness of the gospel. Then we must share this truth with others.

One day while the Master and His disciples were on their way to Caesarea Philippi, they stopped for a rest. And the Master asked them, "Whom do men say that I the Son of man am?

"And they said, Some say that thou art John the Baptist: some, Elias; and others, Jeremias, or one of the prophets."

And then Jesus asked the disciples to bear their testimonies: "But whom say ye that I am?"

I suppose they all bore testimony, but we have only Peter's recorded: "Thou art the Christ, the Son of the living God."

Then the Master replied, "Blessed art thou, Simon Barjona: for flesh and blood hath not revealed it unto thee, but my Father which is in heaven." (Matthew 16:13-17.)

Peter had received a revelation. He knew that Jesus was the Christ, the Savior of the world, the divine Son of God. Now, it could only have been a year or so after this incident that the Master turned to Peter with a rebuke. We do not know what it was that caused Him to rebuke Simon Peter, but He said:

> Simon, Simon, behold, Satan hath desired to have you, that he may sift you as wheat:
>
> But I have prayed for thee, that thy faith fail not: and when thou art converted, strengthen thy brethren. (Luke 22:31-32.)

Can you imagine the Lord saying this to His chief apostle, to the very man who had previously received a revelation as to the divine mission of the Lord? The Lord said to Peter that Satan just about had him, and that he had better go out and get converted. Well we might ask, "What does it mean to become converted?"—especially after we learn the Lord had suggested that Peter was becoming unconverted. In effect, the Lord is saying that the testimony we have today will not be our testimony of tomorrow. Our testimony is either going to grow and grow until it becomes as the brightness of the sun, or it is going to diminish to nothing, depending on what we do about it. Peter, somehow, was losing his testimony.

The greatest responsibility that a member of Christ's church has ever had is to become truly converted—and it is just as important to stay converted. But again I ask, what is conversion? Some clues are given by the Lord. In answering a question as to why He spoke in parables, He quoted a scripture from Isaiah:

> Make the heart of this people fat, and make their ears heavy, and shut their eyes; lest they see with their eyes, and hear with their ears, and understand with their heart, and convert, and be healed. (Isaiah 6:10.)

As you can see, one is converted when he sees with his eyes what he ought to see; when he hears with his ears what he ought to hear; and when he understands with his heart what he ought to understand. And what he ought to see, hear, and understand is truth—eternal truth—and then practice it. That is conversion. But when he fails to see, and fails to hear, and fails to understand truth and apply it in his life for some reason, then that man has lost his faith. He has lost his testimony because of something he has done. Remember, the Lord told Peter to go out and regain what he had lost.

A few years ago a prominent university professor joined the Church. When I asked him to speak before a group of New York businessmen and to explain why he had joined The Church of Jesus Christ of Latter-day Saints, he said to these men, "I'll tell you why I joined this church. I came to a time in my life when my heart told me things that my mind did not know. Then it was that I knew the gospel was true."

When we understand more than we know with our minds, when we understand with our hearts, then we know that the Spirit of the Lord is working upon us.

I once had a visit from a young Catholic priest who came with a stake missionary from Colorado. I asked him why he had come, and he replied, "I came to see you."

"Why?" I asked.

"Well," he said, "I have been searching for certain concepts that I have not been able to find. But I think I am finding them now in the Mormon community."

That led to a half-hour conversation. I told him, "Father, when your heart begins to tell you things that your mind does not know, then you are getting the Spirit of the Lord."

He smiled and said, "I think that's happening to me already."

"Then don't wait too long," I said to him.

A few weeks later I received a telephone call from him. He said, "Next Saturday I am going to be baptized a member of the Church, because my heart has told me things my mind did not know."

He was converted. He saw what he should have seen. He heard what he should have heard. He understood what he should have understood, and he was doing something about it. He had a testimony.

Speaking to persons with a testimony, the Lord has said:

> Therefore, hold up your light that it may shine unto the world. Behold I am the light which ye shall hold up—that which ye have seen me do. (3 Nephi 18:24.)

It is the Savior who provides direction for all who need it. The apostle John said of Him,

> That was the true Light, which lighteth every man that cometh into the world.
>
> In him was life; and the life was the light of men.
>
> And the light shineth in darkness; and the darkness comprehended it not. (John 1:9, 4, 5.)

That is the light that we have. Every one of us has been born with that light, the light of Christ, which lightens all of us who come into the world, and it never ceases to strive with us, to warn us, to guide us, as long as we are keeping the commandments of God. Thus, when we have a testimony, we are expected to use it for the benefit of others, as Peter was instructed: "When thou art converted, strengthen thy brethren."

All of us have so many, many opportunities to strengthen others. It may be our own brothers and sisters. It may be our friends. It may be a neighbor or a new acquaintance. It may even be our own parents. Now that's a great concept, isn't it—parents and youth strengthening one another. Let me show you what I mean.

The president of the Alberta Temple told me this incident. He said, "A group of young people came to the temple for the first time to do baptisms for the dead. After they had participated in two or three baptismal sessions and were about ready to go home, I suggested that they could come down to my office and I would attempt to answer any questions they might have. I talked to them about their own baptisms. I said, 'After your own baptism, you were told to receive the Holy Ghost, which means that the Holy Ghost will guide and bless you if you are worthy. If anyone should oppose you, or bring harm to you, you can overcome that opposition by the influence of the Holy Ghost.'

"I looked around and saw a pleasant young girl sobbing. She said, 'When I was baptized, my mother cursed me. Every time I would go out she was vile and called me wicked names. When I told her I was going to the temple, she profaned and said I was no daughter of hers. I have been fasting ever since I left home that here in the temple I would be given a guide and the power to overcome the opposition of my mother. I was going away disappointed. But now, at the last moment, you have given me the key.' A smile lit up on her face as she said, 'I am going to bring Mother within the influence of the power of the Holy Ghost which I have a right to enjoy.'"

Then the president said, "Weeks went by, and a letter came from this girl that said, 'When I returned home and entered the house, Mother greeted me similarly to the way she had when I left, by profaning. On other occasions I had fought back, but this time I walked over and put my arm around her shoulder and said, "Mother, I am not going to quarrel with you today. I want you to come over on the couch and sit down beside me. I want to tell you something." This surprised Mother. As we sat down, we touched cheeks so that in actuality the Spirit would emanate from me to her, and I bore my testimony. I told her what a wonderful experience I had had in the temple. And to my amazement, Mother burst into tears and begged my forgiveness.'

"The girl closed her letter by saying, 'We are now preparing Mother to be baptized a member of the Church.' "

"When thou art converted, strengthen thy brethren," said the Savior. That is my message to you, because it is the Savior's message. Our number one responsibility is to see that we are converted, and then to convert others.

I would pray that you could feel the love flowing from my soul to yours, and know of my deep compassion toward each of you as you face the problems of today. The time is here when each of you must stand on your own feet. Be converted, because no one can endure on borrowed light. You will have to be guided by the light within yourself. If you do not have it, you will not stand.

May the Lord bless you and clothe you with the armor of righteousness, that you might be able to stand steadfast through whatever trials may be yours in the days that lie ahead.

10

The Abundant Life

WE have a scripture recording the words of the Master: ". . . I am come that they might have life, and that they might have it more abundantly." (John 10:10.)

That scripture has been the text for certain economic philosophies that are with us today, and from that text has been coined the term "the abundant life," which has been used frequently to refer to a condition of plenty or sufficiency or a profuseness of the material things of life. But if we are to strip those philosophies of all their high-sounding phrases and explanations, we might describe them in this language: "Giving more and more to an individual in return for less and less from him."

As I think back over my life, I remember that these philosophies did not begin with the last few years. When I think of the first political campaigns that I, as a young boy, heard about—and fortunately we did not hear as much about them in those days as we hear about them today—I remember that some of the slogans of those days sounded very much like the kinds of philosophy we have today. I remember in one campaign there was one something like this: "We stand for a full dinner pail," and on another occasion, "We stand for a chicken in every pot," and still later, "Two cars in every garage." I remember picking up a magazine and seeing a picture of a family in a beautiful convertible, off to the movies, and underneath it said: "This is the American way of life." And more recently, we have had a philosophy, or slogan: "Full employment for everybody in America and a pint of milk for everybody in the world."

Now, I call these sayings to your attention—and you who are older than I can add other slogans along the same line—not to ridicule, but to call your attention to the fact that in this land, and perhaps other lands, we have been choosing as ideals these material benefits and we have called them the way to an abundant life.

In commenting about these things that seemingly have existed in America, the president of one of our great American universities said this: "But the ideal of comfort which is the best we have been able to think of for ourselves will never do as an aim for a world order. Men can never be comfortable enough: we can never have enough material goods, if material goods are what we want. Any world order with this ideal will be torn to pieces by the divisions to which it leads."

As long as it is assumed, then, that it is the duty of all of us to get all we can and make the ideal of comfort our goal in life, then we may expect a similar fate to that nation, or community, or that family which builds on such an ideal. They will certainly be torn to pieces by the divisions to which such an ideal will lead.

I think I would be safe in saying, and I believe you would agree with me, that perhaps never before in the history of the world has so much been said about the abundant life and so little effort expended in obtaining the essentials that make for an abundant life.

I should like to refer to the parable that preceded the Master's statement on the abundant life. These were His words:

> Verily, verily, I say unto you, He that entereth not by the door into the sheepfold, but climbeth up some other way, the same is a thief and a robber.
>
> Then said Jesus unto them again, Verily, verily, I say unto you, I am the door of the sheep.
>
> I am the door: by me if any man enter in, he shall be saved, and shall go in and out, and find pasture. (John 10:1, 7, 9.)

And then He closed His lesson with this statement:". . . I am come that they might have life, and that they might have it more abundantly." (John 10:10.)

To His disciples on another occasion He said: "I am the way, the truth, and the life: no man cometh unto the Father, but by me." (John 14:6.)

It was the same message that He gave to Nicodemus, who asked what he must do to be saved, and in reply the Master answered: "Except a man be born of water and of the Spirit, he cannot enter into the kingdom of God." (John 3:5.)

Those who seek for the abundant life in any other way, then, but by the way the Master has laid out in the gospel plan is "as a thief and a robber," to use the Master's words. But the tragedy is that he who does so rob is also the victim of his own robbery, and his own house is left to him desolate in the day of his great spiritual need. Such a one is poor indeed.

The scriptures have given us unmistakably a charted way for the living of the abundant life and the preparation therefor. It was the Apostle Paul who said to the Hebrews:

"Therefore leaving the principles of the doctrine of Christ, let us go on unto perfection. . . ." (Hebrews 6:1.)

In explaining what salvation means, the Prophet Joseph Smith declared:

> Salvation is nothing more nor less than to triumph over all our enemies and put them under our feet. And when we have power to put all enemies under our feet in this world, and a knowledge to triumph over all evil spirits in the world to come, then we are saved. . . . (*Teachings of the Prophet Joseph Smith,* p. 297.)

But apparently, as I read the scriptures, the Lord did not intend to convey that a fulness of the abundant life was attainable even in this life, for we find His saying in a revelation to the Prophet Joseph Smith: "Wherefore, fear not even unto death; for in this world your joy is not full, but in me your joy is full." (D&C 101:36.)

The apostle Peter reduced that teaching to a formula, a pattern, a way of life. These are his words:

> And beside this, giving all diligence, add to your faith virtue; and to virtue knowledge;
>
> And to knowledge temperance; and to temperance patience; and to patience godliness;
>
> And to godliness brotherly kindness; and to brotherly kindness charity.
>
> For if these things be in you, and abound, they make you that ye shall neither be barren nor unfruitful in the knowledge of our Lord Jesus Christ.
>
> But he that lacketh these things is blind, and cannot see afar off, and hath forgotten that he was purged from his old sins.
>
> Wherefore the rather, brethren, give diligence to make your calling and election sure: for if ye do these things, ye shall never fall:
>
> For so an entrance shall be ministered unto you abundantly into the everlasting kingdom of our Lord and Saviour Jesus Christ. (2 Peter 1:5-11.)

When I understand the full import of Peter's words, describing that way of life by which we might obtain that abundance, or in other words that "abundant entrance" into the kingdom of our Lord and Savior, Jesus Christ, I am made aware that we cannot obtain it by spiritual gratuities any more than we can obtain a temporal abundant life by receiving temporal gratuities, for the Lord declared: "Not every one that saith unto me, Lord, Lord, shall enter into the kingdom of heaven; but he that doeth the will of my Father which is in heaven." (Matthew 7:21.)

Only can an individual receive that joy and that abundant life whose life is patterned to the standards as laid down in the gospel of Jesus Christ. We have a splendid illustration that I should like to call to your attention as to how this might be obtained.

Saul of Tarsus was one who had been valiant and conscientiously engaged in trying to stamp out Christianity, which he believed to be a sect that was defiling the word of God. He even held the coats of the men who stoned Stephen, and having obtained letters of authority, was on his way to Damascus there to prosecute his work; it was about noonday:

> And as he journeyed, he came near Damascus: and suddenly there shined round about him a light from heaven:
>
> And he fell to the earth, and heard a voice saying unto him, Saul, Saul, why persecutest thou me?
>
> And he said, Who art thou, Lord? And the Lord said, I am Jesus whom thou persecutest: it is hard for thee to kick against the pricks.
>
> And he trembling and astonished said, Lord, what wilt thou have me to do? And the Lord said unto him, Arise, and go into the city, and it shall be told thee what thou must do. (Acts 9:3-6.)

Saul went and found Ananias, a humble man of God, and Ananias taught him the way to an abundant life. He baptized him and then sent him to the apostles, where he received his commission that sent him out to be one of the greatest missionaries among the gentiles, and we know him from that time forth as the Apostle Paul.

The rewards that came from a life of sacrifice and service are also illustrated in an incident in his life. You recall, he was now a prisoner on his way to Rome. As they put out from an island in the Mediterranean Sea, he had the impression that all would not be well, and they were hardly out of sight of land when a furious storm broke, and for fourteen days that frail ship was tossed about, and when, as the scriptures say, "neither sun nor stars in many days appeared, and no small tempest lay on us, all hope that we should be saved was then taken away." (Acts 27:20.)

Then it was that the Apostle Paul went down into a place by himself and prayed, and here are the words that are recorded in the scriptures which describe his experience:

> . . . after long abstinence Paul stood forth in the midst of them, and said, . . .
>
> And now I exhort you to be of good cheer: for there shall be no loss of any man's life among you, but of the ship.
>
> For there stood by me this night the angel of God, whose I am, and whom I serve,
>
> Saying, Fear not, Paul; thou must be brought before Caesar: and, lo, God hath given thee all them that sail with thee.

Then Paul quieted his shipmates with this testimony: "Wherefore, sirs, be of good cheer: for I believe God, that it shall be even as it was told me." (Acts 27:21-25.)

There we might find illustrated the essential steps toward the abundant life of which the Master spoke. The first step is to live the kind of life that permits us to receive the light of heaven, and a testimony that Jesus is a living reality and that He can speak to us. One possessed of such testimony, then, from the depths of his heart will say, as did Paul: "Lord, what wilt thou have me to do?"

Think about that, you who preside in the missions and the stakes of the Church, in the various organizations and priesthood quorums, those of us who sit in places in the presiding councils of the Church: Whenever we come to the selecting of an officer or the determining of policy for the welfare of Zion, how well it would be if always we would say, we who have that testimony of Jesus, "Heavenly Father, what wilt thou have me do?" If only we will remember that as fathers and mothers in dealing with a wayward child, if we will remember that when we sit in judgment upon the sinner, in all our business affairs, and the youth in his love affairs! May we who have the testimony remember that lesson of the Apostle Paul and from our hearts cry out to our Father: "Lord, what wilt thou have me do?"

And if we pray in real sincerity and faith, there will come back to us the answer to that prayerful inquiry. The answer has come oft repeated, time and time again, that all that we do should be done "with an eye single to the glory of God." What is the glory of God? The Lord told Moses, ". . . this is my work and my glory—to bring to pass the immortality and eternal life of man." (Moses 1:39.)

With that goal always before us—seeing every act of our lives, every decision we make, as patterned toward the development of a life that shall permit us to enter into the presence of the Lord, our Heavenly Father, to gain which is to obtain eternal life—how much more wisdom there would be in the many things of life. Cannot you see, mothers, that if yours is the responsibility to teach your little children that there is a Heavenly Father and that life has a purpose—and that purpose is to prepare to go back to His presence in a day not far distant—then when that child comes to a decision in the choice of educational subjects in school or any other decision he may face, he may well choose rightly.

If there should come a problem as to what kind of business a man should be engaged in, whether he should invest in this matter or that, whether he should marry this girl or that one, where he should marry, and how he should marry—when it comes to the prosecuting of the work to which we are assigned, how much more certainly will those decisions be if always we recall that all we do, and all the decisions we make, should be made with that eternal goal in mind: with an eye single to the ultimate glory of man in the celestial world.

If all our selfish motives, then, and all our personal desires and expediency would be subordinated to a desire to know the will of the Lord, one could have the companionship of heavenly vision. If our problems be too great for human intelligence or too much for human strength, we too, if we are faithful and appeal rightly unto the source of divine power, might have standing by us in our hour of peril or great need an angel of God. One who lives thus worthy of a testimony that God lives and that Jesus is the Christ, and who is willing to reach out to Him in constant inquiry to know if his course is approved, is the one who is living life to its full abundance here and is preparing for the celestial world, which is to live eternally with his Heavenly Father.

I bear you my humble testimony, as one of the humblest among you. I know there are powers that can draw close to one who fills his heart with love. I came to a night, some years ago, when on my bed I realized that before I could be worthy of the high place to which I had been called, I must love and forgive every soul that walked the earth. And in that time I came to know, and I received a peace, a direction, a comfort, and an inspiration that told me things to come and gave me impressions that I knew were from a divine source. I know that these things are true and that God lives, that Jesus is the Christ, and that each of us might live the abundant life by drawing thus close to Him.

11

A Sure Sound of the Trumpet

IN the early days of the Church Welfare Program, Elmer G. Petersen, who was then president of Utah State Agricultural College (now Utah State University) was on our agriculture committee with Elder John A. Widtsoe of the Council of the Twelve as the chairman. We had sent Brother Petersen out on some kind of an agricultural assignment, and when he came back he prefaced his report by a rather significant statement: "Well, I have discovered again something that I have already known. The members of this church are like soldiers in the ranks, and all they need is for someone to give them marching orders."

There is a scripture that seems to fit that theme, when the Apostle Paul cautioned the leaders among the Corinthians:

> For if the trumpet give an uncertain sound, who shall prepare himself to the battle?
>
> There are, it may be, so many kinds of voices in the world, and none of them is without signification.

Therefore if I know not the meaning of the voice, I shall be unto him that speaketh a barbarian, and he that speaketh shall be a barbarian unto me. (1 Corinthians 14:8, 10-11.)

Now, I would have you see three important truths from the Apostle Paul's statement. First, those who lead must have a certain, sure trumpet sound to their instructions—no wavering, no compromising, but down the middle of the road of truth. To be a leader, you have to be moving. I cannot conceive of anybody following a leader who isn't going anywhere, and that's what Paul is trying to say.

The second thing he says is that "there may be many kinds of voices in the world, and all of them have meaning or signification." Voices mean different things to different people.

And then the final thought: If I personally know not the meaning of the voice, "I shall be unto him that speaketh as a barbarian, and he that speaketh shall be a barbarian unto me." Leaders with clear, sharp understanding of their jobs, and the ability to give instructions and leadership direction, and those who have the ability to listen are vital in this program. Finally, we must expect that there is going to be confusion, that there always has been, and there always will be until the end of time, and that all these confusing voices mean different things to the different people who hear.

In a stake conference, a serviceman said something about the importance of trumpet calls to a military man. There is reveille at daybreak, which summons men to the day's duties. There is the trumpet call that means assembly, or to assemble or fall into military order. There is the mess call. (I suspect that is probably the first one that military men learn to understand. That's the call to meals.) There is the call that means forward march. There is the call that means a call to arms, to prepare for battle. And then there is taps, a signal to extinguish all lights in military quarters and to go to bed or to preserve silence; it is also used at a military burial.

One can imagine the utter confusion if a military commander were to fail to give correct instructions to the bugler. If the individuals in the military encampment were not taught sufficiently to understand each trumpet call, one can likewise fancy the confusion. It is this confusion in the Babel-like tower of contradictory voices among us today that I would like to make a few comments about and, if possible, to guide the thinking of our leaders and youth.

What is the formula for motivating our choice young men and women to right thinking and proper conduct, to know truth from untruth? What is the simple formula? I think I heard it when I was talking with a stake president about the choice of counselors. He pointed to a certain man and said, "Here is a man who doesn't do things because he wants to, but because they are right. I need that kind of man on my team."

Now, every one of us, so Mormon said, may know by the light of Christ, the spirit of Christ, which is given to every person that he may know good from evil. ". . . it is given unto you to judge," Moroni quotes his father as saying, "that ye may know good from evil; and the way to judge is as plain, that ye may know with a perfect knowledge, as the daylight is from the dark night." (Moroni 7:15.)

As I read that scripture again, I remembered an experience many years ago when a young man under the stress of circumstance with two others planned to falsify the payrolls of a government work project; each of them would get pay by answering the call to the same man's name who appeared on each of these jobs because of the confusion in the registration. When they were found out, this young man came to me, as many youths do after it is almost too late for help, and he wanted to ask some questions. He said, "Now what was the purpose of this money that was being paid out?"

I said, "It was to help the unemployed."

"Well, then I was helping to distribute the money, wasn't I?"

Of course I had to say, "Yes, I suppose you were."

He said, "You know that I needed this. You know that these other boys needed this. Now then, good resulted from my acts, didn't it?"

And I had to say, "Yes."

"Then why should what I did be called a sin or be called a crime if I was merely helping the government and good resulted from my act?"

I looked at him in amazement and replied, "If I did not know you had been raised in a Latter-day Saint home, I would not be surprised; but you have been taught that written by the finger of God on tablets of stone are the divine injunctions, 'Thou shalt not steal. Thou shalt not bear false witness. . . .' [Exodus 20:15-16.] That is what you have done. You have lied, and it is a sin before God; and if it is a sin, it is a crime before the law of this government."

What other confusing voices must we be aware of? Among the most cherished privileges in a free world are freedom of speech, freedom of the press, and freedom of assembly. But I ask you to consider freedom if the authors of one of our university publications, for example, were to attack the Church or to ridicule some of our church leaders, exercising freedom of the press, as they claim. They would be violating another freedom, the freedom to worship, of that church which is so attacked. The right to worship implies protection from those who abuse the freedom of the press or speech or assembly to malign another's religious prerogatives.

It is difficult to justify an unruly band of university students who demand the right to use and write obscene words on the campus, or to display nude and obscene pictures in the name of so-called art. It is hard to justify a professor who delivers a eulogy to an associate in which he takes occasion to make apostate and vulgar references to the Church whose youthful members comprise the majority of the student body, young people whose parents pay the greater part of the taxes that make up this very professor's salary. What an abuse of the right of free speech, the right of assembly, and the right of freedom of the press!

Some time ago I read a very excellent article written by a great educator in this country. This man said: "A medical doctor heading a commission on the study of alcoholism came out with the recommendation that school children be taught to drink liquor. He feels they are going to be drunkards anyway, and therefore they should be taught how to drink properly."

Now, isn't that a bright and wonderful observation from a medical doctor? This educator's answer to such nonsense is the same as every straight-thinking teacher and leader should make. The laws of some states require every teacher to instruct his pupils in the evils of alcohol; that's it, the *evils*—no "ifs," no "buts," no wavering of the "trumpet's sound." It is the evil of the drinking of alcohol that should be taught. Then this educator said, "Schools are not built or maintained to compromise with evil, and teaching children to drink is evil, no matter how you slice it."

We must make certain that in childhood, in family home evening, and in the Church our youth have been taught correct principles. Church doesn't begin with the youth of MIA, but it begins with the three-year-old and sometimes even earlier in the home. It's our experience that those who fall away from the Church might be put in two classes: first, those who are ignorant of the teachings of the doctrines and practices of the Church; and second, those who have sinned so they have lost their faith and their testimony. The Lord said, "And he that repents not, from him shall be taken even the light which he has received; for my Spirit shall not always strive with man, saith the Lord of Hosts." (D&C 1:33.)

The Lord said to another prophet, ". . . the Spirit of the Lord will not always strive with man. And when the Spirit ceaseth to strive with man then cometh speedy destruction, and this grieveth my soul." (2 Nephi 26:11.)

What is the way we must teach our youth to gain a testimony? A classic, one-sentence formula from Cyprian, one of the "apologists" just after the apostolic period, contains it all. Listen to what he said: "Into my heart, purified of all sin, there entered a light that came from on high and then suddenly, and in a marvelous manner, I saw certainty succeed doubt."

At the root of the individual testimony must be a righteous, pure life, else the Spirit cannot witness as to the divinity of the mission of the Lord or of this work in our day.

The Lord said through Amos the prophet, "Surely the Lord God will do nothing, but he revealeth his secret unto his servants the prophets." (Amos 3:7.) In our day he has put it in about the same language. He said: ". . . the arm of the Lord shall be revealed; and the day cometh that they who will not hear the voice of his servants, . . . neither give heed to the words of the prophets and apostles, shall be cut off from among the people." (D&C 1:14.)

We have the standard Church works. Why do we call them standard? If there is any teacher who teaches a doctrine that can't be substantiated from the standard church works—and I make one qualification, and that is unless that one be the President of the Church, who alone has the right to declare new doctrine—then you may know by that same token that such a teacher is but expressing his own opinion. If, on the other hand, you have someone teaching a doctrine that cannot be substantiated by the scriptures, and more than that, if it contradicts what is in the standard Church works, you may know that that person is teaching false doctrine, no matter what his position in this church may be. The President of the Church alone may declare the mind and will of God to His people. No officer nor any other church in the world has this high and lofty prerogative. When the President proclaims any such new doctrine, he will declare it to be a revelation from the Lord.

There have been times when even the President of the Church has not been moved upon by the Holy Ghost. There is, I suppose you'd say, a classic story of Brigham Young in the time when Johnston's army was on the move. The Saints were all inflamed, and President Young had his feelings whetted to fighting pitch. He stood up in the morning session of general conference and preached a sermon vibrant with defiance at the approaching army, declaring an intention to oppose them and drive them back. In the afternoon he rose and said that Brigham Young had been talking in the morning but the Lord was going to talk now. He then delivered an address the tempo of which was the exact opposite of the morning sermon.

Whether that happened or not, it illustrates a principle: that the Lord can move upon His people but they may speak on occasions their own opinions.

In our day the Lord has told us that we must live to enjoy the Spirit of the Lord. The most terrible thing that can happen to any one of us is to have had the Spirit of the Lord once and then to have lost it. So the Lord pleads with us: "The Holy Ghost shall be thy constant companion, and thy scepter an unchanging scepter of righteousness and truth; and thy dominion shall be an everlasting dominion, and without compulsory means it shall flow unto thee forever and ever." (D&C 121:46.)

Beautiful roses don't grow in a garden unless the rosebush has been planted in fertile soil, cultivated, watered, and fertilized by someone who loves roses. Just so, beautiful flowers of honesty, integrity, virtue, and loyalty do not blossom in an individual unless his feet have been planted in a firm, sure testimony of the Lord Jesus Christ.

Leaders, do you have the determination to excel? Are you willing to pay the price for excellence, to work everlastingly at your job whether you like it or not? Do you have faith in the righteous rightness of the thing you are doing? Do you have spiritual motivation? Someone said in a recent publication that men who possess the capacity for leadership are always among us, waiting in the wings, but it sometimes takes a great crisis to bring them to prominence. Selfless dedication, courage and conviction, fortitude, humanity, thorough homework, power of persuasion—these qualities are important, for from the ranks of little leaders come big leaders. We must never urge any young man with ambition to be so hasty in deciding that he doesn't have the stature for high leadership.

12

"Eye Hath Not Seen"

A *FEW* years ago a beautiful girl suffered humiliation and a shocking experience because of the betrayal of a man, and she became a victim of her sins. Shocking as that experience was, she felt she was fortified against a repetition of it, and yet that sin was repeated—not once, but more often. And sadly she recognized that her powers of resistance were diminishing with each experience. Then she added, as she sobbed out her story, "How can I obtain the strength to resist future temptations?"

I cannot think of a more important question. I have had time to think about it, and I am going to try to answer it a little more fully than I was able to when we talked.

A second experience is that of a young couple married a few years ago. The girl, heartbroken because of the unhappiness in her home, had visited an attorney and taken the preliminary steps toward a divorce. She had sought to invite her husband to have an interview with one of the local Church leaders but he had steadfastly refused, and so she came asking if I would meet with them. I invited her and her husband to be at a stake conference where I was to be in attendance, so that we could arrange a time to sit down together. They came up at the close of the conference, where there had been a marvelous spirit. There, with their arms around each other and with my arms about both of them, I heard them say, with tears streaming down their cheeks, "Brother Lee, after the wonderful spirit that we have felt here in this conference today, it is unlikely that we will have need to talk further with you."

It's the comfort of that second incident that I would like the young girl of the first experience to catch; and having found that, she will have found in part the realization of the strength for which she seeks.

"No one," someone has said, "with a heart full of hate can find God." Just so, no one with lust in his heart can experience a pure, fully sacred love. No one who covets what belongs to another can be truly honest, and no one who is envious or jealous can ever enjoy the thrill of sacrificing for the welfare of others. But to get the full meaning of that, may I turn it about and say that no one who knows God can have a heart full of hate. No one can have a pure, sacred, holy love and at the same time have an unholy lust in his heart. No truly honest person can covet what belongs to another, and no one who has the thrill of doing things for others, unselfishly, can ever be envious or jealous of that other person.

The Apostle Paul said something that was in reality a quotation from the prophet Isaiah:

> But as it is written, Eye hath not seen, nor ear heard, neither have entered into the heart of man, the things which God hath prepared for them that love him. (1 Corinthians 2:9.)

Sometimes that has been taken to mean blessings hereafter, and too little thought has been given that those great and wonderful blessings can apply to us here and now. And it is about some of those things and an additional quotation from Isaiah that I would have you keep in mind as I review some of the wonderful experiences and blessings that we here can enjoy that no one, outside of those who do enjoy them, can fully appreciate. This is what Isaiah said:

> But now, O Lord, thou art our father; we are the clay, and thou our potter; and we all are the work of thy hand. (Isaiah 64:8.)

I've read that verse many times but had not received the full significance until I was down in Mexico a few years ago at Telacapaca, where the people mold clay into various kinds of pottery. There I saw them take clay that had been mixed by crude, primitive methods, the molder wading in the mud to mix it properly. Then it was put upon a potter's wheel and the potter began to fashion the intricate bits of pottery, which he was to place on the market. And as we watched, we saw occasionally, because of some defect in the mixing, the necessity for pulling the whole lump of clay apart and throwing it back in to be mixed over again, and sometimes the process had to be repeated several times before the mud was properly mixed.

With that in mind, I began to see the meaning of this scripture. Yes, we too have to be tried and tested by poverty, by sickness, by the death of loved ones, by temptation, sometimes by the betrayal of supposed friends, by affluence and riches, by ease and luxury, by false educational ideas, and by the flattery of the world. A father, explaining this matter to his son, said:

> And to bring about his eternal purposes in the end of man, after he had created our first parents, and the beasts of the field and the fowls of the air, and in fine, all things which are created, it must needs be that there was an opposition; even the forbidden fruit in opposition to the tree of life; the one being sweet and the other bitter. (2 Peter 2:15.)

It was the Prophet Joseph Smith who said, speaking of this refining process, that he was like a huge, rough stone rolling down the mountainside, and the only polishing he got was when some rough corner came in contact with something else, knocking off a corner here and a corner there. But, he said, "Thus will I become a polished shaft in the quiver of the Almighty."

So, we must be refined; we must be tested in order to prove the strength and power that are in us.

Now, what are the blessings that are so great that "eye hath not seen, nor ear heard" the magnitude thereof? I'd like to talk about five wonderful blessings that can be enjoyed by all who have been born into this church or who have come in as baptized members through conversion.

The first endowment of spiritual power that each of us has, as do all who are born upon this earth, is spoken of in the scriptures as the "true light, which lighteth every man that cometh into the world." (John 1:9.) This is what the Lord said in a revelation concerning this spirit:

> And the Spirit giveth light to every man that cometh into the world; and the Spirit enlighteneth every man through the world, that hearkeneth to the voice of the Spirit. (D&C 84:46.)

That means that every soul who walks the earth, wherever he lives, in whatever nation he may have been born, no matter whether he be in riches or in poverty, had at birth an endowment of that first light which is called the Light of Christ, the Spirit of Truth, or the Spirit of God—that universal light of intelligence with which every soul is blessed. Moroni spoke of that Spirit when he said:

> For behold, the Spirit of Christ is given to every man, that he may know good from evil; wherefore, I show unto you the way to judge; for every thing which inviteth to do good, and to persuade to believe in Christ, is sent forth by the power and gift of Christ; wherefore ye may know with a perfect knowledge it is of God. (Moroni 7:16.)

That is the first safeguard we may have. If we live true to that Spirit, we will know with a certainty whether a thing is of God or whether it is of evil. There will be a warning and a preparation to withstand, if we will only give heed to the enlightenment of that Spirit of intelligence.

The next blessing comes when a baby, probably within a few weeks after birth, is taken to the fast meeting in the ward where his parents live, and there his father or others holding the holy priesthool take him in their arms to give a father's blessing. In that blessing perhaps words something like these are used: "You are blessed to receive strength and vitality in body and in mind. You are blessed to have wise and prudent guidance and a desire to advance and grow in the kingdom."

As a child grows older, at the age of eight, when he is judged to have come to the age of accountability, or at the time of a person's conversion and baptism into the Church, he is given the opportunity of being baptized of water and, following that, a baptism of Spirit by the laying on of hands. By this experience three things happen: (1) He has a reclamation from the darkness, or the first death, which has been suffered by all the children of Adam and Eve since the time of the Fall. (2) By that process he gains entrance into the kingdom of God and the initiatory steps necessary for entrance into the celestial kingdom, on condition that he keep himself a fit temple in which the Holy Ghost can dwell. (3) He is also given the right to receive the gift of the Holy Ghost, one of the Godhead, a companionship that can be enjoyed and that gives him special gifts and special endowments of power as he lives and cultivates his worthiness to receive its holy promptings.

Perhaps the next thing, when he grows a little older, if he has listened to counsel and his parents have likewise followed wise counsel, he is taken to a patriarch in the

Church and there given a patriarchal blessing. President Karl G. Maeser spoke of the patriarchal blessings as "paragraphs from the book of your possibilities." If we read our patriarchal blessings, we will see what the spirit of prophecy has held up to us as to what each of us can become.

Another blessing that can come is a father's blessing, which can help us face some of life's greatest challenges. One of the sweetest experiences of my life came to me when my own oldest daughter, then a university student and faced with some of life's greatest decisions, came to my office and asked if I would give her a father's blessing.

Other gifts and blessings have been vouchsafed to us if we are willing to accept responsibility in the Church. We have a process we call setting apart: that is, the commission of certain gifts and endowments of power and the right to enjoy inspiration when one is ordained to the priesthood or set apart for an auxiliary office or set apart to go on a mission. The significance of these blessings is indicated in what the Lord said to Edward Patridge when he was about to have conferred upon him the Holy Ghost: "And I will lay my hand upon you by the hand of my servant Sidney Rigdon, and you shall receive . . . the Holy Ghost. . . ." (D&C 36:2.)

And so, the next thing a person must do if he wants to be safe is to keep active in the Church, and to have, by the setting apart of those who preside over him, the endowment of special gifts that will help to keep him strong in the faith.

The only place on earth where we can receive the fulness of the blessings of the priesthood is in the holy temple. That is the only place where, through holy ordinances, we can receive that which will qualify us for exaltation in the celestial kingdom.

Now may I look on the negative side of this question for a moment? May I call five great prophets of the Book of Mormon to witness to one of the most tragic experiences that can come to individuals—to have the Lord withdraw His Spirit from us. And when he speaks of His Spirit, it isn't just the Holy Ghost, because many of those spoken of by the prophets had not received the gift of the Holy Ghost. This Spirit to which I refer is the Light of Christ. When withdrawn, it becomes difficult for us to pray, to have direction and guidance, to withstand evil. From the prophet Nephi we read:

> For the Spirit of the Lord will not always strive with man. . . . then cometh destruction, and this grieveth the soul. (2 Nephi 26:11.)

The prophet Alma made this comment:

> And thus we can plainly discern, that after a people have been once enlightened by the Spirit of God, and have had great knowledge of things pertaining to righteousness, and then have fallen away into sin and transgression, they become more hardened, and thus their state becomes worse than though they had never known these things. (Alma 24:30.)

From the prophet Helaman:

> Because of the hardness of the hearts of the people of the Nephites, except they repent, I will take away my word from them, and I will withdraw my Spirit from them, and I will suffer them no longer, and I will turn the hearts of their brethren against them. (Helaman 13:8.)

From the prophet Mormon:

> For behold, the Spirit of the Lord hath already ceased to strive with their fathers; and they are without Christ and God in the world; and they are driven about as chaff before the wind. (Mormon 5:16.)

And finally, from the book of Ether:

> And the brother of Jared repented of the evil which he had done, and did call upon the name of the Lord for his brethren who were with him. And the Lord said unto him: I will forgive thee and thy brethren of their sins; but thou shalt not sin any more, for ye shall remember that my Spirit will not always strive with man; wherefore, if ye will sin until ye are fully ripe ye shall be cut off from the presence of the Lord. . . . (Ether 2:15.)

This means the withdrawing of that vital light which all could have enjoyed if they had kept the commandments.

Now, may I take another example to impress how much further one may go. One day there came to my office a man who a few years before had been excommunicated from the Church because of a very serious transgression. After these years of sad, humiliating, tragic experiences, he is wondering how he can find his way back into the Church. One might ask, "Why should he have been excommunicated?"

The more we give to a person in the Church, the more the Lord expects of him. We wouldn't baptize an individual unless we are assured that that individual has repented of his sins. We wouldn't think of conferring the Holy Ghost upon him unless we felt that he was prepared to receive it. We wouldn't give to him the holy priesthood, which would only be a burden he is not prepared to carry, unless he was worthy of it. And so it is when one has sinned so seriously that to hold further membership or to hold the holy priesthood would be as a stumbling block and burden rather than a blessing. In the wisdom of the Lord, these privileges are taken from him that he might be ground as "clay in the hands of the potter," again tried and tested, until he is again worthy to receive these holy blessings.

This man who had been excommunicated had attended a stake conference shortly before he came to see me. One of the General Authorities was there and said, "One of the most terrible things that you can experience is to lose the Spirit of the Lord." This excommunicant said to himself, "How does he know, unless he has sinned as I have? How does a General Authority know?" Well, he reasoned it out in his mind that maybe one in the General Authority's position can know vicariously, and maybe he has had experiences with those who have lost the Spirit, so that he knows. With these things on his mind, he went home and began to write, and he put in my hands the results of his thinking. This statement is one of the saddest things that I have read in a long time. This man had been a teacher, and he said:

> While I was enjoying the Spirit of the Holy Ghost, I could read the scriptures and the unfoldment of truths would come before me, and I was thrilled. That power is gone today. That day . . . I heard that terrible word in the high council trial, 'You are hereby excommunicated,' it was as though a pall of darkness fell, and now instead of light, there is doubt and wavering in my faith. I am wondering and I am struggling without that light. I used to be able to kneel down and get a tremendous lift from my prayer. Even while I was sinning, even up to the point of my excommunication, I god some comfort from it, but now it is as though a dome of steel is over my head, and I seem not to be able to pray. The spirit that leads to the presence of our Father has been lost.
>
> I used to enjoy performing the ordinances of the Church, especially in behalf of my own children—to bless them, to baptize them, to confirm them, to ordain them to the priesthood; and now to have to stand by while some other takes my place has been one of the saddest experiences that has come to me. And, of course, I have been refused the privilege of going to the temple. I no longer can go there and enjoy the sweet peace. I stand as though I had never been within those sacred walls. When I go to sacrament meeting, I can't partake of the sacrament. I have lost the respect of my family. My children, including a son now grown, tolerate me, but I know that deep in their hearts there is a shame because they bear the name of a father who hasn't lived worthily.
>
> But the most serious of all my reflections has come when I have contemplated death. Years ago I used to think of death as a contemplation into a great life—into the presence of the Lord. Now when I think about it, I have a feeling of horror, and for the first time I know what the scripture means when it says: "And it shall come to pass that those that die in me shall not taste of death, for it shall be sweet unto them, And they that die not in me, wo unto them, for their death is bitter." (D&C 42:46-47.)
>
> I had heard the warnings of these and other unpleasant conditions that would result when the Spirit of the Lord was withdrawn because of transgression. The warnings have been given many times by the General Authorities as they have come to our meetings to counsel us. How often I failed to heed their warning! Now I am being taught the correctness of their words by the most costly of all teachers, experience. I know that their warnings were inspired. I know now that the conditions they said would follow in the darkness that comes with the loss of the Spirit to transgressors were as sure as the night follows the day. I add my

warning, as one who is being taught by sorrowful, costly experience, to that of the leaders and give testimony that they know whereof they speak. It is given in hope that someone will be moved to heed the counsel of these wise men before he too has regrets that cannot be overcome and sorrows that cannot be assuaged.

How thankful we should be for the commandments of the Lord and the wonderful guidelines He has given us to help us be worthy of the blessings of the Spirit! Health and happiness are what our Father in heaven wants for us, and that is why He has given us commandments to keep, and not for any other reason. Health and happiness and success are what our parents want for us, and that is why they give us counsel and guidance, and not for any other reason. We have one earthly body that must last for a lifetime. Our Maker planned it that way. He knows what is good for us. He knows what will give us health and happiness and success and peace inside ourselves. That is why He told us how to live, and that is why He has told us how to leave some things alone.

In the book of Psalms we read the prayer of one who had sinned seriously and knew whereof he spoke:

> The law of the Lord is perfect, converting the soul: the testimony of the Lord is sure, making wise the simple.
>
> The statutes of the Lord are right, rejoicing the heart: the commandment of the Lord is pure, enlightening the eyes.
>
> The fear of the Lord is clean, enduring for ever: the judgments of the Lord are true and righteous altogether.
>
> More to be desired are they than gold, yea, than much fine gold: sweeter also than honey and the honeycomb.
>
> Moreover by them is thy servant warned: and in keeping of them there is great reward.
>
> Who can understand his errors? cleanse thou me from secret faults.
>
> Keep back thy servant also from presumptuous sins; let them not have dominion over me: then shall I be upright, and I shall be innocent from the great transgression.

Let the words of my mouth, and the meditation of my heart, be acceptable in thy sight, O Lord, my strength, and my redeemer. (Psalm 19:7-14.)

If those who have transgressed will memorize that and let that be the prayer of their hearts, we will pray for them, we'll uphold them, we'll sustain them; and God in heaven, who hears their pious cry of anguish in the hours of their repentance, will wash clean their sins in the atoning blood of the Lord and Savior of the world.

God grant to all of the youth of Zion the answer to the query of the beautiful girl I spoke of earlier: How can I gain the vital strength necessary to resist temptation? Yes, it is from spiritual experiences such as these that youth may gain the spirit power, the heart power necessary to withstand temptation. And if little troubles come, bitterness overtakes them, differences arise in their homes, if they will only go to the places where the Lord is pouring out His Spirit and will receive the strength necessary to make them love instead of hate, then they will learn a lesson early that perhaps will forestall the future's sad years.

O youth of Zion, the noblest of young manhood and young womanhood who walk the earth today, I beseech you: Be loyal to the royal within you, as children of the saints of the Most High God, for I bear you my solemn testimony that these are the blessings of which the prophet Isaiah spoke and of which the Apostle Paul spoke when he said, "Eye hath not seen, nor ear heard, neither have entered into the heart of man, the things which God hath prepared for them that love him."

Section Three

REVELATION

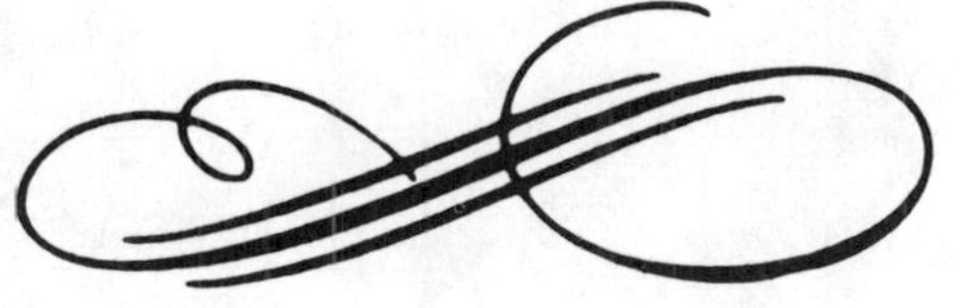

13

The Rock of Revelation

I BELIEVE now I am beginning to understand what the Master meant when He spoke to Peter after Peter had declared his testimony of the divinity of the Savior. The Master had told him that this was a revelation from God, and then added,

> And I say also unto thee, That thou art Peter and upon this rock I will build my church; and the gates of hell shall not prevail against it. (Matthew 16:18.)

There are those with limited or little understanding who believe that that statement rufutes our teaching that there has been an apostasy. They say, "If there was an apostasy, then the gates of hell did prevail against the church, contrary to the words of the Savior to Peter."

As I have thought of the true meaning of that statement, I have said to myself, "Oh, how great is the wisdom of God as contrasted with the foolishness of men!"

What was the purpose of our Father concerning us

and His work? He declared it to Moses: ". . . this is my work and my glory—to bring to pass the immortality and eternal life of man." (Moses 1:39.)

It was John who said that Jesus was "the Lamb slain from the foundation of the world" (Revelation 13:8) or, in other words, Jesus was prepared for an atonement; His sacrifice was to be made as a ransom for all of those who would obey Him and keep His commandments.

The Prophet Joseph Smith, in speaking about this matter, said this:

> The great Jehovah contemplated the whole of the events connected with the earth, pertaining to the plan of salvation, before it rolled into existence, or ever "the stars of morning sang together" for joy; the past, the present, and the future were and are, with Him, one eternal "now". . . . He knows the situation of both the living and the dead, and has made ample provision for their redemption, according to their several circumstances, and the laws of the kingdom of God, whether in this world, or in the world to come. (*Teachings of the Prophet Joseph Smith,* p. 220.)

That plan, which had been laid in the heavens before the foundations of the world were laid, contemplated a testing in the spirit world. It contemplated the plan of salvation given in various dispensations of the gospel here upon the earth.

It was not God who sealed the heavens following a dispensation of the gospel. It was man. Hence, we are to believe that there would have been but one dispensation beginning with Adam and reaching down to now, had it not been for the wickedness of men.

That plan contemplated the preaching of the gospel to those who were in the spirit world and who departed this life without having had ample opportunity of hearing the gospel. It contemplated the vicarious work to be carried on, in behalf of those who died without that knowledge, in holy temples here in order that they might be judged as though they had heard the gospel here in the flesh.

The gates of hell would have prevailed if Satan had been victorious in the war in heaven, and if his plan, which would have nullified free agency, had been the order. The gates of hell would have prevailed had there ever been a time when the power to administer the saving ordinances of the gospel was not in each dispensation of the gospel upon the earth.

The gates of hell would have prevailed had the gospel not been taught to the spirits in prison and to those who had not had ample opportunity to receive the gospel here in its fulness. It would have prevailed if there were not a vicarious work for the dead, and had it not been instituted to provide for those in the spirit world who desire to accept the gospel.

The gates of hell would have prevailed were it not for other vicarious work pertaining to the exaltation that those who accept the gospel might receive, ordinances for both the living and the dead.

Now, as I think of that plan, so perfect in its conception, it is clear that this plan could not have existed except for revelations of the living God. So we begin to understand what the Lord meant when He said to Peter, ". . . upon this rock I will build my church; and the gates of hell shall not prevail against it." He was speaking of the revelation of the Lord to His authorized servants, and all the forces of hell combined could not prevent it.

Several years ago while I was serving as a missionary, I came to the door of a woman who belonged to an apostate faction that fell away after the death of the Prophet Joseph Smith. For a considerable time we had a rather spirited discussion, although not unfriendly, in which she argued her case and stated that we, the Latter-day Saints, and not her faction, were the apostates from the truth.

As we talked on into the afternoon, there came an interesting turn to our conversation. It developed that this couple had had but one child, a little boy, who, when about seven years of age, was stricken with an incurable disease. When he became eight years old, the age of accountability, he was still sick, and at nine or shortly thereafter he passed away, still unable to be taken into the waters of baptism.

Now, they accepted the revelation of the Lord through the Prophet Joseph Smith that at eight years of age, the age of accountability, children are to be baptized, except for which they should not enter into the kingdom of heaven.

"Now," she asked, "what do you think we ought to do for our child?"

I replied: "Oh, that is easy. Have him baptized for in the temple. That is what temples are for."

"But," she said, "we have no temple."

Then there came into my mind a scripture in which the Lord said:

> Now the great and grand secret . . . and the *summum bonum* of the whole subject that is lying before us, consists in obtaining the powers of the Holy Priesthood. For him to whom these keys are given there is no difficulty in obtaining a knowledge of facts in relation to the salvation of the children of men, both as well for the dead as for the living. (D&C 128:11.)

As I thought about her plight, I realized that the gates of hell had prevailed against her church because the keys and the power to reveal knowledge from heaven were not to be found in that church.

In other words, the Lord said to Joseph Smith what He said to Peter and what He has said to every prophet in every dispensation. He has given to each the keys to the kingdom of heaven and the power to receive revelation in order that the gates of hell shall not prevail against His plan.

What He said to Peter was tantamount to saying to Joseph, in essence, "And I say unto thee, thou art Joseph, and upon this rock I will build my church; and the gates of hell shall not prevail against it."

What He said to Joseph might well have been said to Peter: "I give unto thee the keys to the kingdom of heaven, for he to whom these keys are given shall have no difficulty in obtaining a knowledge of both the salvation of the living and the dead."

The importance of revelation on which this church was to be founded was again impressed on the day the Church was organized, when the Lord said, not just to those few who were then members, but also to all of us who have since been members:

> Wherefore, meaning the church, thou shalt give heed unto all his words [meaning the words of the President of the Church, the prophet of the Lord] and commandments which he shall give unto you as he receiveth them, walking in all holiness before me;
>
> For his word ye shall receive, as if from mine own mouth, in all patience and faith.
>
> For by doing these things the gates of hell shall not prevail against you; yea, and the Lord God will disperse the powers of darkness from before you and cause the heavens to shake for your good, and his name's glory. (D&C 21:4-6.)

In other words, the Lord has said it was not only important that there be revelation to the Church through His mouthpiece, the one who held the keys, but His church must also be founded on personal revelation, that every member of the Church who has been baptized and has received the Holy Ghost must be admonished so to live that each might receive a personal testimony and a witness of the divine calling of him who was called to lead as the president of the Church so that he will accept those words and that counsel as if from the mouth of the Lord Himself. Otherwise, the gates of hell would prevail against that individual.

It was exactly that meaning that the Apostle Paul intended to convey when he wrote to the Ephesians, "And he gave some, apostles; and some, prophets; and some, evangelists; and some, pastors and teachers." (Ephesians 4:11.)

In other words, He organized the Church and set up the proper officers, "that we henceforth be no more children, tossed to and fro and carried about with every wind of doctrine, by the sleight of men, and cunning craftiness, whereby they lie in wait to deceive." (Ephesians 4:14.) Upon this rock, the rock of revelation, to individuals who have the power of the Holy Ghost—revelation from God to His church—the Lord in wisdom has designed that therefore the gates of hell shall not prevail against it.

In the midst of travail and suffering the Lord sent this word of comfort to the Prophet Joseph:

> God shall give unto you knowledge by his Holy Spirit, yea, by the unspeakable gift of the Holy Ghost, that has not been revealed since the world was until now;
>
> According to that which was ordained in the midst of the Council of the Eternal God of all other gods before this world was, that should be reserved unto the finishing and the end thereof, when every man shall enter into his eternal presence and into his immortal rest. (D&C 121:26, 32.)

Thus the rock of revealed knowledge has built the Church, and the gates of hell have never prevailed against it. With that overpowering thought that the plan of the Almighty has been so laid that never has Satan been able to shake it, how we should rejoice at the word of the Lord to Joseph when He said:

> . . . What power can stay the heavens? As well might man stretch forth his puny arm to stop the Missouri river in its decreed course, or to turn it up stream, as to hinder the Almighty from pouring down knowledge from heaven upon the heads of the Latter-day Saints. (D&C 121:33.)

I am grateful to realize that this is His church. We have at the head of this church an earthly head who presides as the president thereof, the mouthpiece of God. In this day to those who will believe and will listen to counsel, the gates of hell shall never prevail. Those who die without a knowledge will have the right to hear that truth in the spirit world, and if they accept it, work may be done vicariously that they might be judged and blessed even as though they had accepted it in the flesh.

Thanks be to God that the devil's power has never prevailed against His plan of continued revelation to His servants, and never will prevail so long as the earth shall stand, for the gospel plan was laid in heaven and will continue throughout the eternities for the purpose of bringing about immortality and eternal life.

14

Revelation and You

SEVERAL years ago, we had a visit from an eminent civil engineer from the East who was entertained by a rather prominent man in the Church. After this man had left to go home, our brother said, "Do you know what this civil engineer said to me? Said he, 'You know, I could almost accept membership in this church. I thrill with the things that you are doing, your wonderful education system, the welfare program, your fine community life, wonderful social life, and so with all of your virtues. If you would do without just one thing that you claim, then I could accept everything else.'" Our brother asked, "What is that one thing?" And the man replied, "If you would do away with this principle of revelation which you claim, I could become a member of the Church." Then our brother made a startling remark: "I wonder if we shouldn't do something about that."

Elder John A. Widtsoe of the Council of the Twelve once told of a discussion he had with a group of stake officers. In the course of the discussion someone said to him, "Brother Widtsoe, how long has it been since the Church received a revelation?" Brother Widtsoe rubbed his chin thoughtfully and said in reply, "Oh, probably since last Thursday." I think that surprised the people who asked.

Another example grows out of a discussion I had with one of our brilliant young educators who was rather disturbed by the claims of some that what is spoken by the brethren in presiding authority is the mind and the will of the Lord. He told of having a discussion with one of the teachers at Brigham Young University. They were discussing a talk that had been given at the university shortly before that by President J. Reuben Clark, Jr., on international relations, entitled "Our Dwindling Sovereignty." The teacher had said regarding this talk, according to the young educator's report, "Now that's the mind and the will of the Lord because it came from one of the First Presidency, and if you don't accept what President Clark said, then you're not in harmony with the will of the Lord on this subject."

This had displeased the educator, and he quarreled with it. Later he asked me, "What do you think about it?"

I replied, "Well, I remember President Clark prefaced his remarks that night by saying something to this effect: 'Now I take sole responsibility for what I am going to say to you tonight. I'm not speaking for anyone else.'" I told him that I had had an interview with a prospective Church teacher, preparatory to his going out into one of our seminaries. As I talked to him about his faith and his loyalties, he said, "I don't agree with all that the General Authorities say. For instance, I didn't agree with what President Clark said at the university." I wanted to say to that young man, "Well, I suppose it would be difficult for a pygmy to get the viewpoint of a giant." But I didn't say that—that would have been a little harsh. What I did say was, "You know, when I have the opportunity of sitting under the influence of a great international lawyer, an expert in his field, that's the time when I spend all my time listening and not too much time talking. So far as I'm concerned, I listen. I am not in a position to criticize."

Prefaced by those three incidents, I should like now to have you think through a few matters regarding revelation. Through the scriptures this phrase is often repeated: "He that hath ears to hear, let him hear." All of us are not so blessed to hear all that we ought to hear. Let me recall to your minds a few incidents in the scriptures.

There was an occasion, just before the crucifixion and during what we have styled the "Passion Week" when the Master was in the temple, and the Greeks came among the people, apparently anxious to see Him because He had gained such notoriety. There, in that place sacred to Him, the Master kneeled down and prayed, asking the Lord to let this hour pass, and then He said, "Father, glorify thy name." The answer came, "I have both glorified it, and will glorify it again." (John 12:28.) There were some people who heard it and said that it had thundered; there were a few who said an angel of the Lord had spoken to Him. You see, there were some who had ears to hear, but they didn't hear.

On another occasion you will recall that the Master prayed, "I thank thee, O Father, . . . because thou hast hid these things from the wise and prudent, and hast revealed them unto babes." (Matthew 11:25.) This suggests the same thought, that no matter how wise and prudent in worldly things men may be, yet there may be precious things hidden from their gaze because they do not see, neither do they hear.

 You will recall the occasion when the Apostle Paul

was converted; he was on his way to Damascus with writs of authority to further persecute the saints at that place. Remember how he was stricken down by a bright light that overshadowed him and blinded him, and a voice spoke out of heaven and said, "Saul, Saul, why persecutest thou me?" (Acts 9:4.) And Paul, in telling about the incident, says, "And they that were with me, saw indeed the light, . . . but they heard not the voice of him that spoke to me." (Acts 22:9.) These also had ears to hear but they heard nothing.

As I thought of those scriptures, I remembered an illustration that Brother Widtsoe related in a general conference. He said, "When God speaks, some of us fail to so live that we understand the message that comes from eternity."

I know some people who will say, "How can I conduct my life so as to be responsive to the message that comes from an unseen world?" There's an old illustration that bears on this subject: We may take a rod of iron and place it with some filings without apparently causing any change—the rod is not magnetic. But if we wrap that rod with a wire carrying an electric current, it becomes a magnet. Though the rod has not changed in shape and width and length, it has undergone a deep change. It has become changed so that it attracts iron filings or whatever else is subject to magnetic action. Just so, if each of us could wrap ourselves in obedience to God's love and live as we should, a wonderful change would be effected in us, and we too could then hear the messages from the unseen world.

I had that illustrated some years ago when I served as a stake president. We had a very grievous case that had to come before the high council and the stake presidency that resulted in the excommunication of a man who had harmed a lovely young girl. After a nearly all-night session that resulted in that action, I went to my office rather weary the next morning and was confronted by a brother of this man whom we had had on trial the night before. This man said, "I want to tell you that my brother wasn't guilty of what you charged him with."

"How do you know he wasn't guilty?" I asked.

"Because I prayed, and the Lord told me he was innocent," the man answered.

I asked him to come into the office and we sat down, and I asked, "Would you mind if I ask you a few personal questions?"

He said, "Certainly not."

"How old are you?"

"Forty-seven."

"What priesthood do you hold?"

He said he thought he was a teacher.

"Do you keep the Word of Wisdom?"

"Well, no." He used tobacco, which was obvious.

"Do you pay your tithing?"

He said, "No"—and he didn't intend to as long as that blankety-blank-blank man was the bishop of the Thirty-Second Ward.

I said, "Do you attend your priesthood meetings?"

He replied, "No, sir!" and he didn't intent to as long as that man was bishop.

"You don't attend your sacrament meetings either?"

"No, sir."

"Do you have your family prayers?" and he said no.

"Do you study the scriptures?" He said well, his eyes were bad, and he couldn't read very much.

I then said to him: "In my home I have a beautiful instrument called a radio. When everything is in good working order we can dial it to a certain station and pick up the voice of a speaker or a singer all the way across the continent or sometimes on the other side of the world, bringing them into the front room as though they were almost right there. But after we have used it for a long time, the little delicate instruments or electrical devices on the inside called radio tubes begin to wear out. When one of them wears out, we may get some static—it isn't so clear. Another wears out, and if we don't give it attention, the sound may fade in and out. And if another one wears out—well, the radio may sit there looking quite like it did before, but because of what has happened on the inside, we can hear nothing.

"Now," I said, "you and I have within our souls something like what might be said to be a counterpart of those radio tubes. We might have what we call a 'go-to-sacrament-meeting' tube, a 'keep-the-Word-of-Wisdom' tube, a 'pay-your-tithing' tube, a 'have-your-family-prayers' tube, a 'read-the-scriptures' tube, and, as one of the most important—one that might be said to be the master tube of our whole soul—we have what we might call the 'keep-yourselves-morally-clean' tube. If one of these becomes worn out by disuse or inactivity—if we fail to keep the commandments of God—it has the same effect upon our spiritual selves that a worn-out tube has in a radio.

"Now, then," I said, "fifteen of the best-living men in the Pioneer Stake prayed last night. They heard the evidence and every man was united in saying that your brother was guilty. Now you, who do none of these things, you say you prayed and got an opposite answer. How would you explain that?"

Then this man gave an answer that I think was a classic. He said, "Well, President Lee, I think I must have gotten my answer from the wrong source." And, you know, that's just as great a truth as we can have. We get our answers from the source of the power we list to obey. If we're following the ways of the devil, we'll get answers from the devil. If we're keeping the commandments of God, we'll get our answers from God.

I listened to an inspired sermon at Brigham Young University by President Clark, who had been asked to give an answer to the question, "Was the Welfare Program a Revelation?" His answer to that was interesting, but in the process he analyzed the various kinds of revelation that come. He talked first of a theophany, which he defined as an experience where the Father or the Son or both put in a personal appearance, or speak directly to man. Moses talked with the Lord face to face; Daniel had a theophany, or personal appearance. When the Master came to John the Baptist for baptism, you remember, a voice spoke out of the heavens and said, "This is my beloved Son, in whom I am well pleased." At the conversion of Paul, to which I have made reference, there was also a personal appearance, and an audible voice was heard. At the transfiguration, when Peter, James, and John went with the Master to a high mountain where Moses and Elias appeared before them, again a voice was heard speaking out of the heavens, saying, "This is my beloved Son, in whom I am well pleased. . . ." (Matthew 17:5.)

Perhaps the greatest of all theophanies of our time was the appearance of the Father and the Son to the Prophet Joseph Smith in the grove. Following that there were several appearances, one of which is recorded in the 110th section of the Doctrine and Covenants, when the Savior appeared to Joseph and Oliver.

I have a believing heart that started with a simple testimony that came when I was a child—I think maybe I was around ten or eleven years of age. I was with my father out on a farm away from our home, trying to spend the day busying myself until my father was ready to go home. Over the fence from our place were some tumbledown sheds that would attract a curious boy, and I was adventurous. I started to climb through the fence, and I heard a voice as clearly as you are hearing mine, calling me by name and saying, "Don't go over there!" I turned to look at my father to see if he were talking to me, but he was way up at the other end of the field. There was no person in sight. I realized then, as a child, that there were persons beyond my sight, for I had definitely heard a voice. Since then, when I hear or read stories of the Prophet Joseph Smith, I too have known what it means to hear a voice, because I've had the experience. It was a theophany, in the definition of President Clark.

Another way by which we receive revelation was spoken of by the prophet Enos. He pens this very significant statement in his record in the Book of Mormon: "And while I was thus struggling in the spirit, the voice of the Lord came into my mind. . . ." (Enos 10.)

In other words, sometimes we hear the voice of the Lord coming into our minds, and when it comes, the impressions are just as strong as though He were sounding a trumpet in our ear.

Jeremiah says something like that in the first chapter of the book of Jeremiah: "Then the words of the Lord came unto me, saying. . . ." (Jeremiah 1:4.) The voice of the Lord came into his mind, as Enos said.

In a story in the Book of Mormon, Nephi upbraids his brothers, calling them to repentance, and gives voice to the same thought when he says: ". . . and he hath spoken unto you in a still small voice, but ye were past feeling, that ye could not feel his words. . . ." (1 Nephi 17:45.)

Thus the Lord, by revelation, brings thoughts into our minds as though a voice were speaking. May I bear humble testimony to that fact? I was once in a situation where I needed help. The Lord knew I needed help, as I was on an important mission. I was awakened in the wee hours of the morning and was straightened out on something that I had planned to do in a contrary way, and the way was clearly mapped out before me as I lay there that morning, just as surely as though someone had sat on the edge of my bed and told me what to do. Yes, the voice of the Lord comes into our minds and we can be directed thereby.

We also receive revelation by the power of the Holy Ghost. The Lord said to the Prophet Joseph Smith in the early days of the Church, "Yea, behold, I will tell you in your mind and in your heart, by the Holy Ghost, which shall dwell in your heart. Now, behold, this is the spirit of revelation. . . ." (D&C 8:2-3.) The Master comforted His disciples, you remember, just before His crucifixion when He said, ". . . if I go not away, the Comforter will not come unto you. . . . But when he, the Spirit of Truth [or the Holy Ghost] is come, he will guide you into all truth; . . . he will shew you things to come" (John 16:7, 13), "and bring all things to your remembrance. . . ." (John 14:26.) Thus we see the power of the Holy Ghost. The Prophet Joseph Smith, speaking about this, said, "No man can receive the Holy Ghost without receiving revelations. The Holy Ghost is a revelator." (*Teachings of the Prophet Joseph Smith,* p. 328.)

May I change that about and give it point to the Latter-day Saints and say, Any Latter-day Saint who has been baptized and who has had hands laid upon him from those officiating, commanding him to receive the Holy Ghost, and who has not received a revelation of the spirit of the Holy Ghost, has not received the gift of the Holy Ghost to which he is entitled. Therein lies a very important matter. Let me refer to what the Prophet Joseph Smith said about revelation:

> A person may profit by noticing the first intimation of the spirit of revelation. For instance, when you feel pure intelligence flowing into you, it may give you sudden strokes of ideas so that by noticing it you may find it fulfilled the same day or soon. That is, those things that were presented into your minds by the Spirit of God will come to pass, and thus by learning the Spirit of God, and understanding it, you may grow into the principle of revelation until you become perfect in Christ Jesus.

On what matters may you receive a revelation? Is it startling to you to hear that you—all members of the Church who have received the Holy Ghost—may receive revelation? Not for the president of the Church, not on how to look after the affairs pertaining to the ward, the stake, or the mission in which you live; but every individual within his own station has the right to receive revelation by the Holy Ghost.

Listen to what President Joseph F. Smith said about that:

> I believe that every individual in the Church has just as much right to enjoy the spirit of revelation and the understanding from God which that spirit of revelation gives him, for his own good, as the bishop has to enable him to preside over his ward. (*Conference Report,* April 1912, pp. 9-10.)

Every man has the privilege to exercise these gifts and these privileges in the conduct of his own affairs; in bringing up his children in the way they should go; in the management of his business, or whatever he does. It is his right to enjoy the spirit of revelation and of inspiration to do the right thing, to be wise and prudent, just and good, in everything that he does. I know that is a true principle, and that is the thing that I would like the Latter-day Saints to know. Now then, all of us should try to strive and give heed to the sudden ideas that come to us, and if we'll give heed to them and cultivate an ear to hear these promptings we too—each of us—can grow in the spirit of revelation.

Now there's one more way by which revelations may come, and that is by dreams. Oh, I'm not going to tell you that every dream you have is a direct revelation from the Lord—it may be fried liver and onions that have been responsible for an upset or disorder. But I fear that in this age of sophistication there are those of us who are prone to rule out all dreams as of no purpose, and of no moment. And yet all through the scriptures there were recorded incidents where the Lord, by dreams, has directed His people.

Let us see what Parley P. Pratt said about this matter:

> In all ages and dispensations God has revealed many important instructions and warning to men by means of dreams. When the outward organs of thought and perception are released from their activity, the nerves unstrung, the whole of mortal humanity lies hushed in quiet slumbers in order to renew its strength and vigor, it is then that the spiritual organs are at liberty in a certain degree to assume their wanted functions, to recall some faint outline, some confused and half-defined recollections of that heavenly world, and those endearing scenes of their former estate from which they have descended in order to obtain and mature a tabernacle of flesh. Their kindred spirit, their guardian angels, then hover about them with the fondest affection, the most anxious solicitude. Spirit communes with spirit, thought meets thought, soul blends with soul, in all the raptures of mutual pure and eternal love. In this situation the spiritual organs [and if we could see our spirits, we would know that they have eyes to see, ears to hear, tongues to speak, and so on] are susceptible of converse with Deity, or of communion with angels, and the spirits of just men made perfect. In this situation we frequently hold communion with our departed father, mother, brother, sister, son or daughter, or with the former husband or wife of our bosom whose affections for us, being rooted

and grounded in the eternal elements, issuing from under the sanctuary of love's eternal fountain, can never be lessened or diminished by death, distance of space, or length of years. We may perhaps have had a friend of the other sex whose pulse beat in unison with our own—whose every thought was bright with aspirations, the hope of the bright future in union with our own, whose happiness in time or in eternity would never be fully consummated without that union. Such a one snatched from time in the very bloom of youth lives in the other sphere with the same bright hope—watching our every footstep in our meanderings through the rugged path of life with longing desires for our eternal happiness.

When we begin to understand that beyond sight, as Brigham Young said, the spirit world is right here round about us, and if our spiritual eyes could be open, we could see others visiting with us, directing us. And if we will learn not to be so sophisticated that we rule out that possibility of impressions from those who are beyond sight, then we too may have a dream that may direct us as a revelation.

Speaking of revelation as it pertains to our studies, President Joseph F. Smith has given us some wonderful counsel about how we can avoid the possibility of these studies dimming our spiritual awareness or keeping us from being in tune with the Spirit. This is what he said:

> Our young people are diligent students. They reach out after truth and knowledge with commendable zeal and in so doing they must necessarily adopt for temporary use many theories of men. As long, however, as they recognize them as scaffolding, useful for research purposes, there can be no special harm in them. It is when these theories are settled upon as basic truth that trouble appears and the searcher then stands in grave danger of being led hopelessly from the right way. Philosophic theories of life have their place and use, but they are out of their place in church schools or anywhere else when they seek to supplant the revelations of God.

The revelations of God are the standards by which we measure all learning, and if anything squares not with the revelations, then we may be certain that it is not truth.

I come to you as one who sits in the company of men who live close to their Heavenly Father. I have seen matters come before the First Presidency and the Council of the Twelve in our weekly meetings on which decisions have been reached that were not based upon reasoning, but were based upon an impression which, after that decision had been made, has been found to have been a heaven-sent direction to protect and to guide.

After an important decision has been made, it has been a thrilling thing to hear the president of the Church say, "Brethren, the Lord has spoken."

The thing that all of us should strive for is to so live, keeping the commandments of the Lord, that He can answer our prayers, the prayers of our loved ones, the prayers of the General Authorities, for us. We always pray for the members of the Church, and we thank God when we know that they are praying for us. If we will live worthy, then the Lord will guide us—by a personal appearance, or by His actual voice, or by His voice coming into our mind, or by impressions upon our heart and our soul. And oh, how grateful we ought to be if the Lord sends us a dream in which are revealed to us the beauties of the eternity or a warning and direction for our special comfort. Yes, if we so live, the Lord will guide us for our salvation and for our benefit.

As one of the humblest among you, and occupying the station I do, I want to bear you my humble testimony that I have received by the voice and the power of revelation the knowledge and an understanding that God is.

It was a week following a conference, when I was preparing a radio talk on the life of the Savior and read again the story of His life, crucifixion, and resurrection, that there came to me a testimony, a reality of Him. It was more than just what was on the written page, for in truth, I found myself viewing the scenes with as much certainty as though I had been there in person. I know that these things come by the revelations of the living God.

I bear you my solemn testimony that the Church today is guided by revelation. Every soul in it who has been blessed to receive the Holy Ghost has the power to receive revelation. God help you and me that we will always so live that the Lord can answer the prayers of the faithful through us.

Section Four

THE PROPHET, SEER, AND REVELATOR

15

The Place of the Living Prophet, Seer, and Revelator

PETER, in his great testimony concerning the Master, said, "Thou art the Christ, the Son of the living God." (Matthew 16:16.) The Book of Mormon and the Doctrine and Covenants refer to "living oracles" and admonish us to "believe in the living prophet." The inference is plain that it is easier for people to believe in dead prophets than a living prophet.

At the World's Fair in New York, President G. Stanley McAllister, of the New York Stake, told us of an experience that he had that probably defines the distinction that I am trying to make. He was on a plane returning from a business assignment in St. Louis and his seatmate was a Catholic priest. As they flew toward New York and became acquainted with each other, each discovered the other's identity as to church relationships. As they talked about various things, the Catholic priest said, "Have you been to the World's Fair?" "Yes," Brother McAllister said, "I am on the committee that helped to plan our pavilion." "Well, have you visited our Catholic exhibit?" And again Brother McAllister said yes. The priest said, "Well, I have been to the fair and I have visited your exhibit. At the Catholic exhibit we have the dead Christ—the *Pieta.* But the Mormon Pavilion has the live Christ, or the living Christ." And in that I think there is a distinguishing difference.

I have a banker friend in New York. Years ago when I met him in company with President Theodore M. Jacobsen, who was then presiding over the Eastern States Mission, we had quite a discussion. President Jacobsen had given him a copy of the Book of Mormon which he had read, and he spoke very glowingly of what he called its tremendous philosophies. He invited us to ride to the mission home in his limousine. On the way, as he talked about the Book of Mormon and his reverence for its teachings, I said, "Well, why don't you do something about it? If you accept the Book of Mormon, what is holding you back? Why don't you join the Church? Why don't you accept Joseph Smith, then, as a prophet?" And he said, very thoughtfully and carefully. "Well, I suppose the whole reason is because Joseph Smith is too close to me. If he had lived two thousand years ago, I suppose I would believe. But because he is so close, I guess that is the reason I can't accept."

This man was saying, "I believe in the dead prophets that lived many years ago, but I have great difficulty believing in a living prophet." That attitude is also taken toward God. To say that the heavens are sealed and there is no revelation today is saying we do not believe in a living Christ today, or a living God today—we believe in one long-since dead and gone. So this term "living prophet" has real significance.

We sometimes hear people who talk about the Church

as a democracy. Well, it isn't any such thing. Democracy means a government where the sole authority is vested in the people—the right to nominate, the right to release, to change. The Church is not a democracy. It is more like a kingdom than a democracy—and yet it is not wholly like a kingdom, except that we accept the Lord as the king, who has under His direction an earthly head who operates and becomes His mouthpiece. It is an organization that is defined more accurately as a *theocracy,* which means that it is something like a kingdom as the world would define it, and yet something like a democracy.

The Prophet Joseph Smith said:

> . . . the Melchizedek Priesthood . . . is a perfect law of theocracy, and stands as God to give laws to the people, administering endless lives to the sons and daughters of Adam. . . . The Holy Ghost is God's messenger to administer in all those priesthoods. (*Teachings of the Prophet Joseph Smith,* pp. 322-23.)

Let me read you something by Parley P. Pratt that appeared in the *Millennial Star* in 1845. It was called a "Proclamation."

> The legislative, judicial, and executive power is vested in Him (the Lord). He reveals the laws, and he elects, chooses, or appoints the officers; and holds the right to reprove, to correct, or even to remove them at pleasure. Hence the necessity of a constant intercourse by direct revelation between him and his Church. As a precedent for the foregoing facts, we refer to the examples of all ages as recorded in the Scriptures.
>
> This order of government began in Eden—God appointed Adam to govern the earth, and gave him laws.
>
> It was perpetuated in a regular succession from Adam to Noah to Melchizedek, Abraham, Isaac, Jacob, Joseph, Moses, Samuel, the prophets, John, Jesus, and his apostles. All, and each of which were chosen by the Lord, and not by the people. (*Millennial Star,* 5:150 [March 1843]).

Here Parley P. Pratt is saying something that is fundamental. The leaders are chosen by the Lord and not by the people. The Church is not a democracy. We must not speak of the Church as a democracy. It is true that the people have a voice in the kingdom of God. No officer is to preside over a branch or a stake until he is sustained by a vote of that body over which he is to preside. They may reject, but they do not nominate and they do not release. That is done by a higher authority.

> But they do not confer the authority in the first place, nor can they take it away; for instance, the people did not elect the twelve apostles of Jesus Christ, nor could they by popular vote deprive them of their apostleship.
>
> As the government of the kingdom anciently existed; so is it now restored.
>
> The people did not choose that great modern apostle and prophet, Joseph Smith, but God chose him in the usual way that he has chosen others before him, viz., by open vision, and by his own voice from the heavens. (Ibid.)

This same "Proclamation" in another place states:

> The government of the church and kingdom of God, in this and in all other ages, is purely a Theocracy, that is, a government under the direct control and superintendence of the Almighty. . . .
>
> This last key of the priesthood is the most sacred of all, and pertains exclusively to the first presidency of the church, without whose sanction and approval or authority, no sealing blessing shall be administered pertaining to things of the resurrection and the life to come. (Ibid., pp. 150-51.)

It is very interesting to see the reaction of people. Soon after President David O. McKay announced to the Church that members of the First Council of the Seventy were being ordained high priests in order to extend their usefulness and to give them authority to act when no other General Authority could be present, a seventy I met in Phoenix, Arizona, was very much disturbed. He said to me, "Didn't the Prophet Joseph Smith say that this was contrary to the order of heaven to name high priests as presidents of the First Council of the Seventy?"

And I said, "Well, I have understood that he did, but have you ever thought that what was contrary to the order of heaven in 1840 might not be contrary to the order of heaven in 1960?" He had not thought of that. He again was following a dead prophet, and he was forgetting that there is a living prophet today. Hence the importance of our stressing that word *living*.

Years ago as a young missionary I visited Nauvoo and Carthage with my mission president, and we were holding a missionary meeting in the jail room where Joseph and Hyrum had met their deaths. The mission president related the historical events that led up to the martyrdom and then he closed with this very significant statement: "When the Prophet Joseph Smith was martyred, there were many saints who died spiritually with Joseph." So it was when Brigham Young died: so it was when John Taylor died. Do revelations given to President John Taylor, for example, have any more authority than something that comes from our president and prophet today? Some Church members died spiritually with Wilford Woodruff, with Lorenzo Snow, with Joseph F. Smith, with Heber J. Grant, with George Albert Smith. We have some today willing to believe someone who is dead and gone and to accept his words as having more authority than the words of a living authority today.

As I thought about this matter of a prophet, I added the words "seer and revelator." That narrows the field, you see, to one man. The prophet, seer, and revelator means the president of the Church. There are sixteen men who are sustained as prophets, seers, and revelators, but that does not mean all of them have equal authority. It means that in that body are those who may become seers as well as prophets and revelators. In a broad sense, a prophet is one who speaks, who is inspired of God to speak in His name.

The Prophet Joseph Smith said in answer to a query as to how this church was different from all other churches: "We are different because we have the Holy Ghost." Every one of us who has had hands laid upon his head has been blessed to receive the gift of the Holy Ghost. That was, in a sense, a command for us to so live that we could enjoy the gifts of the Holy Ghost. The Prophet Joseph Smith said, "No man can receive the gift of the Holy Ghost without receiving revelations. The Holy Ghost is a revelator." (*Teachings*, p. 328.)

In a sense, the word *prophet* might apply to all faithful Church members. I do not mean that we have the right to receive revelations as to how this church might be run, or that members may have revelations as to how or who should be named in a stake or ward organization. But I do say that the bishop in his place, the mission president in his place, the stake president in his place, the quorum president, the auxiliary leader, the seminary teacher, the institute teacher, a father and mother in the home, a young person in his or her quest for a proper companion in marriage—each of us has the right to revelation.

No group of people have a gift so widely diffused as the gift of prophecy. You recall the definition as contained in the book of Revelation. John quoted the angelic messenger who came to him as saying, ". . . I am thy fellowservant, and of thy brethren that have the testimony of Jesus: . . . for testimony of Jesus is the spirit of prophecy." (Revelation 19:10.)

Paul wrote to the Corinthians:

> Wherefore I give you to understand, that no man speaking by the Spirit of God calleth Jesus accursed; and that no man can say [and the Prophet Joseph Smith said that should have been translated "no man can know"] that Jesus is the Lord, but by the Holy Ghost. (1 Corinthians 12:3.)

In other words, anyone who enjoys the gift by which he may have God revealed has the spirit of prophecy, the power of revelation, and, in a sense, is a prophet within the sphere of responsibility and authority given to him.

In order for us to get the distinction between a prophet and a seer and a revelator, I refer to what was said of Mosiah that distinguishes the characteristics of one who holds the exalted title of seer and revelator to the Church:

> And the king said that a seer is greater than a prophet.
>
> And Ammon said that a seer is a revelator and a prophet also; and a gift which is greater can no man have, except he should possess the power of God, which no man can; yet a man may have great power given him from God.
>
> But a seer can know things which are past, and also of things which are to come, and by them shall all things be revealed, or, rather, shall secret things be made manifest, and hidden things shall come to light, and things which are not known shall be made known by them, and also things shall be made known by them which otherwise could not be known.
>
> Thus God has provided a means that man, through faith, might work mighty miracles; therefore he becometh a great benefit to his fellow beings. (Mosiah 8:15-18.)

As we read the story of how Aaron was called, we find this classic statement regarding authority: "And no man taketh this honour unto himself, but he that is called by God, as was Aaron." (Hebrews 5:4.) God said, defining the relationship that Moses would have to God and that Aaron would have to Moses:

> And thou shalt speak unto him, and put words in his [Aaron's] mouth: and I will be with thy mouth, . . . and will teach you what ye shall do. And . . . he shall be to thee instead of a mouth, and thou shalt be to him instead of God. (Exodus 4:15-16.)

Now that is as clear a relationship as I think we can find anywhere—the relationship of the prophet of the Lord and the president of the Church, the prophet, seer, and revelator, to others of us to whom he may delegate authority.

Sometimes we have brethren who become a little irritated because they are not consulted and are not asked their opinions on certain high-level matters. I have said to them, rather gently—having had a few years more experience and perhaps lessons that they may have if they live as long as I have—"I choose not to be excited over things that are none of my business." Usually they say, "Well, it is our business." And I have said, "You just think it is your business. It becomes our business when the president of the Church delegates to us some of the keys which he holds in fulness. Until he gives us the authority, it is not our business and we do not have the right to take his place."

The need for revelation has been a matter recognized not only by the people of the Church, but also by some of our great thinkers over the years. I quote the following from Ralph Waldo Emerson:

> Miracles, prophecy, poetry, the ideal life, the holy life, exist as ancient history merely; they are not in the belief nor in the aspiration of society; but when suggested seem ridiculous. . . . It is the office of a true teacher to show us that God is, not was; that He speaketh, not spake. The true Christianity,—a faith like Christ's in the infinitude of man,—is lost.
>
> I look for the hour when that supreme Beauty which ravished the souls of those eastern men, and chiefly of those Hebrews, and through their lips spoke oracles to all time, shall speak in the West also. ("An Address Delivered before the Senior Class in Divinity College, Cambridge," July 15, 1838.)

I suppose he had not heard of the Book of Mormon when he wrote this.

> The Hebrew and Greek scriptures contain immortal sentences, that have been bread of life to missions. But they have no epical integrity; are fragmentary; are not shown in their order to the intellect. I look for the new Teacher that shall follow so far those shining laws

that he shall see them come full circle; shall see their rounding complete grace; shall see the world to be the mirror of the soul. . . .

Nor can the Bible be closed until the last great man is born. Men have come to speak of revelation as something long ago given and done, as if God were dead. (Ibid.)

Do you get that point?—as though God were dead, not speaking as one today. "The injury to faith throttles the preacher; and the goodliest of institutions becomes an uncertain and inarticulate voice." Then Emerson added, "The need was never greater of new revelation than now." (Ibid.)

Speaking as the prophets understood the need, President John Taylor said:

A good many people, and those professing Christians, will sneer a good deal at the idea of present revelation. Whoever heard of true religion without communication with God? To me the thing is the most absurd that the human mind could conceive. I do not wonder, when the people generally reject the principle of present revelation, that skepticism and infidelity prevail to such an alarming extent. I do not wonder that so many men treat religion with contempt, and regard it as something not worth the attention of intelligent beings, for without revelation religion is a mockery and a farce. If I cannot have a religion that will lead me to God, and place me *en rapport* with him, and unfold to my mind the principles of immortality and eternal life, I want nothing to do with it.

The principle of present revelation, then, is the very foundation of our religion. (The *Gospel Kingdom* [Bookcraft, 1964], p. 35.)

Now that means today. Sometimes we get the notion that if something is printed in a book, it is more authentic than if it was spoken in the last general conference. Just because something is written in a book does not make it more of an authority to guide us. President Taylor elaborates on this idea and explains why the scriptures of the past are not sufficient for us today:

The Bible is good; and Paul told Timothy to study it, that he might be a workman that need not be ashamed, and that he might be able to conduct himself aright before the living church [there is that word "living" again], the pillar and ground of truth. The church-mark, with Paul, was the foundation, the pillar, the ground of truth, the living church, not the dead letter. The Book of Mormon is good, and the Doctrine and Covenants, as land-marks. But a mariner who launches into the ocean requires a more certain criterion. He must be acquainted with heavenly bodies, and take his observations from them in order to steer his barque aright. Those books are good for example, precedent, and investigation, and for developing certain laws and principles. But they do not, they cannot, touch every case required to be adjudicated and set in order.

We require a living tree—a living fountain—living intelligence, proceeding from the living priesthood in heaven, through the living priesthood on earth. . . . And from the time that Adam first received his communication from God, to the time that John, on the Isle of Patmos, received his communication, or Joseph Smith had the heavens opened to him, it always required new revelations, adapted to the peculiar circumstances in which the churches or individuals were placed. Adam's revelation did not instruct Noah to build his ark; nor did Noah's revelation tell Lot to forsake Sodom; nor did either of these speak of the departure of the children of Israel from Egypt. These all had revelations for themselves, and so had Isaiah, Jeremiah, Ezekiel, Jesus, Peter, Paul, John, and Joseph. And so must we, or we shall make a shipwreck. (*The Gospel Kingdom,* p. 34.)

Amos gives us that oft-quoted passage:

Behold, the days come . . . that I will send a famine in the land, not a famine of bread, not a thirst for water, but of hearing the words of the Lord:

And they shall wander from sea to sea, and from the north even to the east, they shall run to and fro to seek the word of the Lord, and shall not find it. (Amos 8:11-12.)

Well, that time has come. To quote President Taylor again:

We are living in a world in which the spirits who have dwelt in the bosom of God are coming into it and leaving this state of existence at the rate of about a thousand millions in every thirty-three years; and here are thousands of so-called ministers of religion with an inefficient gospel, that God never ordained, trying to ameliorate the condition of mankind, and sending what they call the gospel to the heathen, and they are continually calling for the pecuniary aid of their fellow Christians to assist them in this enterprise. (*The Gospel Kingdom,* p. 33.)

We have found some who are asking, "How long is it going to be before the Church changes its policy with respect to the Negro?" And I have said, "If you will just change a couple of words so that the question will be, 'How long is it going to be before the Lord (not the Church) changes His (not its) policy,' you will see how utterly silly your question is." When there is to be anything different from that which the Lord has told us already, He will reveal it to His prophet and no one else. Do you suppose that when the Lord has a prophet on the earth, He is going to take some round-about means of revealing things to His children? That is what He has a prophet for, and when He has something to give to this church, He will give it to the president, and the president will see that the presidents of stakes and missions get it, along with the General Authorities, and they in turn will see that the people are advised of any change.

A man came in to see me and said that he had heard that some man appeared mysteriously to a group of temple workers and told them, "You had better hurry up and store for a year, or two, or three, because there will come a season when there won't be any production." He asked me what I thought about it, and I said, "Well, were you in the April conference of 1936?" He replied, "No, I couldn't be there." And I said, "Well, you surely read the report of what was said by the Brethren in that conference?" No, he hadn't. "Well," I said, "at that conference the Lord did give a revelation about the storage of food. How in the world is the Lord going to get over to you what He wants you to do if you are not there when He says it, and you do not take the time to read it after it has been said?"

The Lord is going to keep His people informed, if they

will listen. As President J. Reuben Clark, Jr., said in a classic talk, "What we need today is not more prophets. We have the prophets. But what we need is more people with listening ears. That is the great need of our generation." (*Conference Report*, October 1948, p. 82.)

Going back to what President Taylor was saying:

> The Christian world, by their unbelief, have made the heavens as brass, and wherever they go to declare what they call the gospel they make confusion worse confounded. But who shall debar God from taking care of his own creation, and saving his creatures? Yet this is the position that many men have taken. (*The Gospel Kingdom,* p. 33.)

Again quoting from the prophet Amos, "Surely the Lord God will do nothing, but he revealeth his secret unto his servants the prophets." (Amos 3:7.) Way back in the time of President Wilford Woodruff someone was "prophesying" about the end of the world, and President Woodruff was being asked when the world was coming to an end. He said, "Well, I don't know, but I am still planting cherry trees." He was that unconcerned, as he knew that if the Lord wanted to tell anybody, he would be the first one to know. We must understand this.

I am afraid sometimes our sixth Article of Faith has been wrongly interpreted and wrongly taught. "We believe in the same organization that existed in the Primitive Church, viz., apostles, prophets, pastors, teachers, evangelists, etc."—which has too often been construed and fixed in the minds of our students to mean that there was no church on the face of the earth until it was established by Jesus in the meridian of time. Well, if that was the first time that the Church was upon the earth, what are we going to do about all of those who lived before that time? Why, of course the Church was upon the earth. The kingdom of God was established in the days of Adam, and Abraham, and Moses, the Judges, the Kings, and the Prophets, as well as the meridian of time. And in this, the dispensation of the fulness of times, we have all the essentials of every other dispensation plus things that have been revealed that have never been revealed in other dispensations.

Then we come to the question, "What is the kingdom of God?" Regarding the kingdom of God, the Prophet Joseph Smith said:

> Whenever there has been a righteous man on earth unto whom God revealed His word and gave power and authority to administer in His name, and where there is a priest of God—a minister who has power and authority from God to administer in the ordinances of the gospel and officiate in the priesthood of God, there is the kingdom of God. . . . Where there is a prophet, a priest, or a righteous man unto whom God gives his oracles, there is the kingdom of God; and where the oracles of God are not, there the kingdom of God is not. (*Teachings,* pp. 271-72.)

President Clark said something that startled some folks years ago. He said, "It is my faith that the gospel plan has always been here, that His priesthood has always been here, that His priesthood has been here on the earth, and that it will continue to be so until the end comes." When that conference session was over there were many who said, "My goodness, doesn't President Clark realize that there have been periods of apostasy following each dispensation of the gospel?"

I walked over to the Church Office Building with President Joseph Fielding Smith and he said, "I believe there has never been a moment of time since the creation but what there has been someone holding the priesthood on the earth to hold Satan in check." And then I thought of Enoch's city with perhaps thousands who were taken into heaven and were translated. They must have been translated for a purpose and may have sojourned with those living on the earth ever since that time. I have thought of Elijah—and perhaps Moses, for all we know; they were translated beings, as was John the Revelator. I have thought of the three Nephites. Why were they translated and permitted to tarry? For what purpose? An answer was suggested when I heard President Smith, whom we have considered one of our well-informed theologians, make the above statement. Now that doesn't mean that the kingdom of God has always been present, because these men did not have the authority to administer the saving ordinances of the gospel to the world. But these individuals were translated for a purpose known to the Lord. There is no question but what they were here.

Now, when does a person speak as a prophet? Do you recall that oft-repeated revelation in which the Lord said:

> And, behold, . . . this is an ensample unto all those who were ordained unto this priesthood [and he is talking of General Authorities], whose mission is appointed unto them to go forth—
>
> . . . they shall speak as they are moved upon by the Holy Ghost.
>
> And whatsoever they shall speak when moved upon by the Holy Ghost shall be scripture, shall be the will of the Lord, shall be the mind of the Lord, shall be the word of the Lord, shall be the voice of the Lord, and the power of God unto salvation. (D&C 68:2-4.)

This is so when a General Authority is speaking by the power of the Holy Ghost.

Someone has rightly said that it is not to be thought that every word spoken by our leaders is inspired. The Prophet Joseph Smith wrote in his personal diary: "This morning I . . . visited with a brother and sister from Michigan, who thought that 'a prophet is always a prophet;' but I told them that a prophet was a prophet only when he was acting as such." (*Teachings,* p. 278.)

It is not to be thought that every word spoken by the General Authorities is inspired, or that they are moved upon by the Holy Ghost in everything they write. I don't care what his position is, if he writes something or speaks something that goes beyond anything that you can find in the standard church works, unless that one be the prophet, seer, and revelator—please note that one exception—you may immediately say, "Well, that is his own idea." And if he says something that contradicts what is found in the standard church works, you may know by that same token that it is false, regardless of the position of the man who says it. We can know or have the assurance that they are speaking under inspiration if we so live that we can have a witness that what they are speaking is the word of the Lord. There is only one safety, and that is that we shall live to have the witness to know. President Brigham Young said something to the effect that "the greatest fear I have is that the people of this Church will accept what we say as the will of the Lord without first praying about it and getting the witness within their own hearts that what we say is the word of the Lord."

President Young said something further on this. He said, "It pleases me a little to think how anxious this people are for new revelation." I wish to ask you a question: Do this people know whether they have received any revelation since the death of Joseph, as a people? I can tell you that you receive them continually.

> It has been observed that the people want revelation. This is a revelation; and were it written, it would then be written revelation, as truly as the revelations which are contained in the book of Doctrine and Covenants. I could give you a revelation upon the subject of paying your tithing and building a temple in the name of the Lord; for the light is in me. I could put these revelations as straight to the line of truth in writing as any revelation you ever read. I could write the mind of the Lord, and you could put it in your pockets. But before we desire more written revelation, let us fulfill the revelations that are already written, and which we have scarely begun to fulfill. (*Discourses of Brigham Young,* p. 39.)

In other words, what he is saying is that when we are able to live up to all the revelations he has given, then we may ask why we are not given more.

President George Albert Smith was about to close one of our general conferences, which happened to be at the time of the furor caused by the book *No Man Knows My History*, one of the scurrilous things published against the Church, and there had been different speakers who had said something about these apostate writings with which the Church was being flooded. Just as President Smith was about to finish, he paused—and it was wholly unrelated to what he had been talking about—and he said:

> Many have belittled Joseph Smith, but those who have will be forgotten in the remains of mother earth, and the odor of their infamy will ever be with them; but honor, majesty, and fidelity with God exemplified by Joseph Smith and attached to his name shall never die. (*Conference Report,* April 1946, p. 181.)

I never heard a more profound statement from any prophet.

Yes, we believe in a living prophet, seer, and revelator, and I bear you my solemn witness that we have a living prophet, seer, and revelator. We are not dependent only upon the revelations given in the past as contained in our standard works—as wonderful as they are—but we have a mouthpiece to whom God does reveal and is revealing His mind and will. God will never permit him to lead us astray. As has been said, God would remove him out of his place if he should attempt to do it. You have no concern. Let the management and government of God, then, be with the Lord. Do not try to find fault with the management and affairs that pertain to Him alone and by revelation through His prophet—His living prophet, His seer, and His revelator.

16

"May the Kingdom of God Go Forth"

IN a great revelation of the Lord given to the Church in 1835, the Lord gave specific instructions setting forth the order of the priesthood in the government of the Church and kingdom of God. In this revelation He specified four requisites in the establishment of the First Presidency, or the presidency of the Melchizedek, or High, Priesthood of the Church, as the Lord speaks of it. (D&C 107:22.)

First, it was requisite that there be three presiding high priests.

Second, they were to be chosen by the body (which has been construed to be the Quorum of the Twelve Apostles).

Third, they must be appointed and ordained by the same body—the Quorum of the Twelve.

Fourth, they must be upheld by the confidence, faith, and prayers of the Church.

All of these steps were taken in order that the quorum

of the First Presidency could be formed to preside over the Church.

Those first steps were taken by action of the Twelve and they were attended to in a sacred meeting convened in the temple on July 7, 1972, where the First Presidency was named.

Now, as never before, have I more fully realized the importance of that last requirement: that this presidency, in the Lord's language, must be upheld by the confidence, the faith, and the prayers of the Church—which means, of course, the entire membership of the Church.

We witnessed the outpouring of love and fellowship that was in evidence in the great regional conference of our wonderful Lamanite Saints from Central America and Mexico, assembled in Mexico City. Over 16,000 Saints were gathered together in a great auditorium, where they sustained their General Authorities.

Again, in the mighty demonstration of this solemn assembly [October 6, 1972] I am moved with emotions beyond expression as I have felt the true love and bonds of brotherhood. There has been here an overwhelming spiritual endowment, attesting, no doubt, that in all likelihood we are in the presence of personages, seen and unseen, who are in attendance. Who knows but that even our Lord and Master would be near us on such an occasion as this, for we, and the world, must never forget that this is His church, and under His almighty direction we are to serve! Indeed, I would remind you what He declared in a similar conference of Saints in Fayette, New York, and undoubtedly would remind us again today: "But behold, verily, verily, I say unto you that mine eyes are upon you. I am in your midst and ye cannot see me." (D&C 38:7.)

On the sacred occasion when President Joseph Fielding Smith passed away and I began to sense the magnitude of the overwhelming responsibility which I must now assume, I went to the holy temple. There, in prayerful meditation, I looked upon the paintings of those men of God—true, pure men, God's noblemen—who had preceded me in a similar calling.

A few days ago in the early morning hours, in my private study at home and all alone with my thoughts, I read the tributes paid to each of the presidents by those who had been most closely associated with each of them.

Joseph Smith was the one whom the Lord raised up from boyhood and endowed with divine authority and taught the things necessary for him to know and to obtain the priesthood and to lay the foundation for God's kingdom in these latter days.

There was President Brigham Young, who was foreordained before this world was for his divine calling to lead the persecuted Saints in fleeing from the wrath that threatened the Saints in those early gathering places in Missouri and Illinois and to pioneer the building of an inland commonwealth in the tops of these majestic mountains, to fulfill God's purposes.

To look upon the features of President John Taylor was to gain a realization that here was, as President Joseph F. Smith spoke of him, "One of the purest men I ever knew. . . ."

As I saw the sainted face of President Wilford Woodruff, I was aware that here was a man like Nathanael of old, in whom there was no guile, and susceptible to the impressions of the Spirit of the Lord, by whose light he seemed to almost always walk, "not knowing beforehand the thing he was to do."

While President Lorenzo Snow had but a brief administration, he had a special mission to establish his people on a more solid temporal foundation by the determined application of the law of sacrifice, to relieve the great burdens placed upon the Church because of mistakes and errors that had unwittingly crept in.

When I want to seek for a more clear definition of doctrinal subjects, I have usually turned to the writings and sermons of President Joseph F. Smith. As I looked upon his noble stature, I thought of the nine-year-old boy helping his widowed mother across the plains and the fifteen-year-old missionary on the slopes of Haleakala on the isle of Maui being strengthened by a heavenly vision with his uncle, Joseph Smith. It was he who presided during the stormy days when an antagonistic press maligned the Church, but his was the steady arm by the Lord's appointment to carry off the Church triumphantly.

I suppose I never drew closer to the meaning of a divine calling than when President Heber J. Grant placed his hands upon my shoulders and, with a deep feeling akin to mine, announced my calling to be an apostle of the Lord Jesus Christ. As his picture looked down upon me, there came again to my mind the prophetic words of his inspired blessing when I was ordained in the holy temple under his hands.

President George Albert Smith was a disciple of friendship and love. He was indeed a friend to everyone. My gaze at his likeness seemed to give me a warmth of that radiance which made every man his friend.

Tall and impressive was President David O. McKay, as he now looked at me with those piercing eyes, which always seemed to search my very soul. Never was I privileged to be in his presence but that I felt for a brief moment, as I had done on so many occasions, that I was a better man for having been in his company.

To him who sought no earthly honors, but whose whole soul delighted in the things of the spirit, President

Joseph Fielding Smith was there with his smiling face, my beloved prophet-leader who made no compromise with truth. As "the finger of God touched him and he slept," he seemed in that brief moment to be passing to me, as it were, a sceptre of righteousness as though to say to me, "Go thou and do likewise."

Now I stood alone with my thoughts. Somehow the impressions that came to me were, simply, that the only true record that will ever be made of my service in my new calling will be the record that I may have written in the hearts and lives of those with whom I have served and labored, within and without the Church.

The day after this appointment, following the passing of our beloved President Smith, my attention was called to a paragraph from a sermon delivered in 1853 in a general conference by Elder Orson Hyde, then a member of the Twelve. This provoked some soul-searching in me also.

The subject of his address was "The Man to Lead God's People," and I quote briefly from it:

> . . . it is invariably the case that when an individual is ordained and appointed to lead the people, he has passed through tribulations and trials, and has proven himself before God, and before His people, that he is worthy of the situation which he holds . . . that when a person has not been tried, that has not proved himself before God, and before His people, and before the councils of the Most High, to be worthy, he is not going to step in and lead the Church and people of God. It has never been so, but from the beginning some one that understands the Spirit and counsel of the Almighty, that knows the Church, and is known of her, is the character that will lead the Church. (*Journal of Discourses* 1:123.)

As I have known of the lives of those who have preceded me, I have been made aware that each seemed to have had his special mission for his day and time.

Then, with searching introspection, I thought of myself and my experiences of which Orson Hyde's appraisal had made reference. Then I recalled the words of the Prophet Joseph's characterization of himself, which seemed somewhat analogous to myself. He said:

> I am like a huge, rough stone rolling down from a high mountain; and the only polishing I get is when some corner gets rubbed off by coming in contact with something else, striking with accelerated force against religious bigotry, priestcraft, lawyer-craft, doctor-craft, lying editors, suborned judges and jurors, and the authority of perjured executives, backed by mobs, blasphemers, licentious and corrupt men and women—all hell knocking off a corner here and a corner there. Thus will I become a smooth and polished shaft in the quiver of the Almighty. . . . (*Teachings of the Prophet Joseph Smith,* p. 304.)

These thoughts now running through my mind begin to give greater meaning to some of the experiences in my life, things that have happened which have been difficult for me to understand. At times it has seemed as though I too was like a rough stone rolling down from a high mountainside, being buffeted and polished, I suppose, by experiences, that I too might overcome and become a polished shaft in the quiver of the Almighty.

Maybe it was necessary that I too must learn obedience by the things that I might have suffered—to give me experiences that were for my good, to see if I could pass some of the various tests of mortality.

In the selection of my noble counselors, President N. Eldon Tanner and President Marion G. Romney, I learned that I was not alone with a rich measure of the gift of prophecy. They too had passed the tests, and before the Lord they had not been found wanting. How grateful I am for these noble men of the First Presidency and the Twelve and the other General Authorities.

The morning after my call came, as I knelt with my dear companion in prayer, my heart and soul seemed to reach out of the total membership of the Church with a special kind of fellowship and love which was like the opening of the windows of heaven, to give me a brief feeling of belonging to the more than three million members of the Church in all parts of the world.

I repeat what I have said on other occasions, that I most fervently seek to be upheld by the confidence, faith, and prayers of all the faithful Saints everywhere, and I pledge to you that as you pray for me, I will earnestly try to so live that the Lord can answer your prayers through me. In recent months, there seem to have been awakened in me new wellsprings of spiritual understanding also. I know full well the truth of what the Prophet Joseph told the early missionaries to Great Britain: "The nearer a person approaches the Lord, a greater power will be manifested by the adversary to prevent the accomplishment of His purposes." (Orson F. Whitney, *Life of Heber C. Kimball* [Bookcraft, 1967], p. 131.)

There is no shadow of doubt in my mind that these things are as certain today as in that day, but also I am certain that, as the Lord said, ". . . no weapon that is formed against you shall prosper; And if any man lift his voice against you he shall be confounded in mine own due time." (D&C 71:9-10.)

How grateful I am for your loyalty and your sustaining vote! I bear you solemn witness as to the divine mission of the Savior and the certainty as to His guiding hand in the affairs of His church today, as in all dispensations of time.

I know, with a testimony more powerful than sight, that, as the Lord declared,

> The keys of the kingdom of God are committed unto man on the earth [from the Prophet Joseph Smith through his successors down to the present], and from thence shall the gospel roll forth unto the ends of the earth, as the stone which is cut out of the mountain without hands shall roll forth, until it has filled the whole earth.

Wherefore, may the kingdom of God go forth, that the kingdom of heaven may come. . . . (D&C 65:2, 6.)

I bear testimony with all the conviction of my soul and leave my blessing upon the membership of the Church and the pure in heart everywhere.

17

David O. McKay: "He Lighted the Lamps of Faith"

I *SHOULD* like to take as a text the ninth Article of Faith: "We believe all that God has revealed, all that He does now reveal, and we believe that He will yet reveal many great and important things pertaining to the Kingdom of God."

The distinctive characteristic of the Church over which President David O. McDay presided for nearly nineteen years as its president is expressed in this Article of Faith.

Anciently when the church was established, it was the Apostle Paul who declared it was "built upon the foundation of the apostles and prophets, Jesus Christ himself being the chief corner stone." (Ephesians 2:20.) Anchored by that divine conviction, we often heard our beloved President pray, "O God, we pray that the channel of communication will be always open between Thee and us." That his prayer has been answered has been continually witnessed by those of us who have labored close to him and have heard his profound conviction, "The Lord has spoken!"

A prophet is an inspired and divinely appointed revealer and interpreter of God's mind and will. He has held the keys to the kingdom of God in our day, such as were given to Peter as the earthly head of the church in his day, there being only one man on the earth at a time holding such keys.

The meaning of the title of seer is explained in reputable commentaries and by an ancient prophet. I refer to these so that you may glimpse the spiritual stature of David O. McKay. The *Encyclopedia Britannica* defines seer as follows:

> Seers create the expectation of individuals in mysterious contact with God, standing in his counsel, knowing his secrets, whose words therefore should have absolute authority in times of crisis.

The prophet Ammon declared:

> And the king said that a seer is greater than a prophet.
>
> And Ammon said that a seer is a revelator and a prophet also; and a gift which is greater can no man have, except he should possess the power of God, which no man can; yet a man may have great power given him from God.
>
> But a seer can know of things which are past, and also of things which are to come, and by them shall all things be revealed, or, rather, shall secret things be made manifest, and hidden things shall come to light, and things which are not known shall be made known by them, and also things shall be made known by them which otherwise could not be known.
>
> Thus God has provided a means that man, through faith, might work mighty miracles; therefore he becometh a great benefit to his fellow beings. (Mosiah 8:15-18.)

In those words you have dramatically portrayed the spiritual stature of this great man of God who has been called home to report and to give an accounting of his earthly stewardship.

Someone has written a summation that well expresses the feeling of all of us:

> His love was pure and kind. Though he was gentle, he was firm. Though he was humble, he was not without courage. Though he was forgiving to the truly repentent, he never condoned sin. Though he had seen many changes in the standards of living, and had seen many advancements in science, he never changed any principles of the gospel. He brought honor and respect for the Church and Kingdom of God the world over. He was honored by all respectable people. He was genuine. He talked with God. He was and is a prophet of the Living God. That man and prophet is David O. McKay.

His preparation for this mission began in the pre-mortal world, where Abraham tells us there were great and noble ones, from among whom God said He would make his rulers. To Abraham the Lord declared, as He did to Jeremiah, as well as to others, ". . . thou art one of them; thou wast chosen before thou wast born." (Abraham 3:23.) There is no doubt in the minds of thousands who knew the life of David O. McKay that like Abraham and Jeremiah and others of the prophets, David O. McKay was chosen before he was born.

Joseph Smith, the first prophet of this dispensation, once explained, "A man is only a prophet when he is acting as such." This enlightening declaration doubtless holds true of all prophets, ancient as well as modern men of God. Very likely they receive their polishing by the sometimes refining processes, as Paul declared of the Master: "Though he were a Son, yet learned he obedience by the things which he suffered." (Hebrews 5:8.)

A prophet, then, does not become a spiritual leader by studying books about religion, nor does he become one by attending a theological seminary. One becomes a prophet, a divinely called religious leader, by actual spiritual contacts. He gets his diploma, as it were, directly from God.

Historically most prophet-leaders were chosen from humble walks of life. David O. McKay came of the pioneer, farmer family. He resided in a small hamlet known as Huntsville, nurtured among the hills up Ogden Canyon, isolated in a Bethlehem-like community as related to the larger centers of population. But like others of those pioneers, he and his family, while living in log cabins, dreamed of grand temples of God. Our president was a mighty instrument through which God moved to make that dream come true. During his lifetime as an apostle and as president of the Church, most of our holy temples of today have been constructed. "And by this vision splendid, he was on his way attended," and like Samuel of old, he grew on, and the Lord was with him, and he "was in favour both with the Lord, and also with men." (1 Samuel 2:26.)

President McKay once said, "The poorest shack in which prevails a united family is of far greater value to God and to humanity than any other riches. In such a home God can work miracles and will work miracles. Pure hearts in a pure home are always in whispering distance of heaven." He should know, for the home of his childhood and the one in which he was the father and presided were within "whispering distance of heaven."

The accomplishments of his life have been well documented and need not be further elaborated, but his great love for people urged him to give impetus to the Churchwide welfare movement, designed to give aid to the needy and the unfortunate to be uplifted in the Lord's own way. And in the beginning of that movement, I was called to be close to President McKay, and was called to his office sometimes not once but several times, as he directed the molding of what we call the welfare program of the Church.

As he sensed the decline in family home life in this

and other nations, he directed the establishment of a Churchwide family home evening program, with a well-defined program of weekly religious and moral teachings, an activity designed to draw parents and children together. He said, "One of our most precious possessions in our family home is the school of human virtues. Its responsibilities, joys and sorrows, smiles, tears, hopes and solicitudes form the chief interests of life."

He was alert to the moral decline and mounting juvenile delinquency and the ever-increasing crime wave. He made it clear to all of us that the world was in need of a unifying force, and such an ideal is the gospel of Jesus Christ. Throughout the whole Church, in the family home, and in all Church organizations, these gospel ideals must be constantly impressed, to minimize, if possible, these evils in the world. This has required a lifetime effort on his part to urge us to integrate all lesson materials for all ages and thereby build a solid foundation of faith, that they become an anchor to the many who are floundering and in danger of moral shipwreck.

None of us will ever forget the touchstone of his soul, which was the secret of his nobility, when he declared, "What you think of Christ will determine in large measure what you are. That man is greatest who is most Christlike."

As a special witness of our Lord and Master, he lighted the lamps of faith of many by the intensity of the fire within his own soul. His was the sure world of prophecy that Jesus Christ was indeed our Savior and our Redeemer and literal Son of God, our Heavenly Father.

There could be no doubt but that his calling and election are made sure, and that he is a worthy recipient of the highest privileges accorded to those who live the laws of the celestial kingdom while on this earth. If I were an artist and had been retained to paint a picture of a prophet of God, I could choose no more worthy representative to stand for a picture of that prophet, past or present, than our own beloved President David O. McKay.

Someone remarked, with reference to his passing, "The world was left poorer and heaven richer when he passed away." I would say it differently: "He left the world richer and heaven more glorious by the rich treasures he has brought to each." From one of his "heart petals," as he called them, on his ninetieth birthday, when the General Authorities and the family gathered, he gave us this little verse, addressed in the closing words to one who is dear and precious to him:

Family cares came heavy but not a complaint;
Forty-four children now crown her as saint;
Companion, counselor, adviser alway,
My wife for eternity, my own Emma Ray.
You insist that I'm ninety?
My limbs say you are right,
As I hobble along a pitiable sight;
But I shall always feel young
With the gospel that's true,
With loved ones around me, and friends like you.

As I witnessed the throng of people waiting, waiting, almost around the entire block surrounding the Church Office Building, for the last glimpse of their departed leader, I repeated to myself: That person who has lived best is he who in his passing has taken up most hearts with him. Amidst the turmoil in all the world, we lean upon the assurances that the Lord has given us, that when the devil shall have power over his own dominion, as he said he would in our day, we lean upon the promise of our Heavenly Father that in this day He would reign in the midst of His saints. (See D&C 1:35-36.)

To his beloved family: You bear one of the greatest

family names that has ever been among all the children of men on this earth. Teach your children and your children's children to the last generation to honor that name and never defile it, that the name of the McKay family might be perpetuated through all time.

And to the Church: Cherish his memory, you Church members, by living in your youth, in your marriage, in your homes, as nearly to the perfection that he has demonstrated. He has been called home. New leadership will carry on, not to take his place—no one can take his place—but merely to fill the vacancy caused by his passing. If we look to the leadership that God will place and that will follow thereafter as we have followed President McKay, all will be right with the world; and in the words of some, "stick with the old ship," the kingdom of God, and trust in Almighty God, and He will bring us safely through.

There are evidences today of oppression to the Church and kingdom of God, but like the Apostle Paul we say:

> For we preach not ourselves, but Christ Jesus the Lord; and ourselves your servants for Jesus' sake.
>
> We are troubled on every side, yet not distressed; we are perplexed, but not in despair;
>
> Persecuted, but not forsaken; cast down, but not destroyed. (2 Corinthians 4:5, 8-9.)

Along with Job in the midst of his suffering, we declare, "For I know that my redeemer liveth, and that he shall stand at the latter day upon the earth: And though after my skin worms destroy this body, yet in my flesh shall I see God. . . ." (Job 19:25-26)—if I am worthy and hopefully to stand by the side of this noble leader, whom we have loved so much in life.

"In my Father's house are many mansions: if it were not so, I would have told you. I go to prepare a place for you. . . . that where I am, there ye may be also." (John 14:2-3.) I can imagine his wanting to say that to us now. There are many mansions in our Father's kingdom beyond this. "I go to prepare a place for you. . . . that where I am, there ye may be also. And whither I go ye know, and the way ye know." ". . . Let not your heart be troubled, neither let it be afraid." (John 14:2-4, 27.)

And so as one who bears the responsibility of being a special witness, as was President McKay, and as we have come one by one into the Council of the Twelve, we have been enjoined to remember that our greatest responsibility is to bear a true witness of the divine mission of our Lord and Savior Jesus Christ. And so with all the fervor of my soul, I join with my fellow members of the apostleship. We know, as President McKay knew, that Jesus lives, that He is the Redeemer of the world, and that comfort will come to all who mourn, to the extent that they too can receive that divine witness that Jesus is the Savior of this world, and that this life is but a schooling to prepare us for the life beyond this. To this I bear humble testimony. May we cling to the iron rod lest we in an evil moment fall prey to the wiles of the evil one and miss the golden opportunities that are ours if we remain true to the faith.

Section Five

BASIC PRINCIPLES AND ORDINANCES OF THE GOSPEL

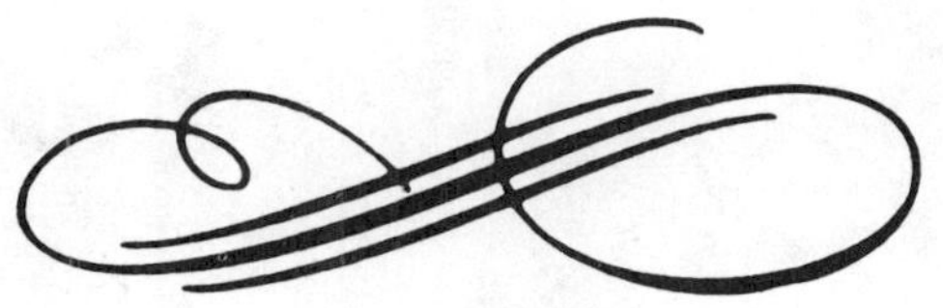

18

"Stand Ye in Holy Places"

If you want to know what the Lord has for this people at the present time, I would admonish you to get and read the discourses that are delivered at general conference; for what the Brethren speak by the power of the Holy Ghost is the mind of the Lord, the will of the Lord, the voice of the Lord, and the power of God unto salvation. I am sure all who listen, if they are in tune, feel the sincerity and the deep conviction from those who speak so appropriately and so effectively.

My soul is filled with joy as I think of the great men whom the Lord has brought to the service of the Church as General Authorities and all others who serve—our Regional Representatives of the Twelve, our Mission Representatives of the Twelve and the First Council of the Seventy, and all who serve in the various organizations. As we have seen them being brought into key positions, we have marveled as to how, when we have need of a man or person for a particular office, the man of the hour seems to be brought to us, almost in a miraculous way.

I remember the instruction that was given by the prophet Alma as a group who had been converted waited on the banks for baptism; and as he explained to them the nature of the covenant in which they were to enter as baptized members, he said:

> . . . as ye are desirous to come into the fold of God, and to be called his people, and are willing to bear one another's burdens, that they may be light;
>
> Yea, and are willing to mourn with those that mourn; yea, and comfort those that stand in need of comfort, and to stand as witnesses of God at all times and in all things, and in all places that ye may be in. . . .
>
> Now I say unto you, if this be the desire of your hearts, what have you against being baptized in the name of the Lord, as a witness before him that ye have entered into a covenant with him, that ye will serve him and keep his commandments, that he may pour out his Spirit more abundantly upon you? (Mosiah 18:8-10.)

If I were to ask you what is the heaviest burden one may have to bear in this life, what would you answer? The heaviest burden that one has to bear in this life is the burden of sin. How do you help one to bear that great burden of sin, in order that it might be light?

Some years ago, President Marion G. Romney and I were sitting in my office. The door opened and a fine young man came in with a troubled look on his face, and he said, "Brethren, I am going to the temple for the first time tomorrow. I have made some mistakes in the past, and I have gone to my bishop and my stake president, and I have made a clean disclosure of it all; and after a period of repentance and assurance that I have not returned again to those mistakes, they have now adjudged me ready to go to the temple. But, brethren, that is not enough. I want to know, and how can I know, that the Lord has forgiven me also."

What would you answer one who might come to you

asking that question? As we pondered for a moment, we remembered King Benjamin's address contained in the book of Mosiah. Here was a group of people asking for baptism, and they said they viewed themselves in their carnal state:

> . . . And they all cried aloud with one voice, saying: O have mercy, and apply the atoning blood of Christ that we may receive forgiveness of our sins, and our hearts may be purified; . . .
>
> . . . after they had spoken these words the Spirit of the Lord came upon them, and they were filled with joy, having received a remission of their sins, and having peace of conscience. . . . (Mosiah 4:2-3.)

There was the answer.

If the time comes when you have done all that you can to repent of your sins, whoever you are, wherever you are, and have made amends and restitution to the best of your ability; if it be something that will affect your standing in the Church and you have gone to the proper authorities, then you will want that confirming answer as to whether or not the Lord has accepted of you. In your soul-searching, if you seek for and you find that peace of conscience, by that token you may know that the Lord has accepted of your repentance. Satan would have you think otherwise and sometimes persuade you that now having made one mistake, you might go on and on with no turning back. That is one of the great falsehoods. The miracle of forgiveness is available to all of those who turn from their evil doings and return no more, because the Lord has said in a revelation to us in our days: ". . . go your ways and sin no more; but unto that soul who sinneth [meaning again] shall the former sins return, saith the Lord your God." (D&C 82:7.) Have that in mind, all of you who may be troubled with a burden of sin.

And to you who are teachers, may you help to lift that

great burden from those who are carrying it, and who have their conscience so seared that they are kept from activity, and they don't know where to go to find the answers. You help them to that day of repentance and restitution, in order that they too may have that peace of conscience, the confirming of the Spirit of the Lord that He has accepted of their repentance.

The great call comes in the sermons of the brethren to aid those who are in need of aid—not just temporal aid, but spiritual aid. The greatest miracles I see today are not necessarily the healing of sick bodies, but the greatest miracles I see are the healing of sick souls, those who are sick in soul and spirit and are downhearted and distraught, on the verge of nervous breakdowns. We are reaching out to all such, because they are precious in the sight of the Lord, and we want no one to feel that he is forgotten.

I read again and again the experience of Peter and John, as they went through the gate beautiful on the way to the temple. Here was one who had never walked, impotent from his birth, begging alms of all who approached the gate. And as Peter and John approached, he held out his hand expectantly, asking for alms. Peter, speaking for this pair of missionaries—church authorities—said, "Look on us." And, of course, that heightened his expectation. Then Peter said, "Silver and gold have I none; but such as I have give I thee: In the name of Jesus Christ of Nazareth rise up and walk." (Acts 3:4, 6.)

Now in my mind's eye I can picture this man and what was in his mind. "Doesn't this man know that I have never walked? He commands me to walk." But the biblical record doesn't end there. Peter just didn't content himself by commanding the man to walk, but he "took him by the right hand, and lifted him up. . . ." (Acts 3:7.)

Will you see that picture now of that noble soul, that chiefest of the apostles, perhaps with his arms around the shoulders of this man, and saying, "Now, my good man, have courage. I will take a few steps with you. Let's walk together, and I assure you that you can walk, because you have received a blessing by the power and authority that God has given us as men, his servants." Then the man leaped with joy.

You cannot lift another soul until you are standing on higher ground than he is. You must be sure, if you would rescue the man, that you yourself are setting the example of what you would have him be. You cannot light a fire in another soul unless it is burning in your own soul. You teachers, the testimony that you bear, the spirit with which you teach and with which you lead, is one of the most important assets that you can have, as you help to strengthen those who need so much, wherein you have so much to give. Who of us, in whatever station we may have been in, have not needed strengthening?

May I impose upon you for a moment to express appreciation for something that happened to me some time ago. I was suffering from an ulcer condition that was becoming worse and worse. We had been touring a mission; my wife, Joan, and I were impressed the next morning that we should get home as quickly as possible, although we had planned to stay for some other meetings.

On the way across the country, we were sitting in the forward section of the airplane. Some of our Church members were in the next section of the airplane. As we approached a certain point en route, someone laid his hand upon my head. I looked up; I could see no one. That happened again before we arrived home, again with the same experience. Who it was, by what means or what medium, I may never know, except I knew that I was receiving a blessing that I came a few hours later to know I needed most desperately.

As soon as we arrived home, my wife very anxiously called the doctor. It was now about 11 o'clock at night. He called me to come to the telephone, and he asked how I was; and I said, "Well, I am very tired. I think I will be all right." But shortly thereafter, there came massive hemorrhages which, had they occurred while we were in flight, I wouldn't be here today talking about it.

I know that there are powers divine that reach out when all other help is not available. We see that manifest down in the countries we speak of as the underprivileged countries where there is little medical aid and perhaps no hospitals. If you want to hear of great miracles among these humble people with simple faith, you will see it among them when they are left to themselves. Yes, I know that there are such powers.

As I came to realize the overwhelming magnitude of the responsibility that now has been given to me to serve, as president of the Church, if I were to have sat down and tried to think of the burden, I would have been devastated and wholly incapable of carrying it. But when I was guided by the Spirit to name as counselors in the First Presidency two noble men, President N. Eldon Tanner and President Marion G. Romney, I realized that mine was not the responsibility to carry these responsibilities alone. And then as we meet week by week in the temple and look across the room and see twelve stalwart men, men chosen from out the world and given the power of the holy apostleship, I am aware that no greater men walk the earth than these men.

Newly baptized members who know little about the gospel and much less about the disciplines of the Church must be taught if the Church is to be safely led. And we have serving with us some of the strongest men in the Church, our Regional Representatives and Mission Representatives. They are going out to the humblest everywhere and teaching them these fundamental principles, teaching them, as the Prophet Joseph answered when asked, "How do you govern your people?" He answered, "I teach them correct principles, and they govern themselves."

They are not going out to do the work themselves. As we have said to them, they are standing as "coaches" rather than as "quarterbacks" on the football team, teaching the quarterbacks how to direct, teaching them correct principles. They are men of faith. And how grateful we are for all these general auxiliary workers who go out, likewise at great expense, great travel, and sacrifice on the part of their businesses and their families.

To you great leaders, stake presidencies, mission presidencies, bishoprics, priesthood quorum leaders, all of you, the faithful Saints everywhere, you who pray for us, I want you to know that we pray earnestly at the altars of the temple for all of you faithful who pray for us. How grateful we are for you!

Just before the dedication of the Los Angeles Temple, something new happened in my life when, along about three or four o'clock in the morning, I enjoyed an experience that I think was not a dream, but it must have been a vision. It seemed that I was witnessing a great spiritual gathering, where men and women were standing up, two or three at a time, and speaking in tongues. The spirit was so unusual. I seemed to hear the voice of President David O. McKay say, "If you want to love God, you have to learn to love and serve the people. That is the way to show your love for God." And there were other things then that I saw and heard.

And so today there is no shadow of doubting in my

mind that I know the reality of the person who is presiding over this church, our Lord and Master, Jesus Christ. I know that He is closer to us than many times we have any idea. He and the Father are not an absentee Lord and Father. They are concerned about us, helping to prepare us for the advent of the Savior, whose coming certainly isn't too far away because of the signs that are becoming apparent.

All you need to do is to read the scriptures, particularly the inspired translation of Matthew, the twenty-fourth chapter, found in the writings of Joseph Smith in the Pearl of Great Price, where the Lord told His disciples to stand in holy places and be not moved, for He comes quickly, but no man knows the hour nor the day. That is the preparation.

In your homes, I pray you, say as did Joshua of old, ". . . as for me and my house, we will serve the Lord." (Joshua 24:15.) Teach your families in your family home evening; teach them to keep the commandments of God, for therein is our only safety in these days. If they will do that, the powers of the Almighty will descend upon them as the dews from heaven, and the Holy Ghost will be theirs. That can be our guide, and that Spirit shall guide us and direct us to His holy home.

And so, as it is my privilege to do, I give you faithful members of the Church everywhere my blessing. God bless you, take care of you, and preserve you. Our love extends not only to those of our Father's children who are already members of the Church, but to all those who are our Father's children to whom He would have us bring the gospel of truth; make them also to enjoy the blessings that we now have.

May the Lord help us so to understand and do, and fill our stations, and not be found wanting in the day of judgment that we have not done all we know how to do to advance

His work in righteousness, I humbly pray in the name of the Lord Jesus Christ.

19

Testimony Is a Divine Witness

IN an address to a conference of Primary workers, I quoted the following statement from President Joseph F. Smith to impress the necessity of a testimony as a requisite for a Latter-day Saint teacher: "Any man who will question the divinity of the mission of the Lord Jesus Christ, or will deny the so-called miracles of the scriptures is unfit to be a teacher of Latter-day Saint children."

I also made the statement in concluding my remarks that you cannot kindle a fire in another heart until it is burning in your own, and called attention to what the Lord had plainly said: "And the Spirit shall be given unto you by the prayer of faith; and if ye receive not the Spirit ye shall not teach." (D&C 42:14.)

A few days thereafter I was challenged by a prominent attorney, not a member of the Church, to prove from the scriptures my statement as to the importance of a testimony.

He argued: "We have faith and we believe, but we do

not know; we have faith when we cannot prove for a moral certainty that what we have faith in and believe in is absolutely true. It seems to me that a testimony puts an end to faith because faith is no longer necessary when the truth is established, so far as the individual is concerned. I have faith in many things, but I cannot prove them; and the reason I have faith is because I cannot prove them and therefore have faith they are true."

I invite my reader to think with me as I attempt a satisfactory answer to our truth-seeking friend.

First, it would seem necessary to define what is meant by faith and testimony. Webster defines faith as—

> the fact of accepting or the disposition to accept as real, true or the like, that which is not supported by sensible evidence or rational proofs or which is undemonstrable . . . an act or state of acknowledging unquestioningly the existence, power, etc., of a supreme being and the reality of a divine order.

The Apostle Paul's classic definition of faith reads: ". . . the substance [or assurance, as some versions have it] of things hoped for, the evidence of things not seen." (Hebrews 11:1.)

A brilliant scholar observed: "To believe only possibilities is not faith, but mere philosophy."

Testimony may be defined simply as divine revelation to the man of faith. The psalmist echoes the same thought: ". . . the testimony of the Lord is sure. . . ." (Psalm 19:7.) Paul, the apostle, declared ". . . no man can say [or know] that Jesus is the Lord, but by the Holy Ghost." (1 Corinthians 12:3.) The prophets have further taught that if you were to

> ask with a sincere heart, with real intent, having faith in Christ, he will manifest the truth of it unto you, by the power of the Holy Ghost. And by the power of the Holy Ghost ye may know the truth of all things. (Moroni 10:4-5.)

So it was with Peter. After his inspired testimony of the divine mission of his Lord, the Master explained: ". . . flesh and blood hath not revealed it unto thee, but my Father which is in heaven." (Matthew 16:17.) A prophet has further said that you "receive no witness until after the trial of your faith." (Ether 12:6.)

With these truths made clear, then—first, that a testimony follows the exercise of faith, and second, that revelation by the power of the Holy Ghost is required for one to receive a testimony—the next question of our truth-seeking friend would naturally be, "Just how does one prepare himself to receive that divine witness called testimony?"

The prophet Alma presents an excellent explanation of the progressive steps by which one proceeds in his search for truth from a desire to experiment upon the words of the Lord to the "exercise [of] a particle of faith, yea, even . . . no more than [a] desire to believe, let this desire work in you, even until ye believe in a manner that ye can give place for a portion" of the words of the Lord; then by spiritual processes within one's own soul his knowledge and testimony is made "perfect in that thing, and [his] faith is dormant. . . ." (Alma 32:27, 34.)

As one reads this whole text, he finds clearly prescribed the way by which all may receive a testimony or "knowledge by revelation" as defined above: first, desire; second, belief; third, faith; fourth, knowledge or testimony.

That a testimony can be received only upon certain conditions is clearly pointed out by the Master, who told His disciples that the Comforter, the Spirit of Truth or the Holy Ghost, would be given to those who were His disciples, but "whom the world cannot receive, because it seeth him not, neither knoweth him. . . ." (John 14:17.) He had previously declared to the unbelieving Jews, "If any man will do his will, he shall know of the doctrine, whether it be of God, or whether I speak of myself." (John 7:17.)

Thus may one make of himself "a temple of the Holy Ghost," as the Apostle Paul taught, and be prepared to receive its gift of revelation.

The Prophet Joseph Smith declared that "no man can receive the Holy Ghost without receiving revelations. The Holy Ghost is a revelator." As to the unexplainable process by which a person receives that "birth of the Spirit" or the witness of testimony, the Master has this to say:

> The wind bloweth where it listeth, and thou hearest the sound thereof, but canst not tell whence it cometh, and whither it goeth; so is every one that is born of the Spirit. (John 3:8.)

But now we must understand one thing more: Faith necessary to knowledge comes by "hearing the word of God," as Paul said. In our day, we have an invaluable scripture given to us in the Book of Mormon, in which the Lord has told us is contained the "fulness of the gospel." (D&C 20:9.) Of the importance in building testimony the Prophet Joseph wrote in his private journal:

> I spent the day in the council with the Twelve Apostles at the house of President (Brigham) Young, conversing with them upon a variety of subjects. . . . I told the brethren that the Book of Mormon was the most correct of any book on earth and the keystone of our religion, and a man would get nearer to God by abiding its precepts than by any other book. (*DHC* 4:461.)

One of our former mission presidents bears a remarkable testimony to the importance of this sacred record. He, in company with brethren of the General Authorities, several years ago was negotiating the purchase of properties in the vicinity of the Hill Cumorah in New York. At an early morning hour and alone he walked to a point on the hill near where the monument now stands. As he stood there reverently, he heard distinctly a voice that said to him: "Push the distribution of the record taken from this hill. It will help bring the world to Christ."

God lives! Jesus is the Savior of this world! The gospel of Jesus Christ as contained in fulness in the ancient and modern scriptures is true! These things I know by the witness of the Spirit to my spirit.

As I know, so may all who do the will of God know by the power of the Holy Ghost, even as the Lord promised in another dispensation: "I will visit thy brethren according to their diligence in keeping my commandments. . . ." (Enos 10.)

20

"Search Diligently, Pray Always, and Be Believing"

"*SEARCH* diligently, pray always, and be believing, and all things shall work together for your good, if ye walk uprightly and remember the covenant wherewith ye have covenanted one with another." (D&C 90:24.)

This quotation was from one of the revelations given when the Church was less than three years old, given in March 1833. Enemies of the Church from without were bringing persecution upon all who professed to be members of the Church of Jesus Christ. Under withering and merciless persecution, they were seeing in our day an interpretation of the Master's interpretation of the parable of the sowers. Some of the new members brought forth only thirtyfold; some brought forth sixtyfold; and a small percentage only, an hundredfold. (See Mark 4:8.)

With little or no experience in church administration among the Church leaders at that time, there was occasionally confusion and disunity, and the immaturity of the members was evidenced in quarrelings and bickerings and factional disputes, and there was a spirit of apostasy in various places, which threatened at times to destroy the very structure of the Church.

It was important, then, that the Lord should send this important warning and instruction that they should search diligently, pray always, and be believing, so that all things would work to their good. Diligence means to be industrious, the opposite of being lazy or careless or indifferent. In other words, they must search to know the doctrines of the Church, and they must search to know the instructions that had been given concerning Church procedures. They were to pray always.

Our missionaries after over a hundred years of experience have learned that no one is truly converted until he prays on his knees to know that Joseph Smith is a prophet of God and that the Church is indeed the Church of Jesus Christ on earth. And the four essentials that the missionaries teach to one who has never prayed before are: he first must thank; he next must ask; he must do it in the name of Jesus Christ; and then he must conclude it with amen. And with that simple instruction the beginning inquirer after truth is taught to pray. In praying, he is enjoined as the father said to his son, after listening to his son's prayers, "Son, don't give the Lord instructions. You just report for duty."

It is a wonderful thing for us in our younger years to remember what old age brings. Chauncey Depew, a United States Congressman, was asked on his ninetieth birthday about his philosophy of life. He replied that when he was a young man his greatest amibition had been to display his intelligence, but the older he grew the greater was his anxiety to conceal his ignorance. It was indeed the beginning of learning when Moses said, after the great and soul-stirring revelation of the personality of God, "Now, for this cause I know that man is nothing, which thing I never had supposed." (Moses 1:10.) That was in the beginning of his wisdom.

To be believing means first to obtain a testimony and then strive to retain it. The testing must precede the testimony, for one will "receive no witness until after the trial of their faith." As the Master said,

> . . . that which is born of the Spirit is spirit.
>
> The wind bloweth where it listeth, and thou hearest the sound thereof, but canst not tell whence it cometh, and whither it goeth: so is every one that is born of the Spirit. (John 3:6, 8.)

The power of the Spirit was more definitely defined in an early revelation to these new Saints when the Lord said:

> . . . I say unto you that assuredly as the Lord liveth, who is your God and your Redeemer, even so surely shall you receive. . . .
>
> Yea, behold, I will tell you in your mind and in your heart, by the Holy Ghost, which shall come upon you and which shall dwell in your heart. (D&C 8:1-2.)

He said further that if they would walk uprightly and remember their covenant, then they would have all things that would work to their good. To walk uprightly means to be morally correct, to be honest, to be just, to be honorable. As the Lord told Enos, the grandson of Lehi, "I will visit thy brethren according to their diligence in keeping my commandments" (Enos 10), which was repeated in substance when the Lord revealed this great truth: "I, the Lord, am bound when ye do what I say; but when ye do not what I say, ye have no promise." (D&C 82:10.) The nature of the covenant that we enter into when we become members of the Church was fully explained when the Lord said:

> *And again, by way of commandment to the church concerning the manner of baptism*—All those who humble themselves before God, and desire to be baptized, and come forth with broken hearts and contrite

spirits, and witness before the church that they have truly repented of all their sins, and are willing to take upon them the name of Jesus Christ, having a determination to serve him to the end, and truly manifest by their works that they have received of the Spirit of Christ unto the remission of their sins, shall be received by baptism into his church. (D&C 20:37.)

The people in the Book of Mormon days were instructed with a similar explanation. "And now I speak," Moroni said,

> concerning baptism, Behold, elders, priests, and teachers were baptized; and they were not baptized save they brought forth fruit meet that they were worthy of it.
>
> Neither did they receive any unto baptism save they came forth with a broken heart and a contrite spirit, and witnessed unto the church that they truly repented of all their sins. (Moroni 6:1-2.)

King Benjamin explained it this way:

> And now, because of the covenant which ye have made ye shall be called the children of Christ, his sons, and his daughters; for behold, this day he hath spiritually begotten you; for ye say that your hearts are changed through faith on his name; therefore, ye are born of him and have become his sons and his daughters. (Mosiah 5:7.)

Others of the prophets asked this soul-searching question of those who were candidates for baptism: "Are you willing to stand as witnesses of God at all times and in all things, and in all places that you might be in, even until death?" (See Mosiah 18:9.) To the first one of those who was baptized, the prophet who officiated said, as he was directed under inspiration,

> Helam, I baptize thee, having authority from the Almighty God, as a testimony that ye have entered into a covenant to serve him until you are dead as to the mortal body; and may the Spirit of the Lord be poured out upon you; and may he grant unto you eternal life, through the redemption of Christ, whom he has prepared from the foundation of the world. (Mosiah 18:13.)

Never was there a time when Church members generally, and newly baptized converts particularly, throughout the stakes and missions, needed more to be reminded of the Lord's admonition that they should search diligently, and pray always, and be believing, that all things should work to their good if they would walk uprightly and remember the covenant wherewith they had covenanted one with another, as the scriptures to which I have referred have so well explained.

Thousands of new members have built upon the foundation of their faith at the time of their baptism, but there are wolves in sheep's clothing among them. Older members by bad example could wound their weak conscience, and make their weaker brethren to offend. (See 1 Corinthians 8:11-13.) Dissension and confusion could result from lack of experience, and the tide of persecution from the outside could roll in upon them and engulf them in a flood of apostasy unless they heed the Lord's warnings.

I was in Australia some time ago, and after I had spent a long evening instructing the stake leaders in their duties, one of the brethren raised his hand and said, "Now, Brother Lee, you have spent the evening telling us what to do. Now answer us one more question. Just how do we obtain the spiritual power necessary for us to lead this people and to instruct them?"

Perhaps a few illustrations will serve to suggest the answer.

I once received a letter from a patriarch who had been instructed that what he should speak in blessings upon the people should be that which the Lord inspired and not of himself. In the struggle that followed his ordination, he sought to know how he could distinguish between what the Lord inspired and that which was just his own thinking. He remembered, he said, what the Lord admonished in an early revelation to Joseph Smith and Oliver Cowdery: ". . . you cannot write [which to him meant you cannot say] that which is sacred save it be given you from me." (D&C 9:9.)

"So my personal problem finally was resolved," he wrote me, "by making this conclusion: You have been called and ordained to this work by an authorized servant of the Lord. You have the authroity to proceed. You must live as closely to the Lord as you know how. You must constantly seek and pray for guidance and inspiration, then perform your duties in humility and rest content in the knowledge that you have done all you could, and in the firm belief that what you have said in giving blessings was indeed inspired."

The Lord's formula for new and untried leaders was this:

> Again I say unto you, that it shall not be given to any one to go forth to preach my gospel, or to build up my church, except he be ordained by some one who has authority, and it is known to the church that he has authority and has been regularly ordained by the heads of the church.
>
> And again, the elders, priests and teachers of this church shall teach the principles of my gospel, which are in the Bible and the Book of Mormon, in the which is the fulness of the gospel.
>
> And they shall observe the covenants and church articles to do them, and these shall be their teachings, as they shall be directed by the Spirit.
>
> And the Spirit shall be given unto you by the prayer of faith; and if ye receive not the Spirit ye shall not teach. (D&C 42:11-14.)

Summarized, this means that there are four essentials for service in the kingdom of God: (1) We must be ordained, (2) we must teach from the standard church works, (3) we must live as we preach, and, (4) we must teach by the Spirit. ". . . when a man speaketh by the power of the Holy Ghost the power of the Holy Ghost carrieth it unto the hearts of the children of men." (2 Nephi 33:1.)

So the Lord has told us in plain language how His servants can be inspired. It was as Alma observed in the sons of Mosiah who were great and successful missionaries: "They were strong in the knowledge of the truth, for they were men of a sound understanding." They fasted and prayed often, and they cultivated "the spirit of prophecy, and the spirit of revelation," so that "when they taught, they taught with power and authority of God." (See Alma 17:2-3.)

I met a man in his late seventies down in Brisbane, Australia, who said that all his lifetime he had been searching for a church that could answer satisfactorily his question, "Are God and his Son, the Savior of the world, living with your church today?" And always the answer to his question was negative. "The scriptures are closed," he had been told. "There is no prophet through whom the Lord speaks today. God does not reveal himself to man."

He was convalescing from a painful accident when two young men—missionaries of The Church of Jesus Christ of Latter-day Saints—called. In their opening testimony, they bore witness that the Lord had appeared with His Heavenly Father to Joseph Smith, and in answer to Joseph's question as to which church they should join, he was told to join none of them, for they were all wrong, that "they draw near to me with their lips, but their hearts are far from me, they teach for doctrines the commandments of men, having a form of godliness, but they deny the power thereof." (Joseph Smith 2:19.)

Here was the answer he had been seeking, and the Spirit bore witness that this was in truth the true Church of Jesus Christ, with which the Father and the Son were living today.

Brigham Young, in speaking about the same things, said,

If all the talent, tact, wisdom, and refinement of the world had been sent to me with the Book of Mormon, and had declared, in the most exalted of earthly eloquence the truth of it, undertaking to prove

> it by learning and worldly wisdom, they would have been to me like the smoke which rises only to vanish away. But when I saw a man without eloquence, or talent for public speaking, who could only say, "I know, by the power of the Holy Ghost, that the Book of Mormon is true, that Joseph Smith is a Prophet of the Lord," the Holy Ghost proceeding from that individual illuminated my understanding, and light, glory, and immortality were before me. I was encircled by them, filled with them, and I knew for myself that the testimony of that man was true. (*Journal of Discourses* 1:90.)

We must teach with that in mind. If the Holy Ghost does not bear witness to the things we say, we cannot and we will not be successful in our missionary work.

I heard a missionary telling about President David O. McKay's visit to Glasgow, Scotland, when a young reporter looked at him and asked, "Are you a prophet of God?" And the young man said President McKay looked at the reporter and replied: "Young man, you look me in the eye and answer your own question." This young man in telling me the story said, "I looked President McKay in the eye, and I received my answer and my witness that he is in truth a prophet of the Living God," to which I also bear humble testimony in the name of the Lord Jesus Christ.

"Except the Lord build the house, they labour in vain that build it. . . ." (Psalm 127:1.)

Today the servants, many unschooled and inexperienced like the disciples of old, must "go forth"—"the Lord working with them, and confirming the word with signs following." (Mark 16:20.)

Except we do walk uprightly and remember our covenants and have an unshakable testimony of the divinity of this church, then, in the language of an eminent businessman and financier, the various activities of the Church would be but a shambles.

May the Lord help us to search diligently and walk

uprightly and remember the covenant wherewith we have covenanted one with another.

21

"What Lack I Yet?"

WE hear much about love as an element in teaching. This recalls an experience when our first little five-year-old trudged off alone to a great big school. I myself had been a principal of schools before, but somehow that morning was a very difficult morning for me. I went home for lunch; and, on some pretext or other, I went over to the school. And as I stood before the kindergarten teacher, embarrassed now that I was there and wondering what I was going to say to her, I finally blurted out, "Miss Sanders, we have sent to you today the most precious thing we have in all the world—our first little five-year-old. We are not concerned about the details of what you teach her—numbering, lettering, writing, and so on. There is only one thing that is in our hearts. We want you to love our little girl, and we want you to teach her to love you. If you'll do that, that's all we ask of you for our little girl."

The more I have seen of teaching, the more I think

that this is the great demand upon those who teach our children. You love them and teach them to love you, and I will take a chance on the outcome of your instruction.

Our responsibility in teaching the gospel is to inspire others to Christlike living. I know this is an all-inclusive statement, one so broad in its concepts that I would almost continue to the limit of my understanding of the gospel and I would not exhaust the possibilities of the subject. To put that statement more in the language of the scriptures would be to say, taking a declaration from the Master's great Sermon on the Mount, "Be ye therefore perfect, even as your Father which is in heaven is perfect." (Matthew 5:48.)

"Christlike living" is a phrase that I think we borrowed from other sources and is one not commonly found in scriptural references. Another scripture that might help explain it is relative to the incident of the splendid young man who came to the Master, as many inquiring youth have come to good teachers, asking, "Good Master, what good thing shall I do, that I may have eternal life?" In other words, what must I have in order to become perfect or to live a Christlike life? The Master answered him:

> . . . if thou wilt enter into life, keep the commandments. He saith unto him, Which? Jesus said, Thou shalt do no murder, Thou shalt not commit adultery, Thou shalt not steal, Thou shalt not bear false witness, Honour thy father and thy mother: and, Thou shalt love thy neighbour as thyself.

In other words, He had said to the young man: "Keep the Ten Commandments if you would enter into life."

The young man said unto Him, "All these things have I kept from my youth up: what lack I yet?"

And then the Master's reply: ". . . go and sell that thou hast, and give to the poor, and thou shalt have treasure in heaven: and come and follow me." Then Jesus told His disciples, as the young man turned sorrowfully away because he possessed many riches, how hard it is for them that trust in riches "to enter into the kingdom of God." (See Matthew 19:16-24.)

What must I do to be saved? As I pondered these words, I thought of three essentials that are necessary to inspire one to live a Christlike life—or, speaking more accurately in the language of the scriptures, to live more perfectly as the Master lived. The first essential I would name in order to qualify is: There must be awakened in the individual who would be taught or who would live perfectly an awareness of his needs.

The rich young ruler did not need to be taught repentance from murder nor from murderous thoughts. He did not have to be schooled in how to repent from adultery, nor from stealing, lying, defrauding, or failing to honor his mother. All these he said he had observed from his youth; but his question was, "What lack I yet?"

The Master, with His keen discernment and the power of a Great Teacher, diagnosed the young man's case perfectly: His need and his lack were to overcome his love for worldly things, his tendency to trust in riches. And then Jesus prescribed the effective remedy: "If thou wilt be perfect, go and sell that thou hast, and give to the poor, and thou shalt have treasure in heaven: and come and follow me." (Matthew 19:21.)

In the Apostle Paul's dramatic conversion, when he was physically blinded by the light while on his way to Damascus with letters of authority to persecute and stamp out that sect which he thought was perpetrating a serious heresy, he heard a voice that said to him: "Saul, Saul, why persecutest thou me?" And from the depths of this humbled Saul's soul there came the question that is always asked by the one who senses that he needs something: "Lord, what wilt thou have me to do?"

Now the Master knew what Paul's great trouble was. He was one of the most brilliant scholars of that community. He had studied under some of the greatest teachers. He was what we would call "worldly wise." He thought he was doing God's service. His energies were misdirected. But the Master knew his heart, and He knew his righteous zeal. Paul's need was a cure for that arrogance because of his superior (as he may have thought) intellectual abilities beyond the humble and unlearned among the early apostolic leaders. So the Master not only diagnosed what his need was, but He supplied a startling and most effective remedy. The Lord did not tell him now to go and be baptized, but He told him to go into the city, where Ananias would instruct him. (This was the very man whom Paul had letters of authority to go to persecute!) (See Acts 9:1-20.)

Alma warned Shiblon, his son:

> Do not pray as the Zoramites do, for ye have seen that they pray to be heard of men, and to be praised for their wisdom.
>
> Do not say: O God, I thank thee that we are better than our brethren; but rather say: O Lord, forgive my unworthiness, and remember my brethren in mercy—yea, acknowledge your unworthiness before God at all times.
>
> . . . Now go, my son, and teach the word unto this people. Be sober. . . . (Alma 38:13-15.)

Enos, the grandson of Lehi, tells of the wrestle he had before God, before he received a remission of his sins. We are not told what his sins were, but he apparently confessed them very freely. And then he said, "And my soul hungered. . . ." (Enos 4.) You see, that awareness and feeling of great need, and that soul-searching, brought him face to face with his lack and his need.

This quality of sensing one's need was expressed in the great Sermon on the Mount when the Master said, "Blessed are the poor in spirit: for theirs is the kingdom of heaven." (Matthew 5:3.) The poor in spirit, of course, means those who are spiritually needy, who feel so impoverished spiritually that they reach out with great yearning for help.

To those who think they are wise, such as the Apostle Paul, Nephi said: ". . . When they are learned they think they are wise, . . . But to be learned is good if they hearken unto the counsels of God. But wo unto the rich, who are rich as to the things of the world. . . ." (2 Nephi 9:28-30.) He had an effective remedy when he found one who needed help.

Every one of us, if we would reach perfection, must one time ask ourselves this question, "What lack I yet?" if we would commence our climb upward on the highway to perfection. The effective leader is one who helps the learner to discover that lack, to diagnose his basic difficulties, and then to prescribe his spiritual remedies.

The second essential for perfection that I would name is found in the conversation the Master had with Nicodemus. He discerned as Nicodemus came to Him that he was seeking to have the answer to what many others had asked Him: "What must I do to be saved?" And the Master answered, "Verily, verily, I say unto thee, Except a man be born again, he cannot see the kingdom of God." Then Nicodemus said, "How can a man be born when he is old? . . ." Jesus answered, "Verily, verily, I say unto thee, Except a man be born of water and of the Spirit, he cannot enter into the kingdom of God." (John 3:3-5.)

A man must be "born again" if he would reach perfection, in order to see or enter into the kingdom of God. And how is one born again? That is the same question that Enos asked. And you remember the simple answer that came back: "Because of thy faith in Christ, whom thou hast never before heard nor seen. And many years pass away before he shall manifest himself in the flesh; wherefore, go to, thy faith hath made thee whole." (Enos 8.)

Brother Marion D. Romney and I were sitting in the office one day when a young man came in. He was getting ready to go on a mission, and he had been interviewed in the usual way and had made confessions of certain transgressions of his youth. But he said to us, "I'm not satisfied by just having confessed. How can I know that I have been forgiven?" In other words, "How do I know that I am born again?" He felt he could not go on a mission in his present state.

As we talked, Brother Romney said: "Son, do you remember what King Benjamin said? He was preaching to some who had been pricked in their hearts because of 'their own carnal state, even less than the dust of the earth. And they all cried aloud with one voice, saying: O have mercy, and apply the atoning blood of Christ that we may receive forgiveness of our sins, and our hearts may be purified; for we believe in Jesus Christ, the Son of God, who created heaven and earth, and all things; who shall come down among the children of men. And it came to pass that after they had spoken these words the Spirit of the Lord came upon them, and they were filled with joy, having received a remission of their sins, and having a peace of conscience, because of their exceeding faith which they had in Jesus Christ. . . .' " (Mosiah 4:2-3.)

Brother Romney said to him, "My son, you wait and pray until you have the peace of conscience because of your faith in Jesus Christ's atonement, and you will know that your sins then have been forgiven." Except for that, as Elder Romney explained, any one of us is impoverished, and we are wandering in a fog until we have had that rebirth.

In the Master's farewell sermon to the Nephites, He said, "And my Father sent me that I might be lifted up upon the cross; and after that I had been lifted up upon the cross, that I might draw all men unto me. . . ." (3 Nephi 27:14.) Nephi had written, "For we labor diligently to write, to persuade our children, and also our brethren, to believe in Christ, and to be reconciled to God; for we know that it is by grace that we are saved, after all we can do." (2 Nephi 25:23.)

Almost the last thing that the Master said to the Nephites was, "And no unclean thing can enter into his kingdom. . . ." (3 Nephi 27:19.)

Now let us confess it, all of us are "sinners anonymous." All of us have done things we ought not to have done, or we have neglected things we should have done; and every one of us has need for repentance. So let us not, as President Woodruff said, spend too much time confessing the other fellow's sins. Ours is the responsibility to find our own need for repentance.

> . . . no unclean thing can enter into his kingdom; therefore nothing entereth into his rest save it be those who have washed their garments in my blood, because of their faith, and the repentance of all their sins, and their faithfulness unto the end.

And then the Savior added,

> Now this is the commandment; Repent, all ye ends of the earth, and come unto me and be baptized in my name, that ye may be sanctified by the reception of the Holy Ghost, that ye may stand spotless before me at the last day. (3 Nephi 27:19-20.)

After they had pondered His words, He added: ". . . Therefore, what manner of men ought ye to be? Verily I say unto you, even as I am." (3 Nephi 27:27.) "Be ye therefore perfect," He was saying to them, "even as your Father which is in heaven is perfect."

You cannot have a Christlike life, as the test would have it, without being born again. One would never be happy in the presence of the Holy One of Israel without this cleansing and purifying. Moroni said, ". . . I say unto you that ye would be more miserable to dwell with a holy and just God, under a consciousness of your filthiness before him, than ye would to dwell with the damned souls in hell." (Moroni 9:4.)

And then finally the third essential: to help the learner to know the gospel by living the gospel. Spiritual certainty that is necessary to salvation must be preceded by a maximum of individual effort. Grace, or the free gift of the Lord's atoning power, must be preceded by personal striving. Repeating again what Nephi said, "By grace . . . we are saved, after all we can do."

I listened to a mission president a few years ago tell of an interesting experience. He was at a district conference, and as usual he was interviewing a number of men who had been recommended to be ordained elders. The district president had written on one recommendation: "This man is still having a problem with tobacco."

So the mission president said to the man, "Tell me about this problem with tobacco."

The man answered, "Oh, president, more than all else in the world I want to stop this ugly habit so that I can be ordained an elder and take my wife and children to the temple."

"Well," the president said, "it ought to be very simple, then, if you mean what you say. Are you prepared to stand up and take me by the right hand, look me square in the eye, and tell me that from this time on you'll never again touch tobacco?"

"Oh, well, no," the man said, "I'm not prepared to do that."

"Well, then," said the president, "you didn't mean what you said." Then the president talked a little bit more and concluded: "The beginning of repentance is to make up your mind, and you haven't made up your mind you are going to stop smoking. Now I'll be back here in three months; and if in that time you can make up your mind, we'll talk about ordaining you an elder."

The man was crestfallen because he had failed again. The next afternoon as the president was preparing to leave at the conclusion of the conference, this man came to him and said, "President, I have been fasting and praying since you talked with me yesterday; and now I have made up my mind. I'm prepared now to take you by the right hand and look you square in the eye and tell you that from now on I'll never touch tobacco."

Then the mission president said a thrilling thing: "And down in my heart I knew he would do what he said, and I ordained him." Now, that is one of the essentials if you would live a perfect life. One must "make up his mind" to live the commandments.

The Master answered a question of the Jews as to how they could be certain as to whether His mission was of God or whether He was just another man. He said: "If any man will do his will, he shall know of the doctrine, whether it be of God, or whether I speak of myself." (John 7:17.)

The testimony of truth never comes to him who has an unclean tabernacle. The Spirit of the Lord and uncleanliness cannot dwell at the same time in a given individual. "I, the Lord, am bound when ye do what I say; but when ye do not what I say, ye have no promise." (D&C 82:10.) ". . . except ye abide my law ye cannot attain to this glory."

(D&C 132:21.) Again and again that truth is repeated in the scriptures.

All the principles and ordinances of the gospel are in a sense but invitations to learning the gospel by the practice of its teachings. No person knows the principle of tithing until he pays tithing. No one knows the principle of the Word of Wisdom until he keeps the Word of Wisdom. Children, or grownups for that matter, are not converted to tithing, the Word of Wisdom, keeping the Sabbath day holy, or prayer by hearing someone talk about these principles. We learn the gospel by living it.

Be virtuous. This is one of the greatest of the commandments.

> Let thy bowels also be full of charity towards all men, and to the household of faith, and let virtue garnish thy thoughts unceasingly; then shall thy confidence wax strong in the presence of God; and the doctrine of the priesthood shall distil upon thy soul as the dews from heaven.
>
> The Holy Ghost shall be thy constant companion, and thy scepter an unchanging scepter of righteousness and truth; and thy dominion shall be an everlasting dominion, and without compulsory means it shall flow unto thee forever and ever. (D&C 121:45-46.)

But never in the world will we have that dominion, that power, that companionship of the Holy Ghost unless we have learned to be virtuous in thought, in habit, and in our actions.

May I say in summary: We never really know anything of the teachings of the gospel until we have experienced the blessings that come from living each principle. "Moral teachings themselves," someone has said, "have only a superficial effect upon the spirit unless they are buttressed by acts." The most important of all the commandments in the gospel to you and to me is that particular commandment which for this moment requires in each of us the greatest soul-searching to obey. Each of us must analyze his needs and begin today to overcome, for only as we overcome are we granted a place in our Father's kingdom.

President Karl G. Maeser said, "School is a drill in the battle of life; but if we fail in the drill, we will fail in the battle." "Education is not play," as some wise teacher has said, "and cannot be made to look like play. It is hard, hard work, but it can be made interesting work." Likewise education that pertains to the kingdom of God is not play, and it cannot be made to look like play. It is hard, hard work; but it can be intensely interesting work.

You and the lessons you teach are merely the tools by which the Holy Ghost converts the souls of men. James said it in more meaningful language than I can command:

> Brethren, if any of you do err from the truth, and one convert him;
>
> Let him know, that he which converteth the sinner from the error of his way shall save a soul from death, and shall hide a multitude of sins. (James 5:19-20.)

President J. Reuben Clark, Jr., said,

> Youth of the Church are hungry for the words of the Lord. Teachers, be sure you are prepared to feed them the bread of life which are the teachings of Jesus Christ. If they will live up to His teachings, they will have more happiness than they have ever before dreamed of.

Within the revealed gospel of Jesus Christ and from the teachings of our church leaders in this dispensation may be found the answer to every question and the solution of every problem essential to the social, temporal, and spiritual welfare of human beings who are all the children of God our Heavenly Father. I so declare unto you, I know it is true.

22

Successful Sinners?

ARE there actually any successful sinners? Well, perhaps you are thinking about the man of independence who, despite the fact that his money may not always have come to him from honest toil or from legitimate enterprise, lives a life of luxury and ease. He spends his Sundays playing golf, at a baseball game, or at the races instead of worrying about difficult Church problems as a responsible Church officer, or otherwise keeping the Sabbath day holy. He takes long excursions to interesting places by spending money, a part of which, at least, he could have paid in tithing contributions or in donations for the building up of the Church or for the care of the needy. He hasn't time to fill a mission for the Church at his own expense. Because of the worldly company he keeps, he has no scruples about drinking or gambling. Even immorality is winked at by his crowd, who absent themselves from Church contacts where such conduct, measured by gospel standards, would be vigorously condemned.

At the same time, you may have observed that the woman who lives at his house, whom he calls his wife, has completely ignored the first commandment "to multiply and replenish the earth." She can't be bothered with children; they might interfere with her career or her social activities. She thinks herself beyond the pale of the Church and quiets her conscience with the constant expression that after all, religion and the Church are only for the poor and the unsophisticated. The expenditure of her husband's wealth has freed her from home responsibilities so that her days must be kept from monotony by bridge parties and other functions where smoking and drinking are indulged in, with little or no regard for Church injunctions to the contrary. She is able to dress in the latest and most expensive fashions; she avoids the telltale marks of a mother's home duties, including worries about children.

Perhaps as you look at such pictures of seeming success by sinners against the Lord's commandments, you may, from lack of perspective of the entire span of life and its purposes, conclude that such have chosen the better way. You may think that by comparison the life of one active in the Church is not easy, with its constant inhibitions and constraints, with the service and sacrifice entailed that require time, talent, and money, and the disquieting shocks that come to the conscience when one acts below the standards he professes. You may think that energies expended in other endeavors might pay greater dividends and that religion should be left to those who can't afford anything better. But before you make your final decision as to the course you will take, let me help you lift your vision to a higher vantage point so you can see things as they really are.

Beautiful, luscious fruit does not grow unless the roots of the parent tree have been planted in rich, fertile soil and unless due care is given to proper pruning, cultivation, and irrigation. So likewise the luscious fruits of virtue and chastity, honesty, temperance, integrity, and fidelity are not to be found growing in that individual whose life is not founded on a firm testimony of the truths of the gospel and of the life and the mission of the Lord Jesus Christ. To be truly righteous, there is required a daily pruning of the evil growth of our characters by daily repentance from sin.

Who is the author of the program that thus dresses up evil and the wrong to become so desirable to our appetites? When there was war in heaven, Lucifer, a son of God in the spirit world before the earth was formed, proposed a plan under which mortals would be saved without glory and honor of God. The plan of our Savior, Jehovah, was to give to each the right to choose for himself the course he would travel in earth life, and all was to be done to the honor and glory of God our Heavenly Father. Jehovah's plan was accepted; Satan's plan was rejected.

But, you ask, why does God, if He truly loves his children, permit Satan to tempt us and thereby jeopardize our chances to gain the best experiences in mortality and return to enjoy eternal life in His presence? The answer is given by a great prophet-teacher:

> Wherefore, the Lord God gave unto man that he should act for himself. Wherefore, man could not act for himself save it should be that he was enticed by the one [which is evil] or the other [which is good]. (2 Nephi 2:16.)

Think about that for a moment. If there were no opposition to good, would there be any chance to exercise your agency or right to choose? To deny you that privilege would be to deny you the opportunity to grow in knowledge, experience, and power. God has given laws with penalties affixed so that man might be made afraid of sin and be guided into paths of truth and duty. (See Alma 42:20.)

And because there is this choice between good and evil, the Lord has provided a means for the return of those who go astray.

Before I attempt to explain this precious refining process of the human soul called repentance, may I state two simple but fundamental truths. First, Satan with all his cunning cannot overthrow you if you strive with all your might to keep the commandments of the Lord. And second, with the first breaking of one of these commandments you have taken your first step into Satan's territory.

Now what are the steps to be taken for repentance—the steps we must take in order to be worthy of God's forgiveness through the redemption of the Master's atoning sacrifice and to eventually enjoy the privileges of eternal life in the world to come? An all-wise Father, foreseeing that some would fall in sin and all would have need to repent, has provided the plan of salvation, which defines the clear-cut way of repentance.

First, those in sin must confess. "By this ye may know if a man repenteth of his sins—behold, he will confess them and forsake them." (D&C 58:43.) That confession must be made first to the person who has been most wronged by your acts. A sincere confession is not merely admitting guilt after the proof is already in evidence. If you have offended many persons openly, your acknowledgment is to be made openly and before those whom you have offended, that you might show your shame and humility and willingness to receive a merited rebuke. If your act is secret and has resulted in injury to no one but yourself, your confession should be in secret, that your Heavenly Father who hears in secret may reward you openly. Acts that may affect your standing in the Church, or your right to privileges or advancement in the Church, are to be promptly confessed to the bishop, whom the Lord has appointed as a shepherd over every flock and whom the Lord has commissioned to be a common judge in Israel.

The unbaptized person who is in sin may, by following a similar course, receive at the hands of an authorized elder of the Church, if otherwise prepared by an understanding of the gospel, baptism for the remission of his sins. Following confession, one in sin must show forth the fruits of his repentance by good deeds, which are weighed against the bad. He must make proper restitution to the limit of his power to restore that which he has taken away, or he must repair the damage he has done. He who thus repents of his sins and altogether turns away therefrom, to return no more to a repetition thereof, is entitled to the promise of a forgiveness of his sins if he has not committed the unpardonable sin; as it was declared by the prophet Isaiah: ". . . though your sins be as scarlet, they shall be as white as snow; though they be red like crimson, they shall be as wool." (Isaiah 1:18.)

But please do not misunderstand the true meaning of the scriptures. One may not wallow in the mire of filth and sin and conduct his life in a manner unlawful in the sight of God and then suppose that repentance will wipe out the effects of his sin and place him on the level he would have been on had he always lived a righteous and virtuous life. The Lord extends loving mercy and kindness in forgiving you of the sins you commit against Him or His work, but He can never remove the results of the sin you have committed against yourself in thus retarding your own advancement toward your eternal goal.

There are no successful sinners. All must one day stand before God and be judged, each according to the deeds done in the flesh. What do you think now? Is the burden of the sinner lighter than that of the saint?

May you be blessed and guided always in your search for the best in life.

23

True Brotherhood

IN sacred Jewish writing, a parable is told of a man who saw in the distance an object that he supposed was a beast. As the object drew nearer he saw it was a man, and as it came still nearer he exclaimed, "It is my brother!" Seldom do we see as the beast the man we really understand, for with closer association and a clearer understanding of the impulses and the circumstances that impel men to action, we become more tolerant and more forgiving.

If we could learn the lesson taught by that parable, there surely would be less misunderstanding and fault-finding, less hatred and contention, less strife and blood-shed, but more sympathy and forgiveness extended toward him who errs.

The word *brotherhood* in common usage suggests a society or a fraternity of individuals or of groups banded together for a common purpose. More often than other-wise such purpose is selfish and the benefits of the society are limited to only those who comprise the group, and frequently the objective of the society, if achieved, works to the disadvantage or to the actual detriment of those outside that brotherhood. Whether it be of individuals or of nations, the principle is the same.

We often see the awful spectacle of devastating wars between groups of nations, bound to each other within their own allied councils by solemn agreements, prompted not by mutual respect or admiration for each other, but impelled by a fear of each other or by a hope for selfish gains as the result and in the event of ultimate victory to their side.

It should be clear to any thinking person that the promotion of such brotherhoods usually serves only to perpetuate strife, and decisions arrived at between such groups are dictated by the force of might rather than on the basis of justice and equity. The establishment of a peace in the world that will be everlasting and desirable will be possible if and when mankind unites together in a fraternity where such brotherly relationships are characterized by love and affection.

Some time ago there appeared in the *New York Times* a scholarly article prepared by a conference of eminent Catholic bishops entitled "Pronouncement by Catholic Bishops on Church and Social Welfare." The article dealt with the contending views of capital and labor and boldly criticized each faction for the evident selfishness and short-sightedness in their present plans and policies. Then it outlined a suggested course to be followed to overcome the conflicting views that presently exist. Here are the concluding words: "There must be a reform of morals and a profound renewal of Christian spirit. . . . To do that it is argued that our economic life must be reorganized, and selfishness must be replaced by justice and charity."

The answer of the Master to the question, "Master,

which is the great commandment in the law?" runs to the same conclusion.

> Jesus said unto him, Thou shalt love thy Lord thy God with all thy heart, and with all thy soul, and with all thy mind.
>
> This is the first and great commandment.
>
> And the second is like unto it, Thou shalt love thy neighbour as thyself. (Matthew 22:36-39.)

A brotherhood that seeks to establish the common good is as "sounding brass or a tinkling cymbal," except it be founded upon the divine principle of love of God and our neighbor as ourselves. One who says he loves God and is a follower of Jesus and yet hates his brother is false to himself and before the world, for no one can love God whom he has not seen and yet love not his brother whom he has seen. (See John 4:20.) The truest evidence that one loves God is that he keeps His commandments. (See John 2:3-4.)

And if the loving of one's neighbor is the "second great commandment," then a brotherly relationship with our fellowmen must be the measure of one's Christian standing. The logic of this reasoning is amply supported by the scriptures, where the Lord is declared to be "the God of the spirits of all flesh" (Numbers 27:16), and is compared, as the Father of our spirits, to the fathers of our flesh to whom we give reverence. (Hebrews 12:9.)

Such a conception of the Fatherhood of God declares also a universal brotherhood of man. In such a family relationship, a love of a son for the Father and hatred of that son for others of his Father's offspring is hardly conceivable to the reasoning mind. To understand that man is created in the image of God is a soul-stirring contemplation, and every soul "that hath this hope in him purifieth himself." (See 1 John 3:3.)

But what is necessary for one to discharge his responsibility toward his fellowmen? This same question was undoubtedly in the mind of the lawyer who asked Jesus, "And who is my neighbour?" In reply Jesus gave the parable of the good Samaritan:

> And Jesus answering said, A certain man went down from Jerusalem to Jericho, and fell among thieves, which stripped him of his raiment, and wounded him, and departed, leaving him half dead.
>
> And by chance there came down a certain priest that way: and when he saw him, he passed by on the other side.
>
> And likewise a Levite, when he was at the place, came and looked on him, and passed by on the other side.
>
> But a certain Samaritan, as he journeyed, came where he was: and when he saw him, he had compassion on him.
>
> And went to him, and bound up his wounds, pouring in oil and wine, and set him on his own beast, and brought him to an inn, and took care of him.
>
> And on the morrow when he departed, he took out two pence, and gave them to the host, and said unto him, Take care of him; and whatsoever thou spendest more, when I come again, I will repay thee.
>
> Which now of these three, thinkest thou, was neighbour unto him that fell among the thieves?
>
> And he said, He that shewed mercy on him. Then said Jesus unto him, Go, and do thou likewise. (Luke 10:30-37.)

The moral of the Master's lesson is clear: He only is neighbor who does good to him who is in need.

The influx of many strangers within our gates and the industrialization and militarization of many of our pastoral communities might well cause us to ponder the question as to our responsibility as neighbors to these strangers. Our pioneer parents, led by inspired leaders, came to this western land to establish the mountain of the Lord's house in the top of the mountains. A prophet had declared that many people should say, "Come ye, And let us go up to the mountain of the Lord, . . ." and also that the inhabitants of the house of the God of Jacob were to teach these newcomers of His ways and to walk in His paths. (See Isaiah 2:2-3.)

To the Latter-day Saints the Lord has entrusted a great responsibility as the keepers of the house of the Lord thus established. Paul, the great missionary apostle, defined the purpose of the establishment of the Church of Christ as being "for the perfecting of the saints, for the work of the ministry, and for the edifying of the body of Christ: Till we all come in the unity of the faith. . . ." (Ephesians 4:12-13.)

Since the time when Moses led the children of Israel out of Egypt, the principle of gathering the members of the Church into communities has been taught. The Latter-day Saints have been taught this principle by revelations from the Lord. Here, in such communities, without hindrance or molestation from those who refuse to accept fellowship in the church and kingdom of God, it has been found that the members of the Church thus established can better work out their social, economic, and religious problems than would be possible without such a gathering.

If, to satisfy the critics of the practice of the Latter-day Saints in gathering together for mutual improvement, we were to encourage promiscuous social intercourse with the stranger regardless of his standards and by so doing sacrifice the ideals of morality, of marriage, and of family for which our parents sacrificed much, we would not only be untrue to our heritage, but we would thereby decrease immeasurably our power to do good to him that is in need.

Obedient to the command of the Master, reiterated in our generation, we have sent and will continue to send missionaries to carry the gospel to the stranger within our gates and to "every nation, kindred, tongue and people." And for what purpose? To welcome all "who fear God and give glory to him" to accept membership in the greatest brotherhood in the world, the Church of Chirst established in the last days. Can one conceive of a greater service to be rendered to those who may come to us than to bring to them the opportunities and privileges of the gospel and to fellowship those who live righteous lives?

To you who would administer succor and be a neighbor to the poor and the needy, I would bid you heed the inspired admonition, "And though I bestow all my goods to feed the poor, . . . and have not charity, it profiteth me nothing." (1 Corinthians 13:3.) It would be well if all who dispense charity would do so with a reverent appreciation of their divine relationship to that one so assisted and do it in a manner suggested by the Savior's declaration, that as you would do it unto one such needy, you would do it as a service to Him. (See Matthew 25:40.)

In all such ministering it is well to remember that there are broken hearts and wounded souls among us that need the tender care of a brother who has an understanding heart and is kind. Today there may be heard again in Israel the voice of a Rachel "weeping for her children, and would not be comforted because they are not" (Matthew 2:18) when the cruel blasts of war shall bring the sad news of disaster. She must be soothed with tenderness by sisters worthy to bear the name of this great brotherhood of Saints.

" . . . may the kingdom of God go forth, that the kingdom of heaven may come" (D&C 65:6), that God's "will be done in earth, as it is in heaven." (Matthew 6:10.) May we let our lights so shine as members of the Church of God that others seeing our good works and that we are not of the world will come to seek membership therein. May we sense the fact that true love for our neighbor consists not in descending to his level but rather in so living that we aid him in an upward climb. May we never forget that in this great fellowship, our ears must ever be inclined to hear the cry of the widow and the orphan and that in our ministrations to all such, we do as we think the Master would have us do.

Thus, if we do, and if we teach others to do likewise, ours will be the brotherhood to fill the whole earth and bring about that peace on earth when the powers of darkness will be eternally bound with the everlasting chains of righteousness at the hands of God's children.

24

Time to Prepare to Meet God

A *FEW* years ago, millions of watchers and listeners over the world waited breathlessly and anxiously the precarious flight of Apollo 13. The whole world, it seemed, prayed for one significant result: the safe return to earth of three brave men.

When one of them with restrained anxiety announced the startling information, "We have had an explosion," the Mission Control in Houston immediately mobilized all the technically trained scientists who had, over the years, planned every conceivable detail pertaining to that flight.

The safety of those three now depended on two vital qualifications: on the reliability of the skills and the knowledge of those technicians in the Mission Control center at Houston, and upon the implicit obedience of the men in the "Aquarius" to every instruction from the technicians, who, because of their understanding of the problems of the astronauts, were better qualified to find the essential solutions. The decisions of the technicians had to be perfect or the "Aquarius" could have missed the earth by thousands of miles.

This dramatic event is somewhat analogous to these troublous times in which we live. The headlines in the public press make a startling announcement by a presidential commission to the President of the United States: "U.S. Society Is in Peril." Many are frightened when they see and hear of unbelievable happenings the world over—political intrigues, wars and contention everywhere, frustrations of parents who are endeavoring to cope with social problems that threaten to break down the sanctity of the home, the frustrations of children and youth as they face challenges to their faith and their morals.

Only if *you* are willing to listen and obey, as did the astronauts on the "Aquarius," can you and all your households be guided to ultimate safety and security in the Lord's own way.

There are, in these troubled times, agonizing cries of distress among the peoples of the earth. There are intense feelings of a need for some way to find a solution to overwhelming problems and to ease this distress from all that affects mankind.

To one who is acquainted with and well versed in the prophetic teachings of the past generations, there should be little question as to the meaning of all that is going on among us today, when it seems as though everything is in turmoil.

Prophecy may well be defined as histroy in reverse. Before our very eyes we are witnessing the fulfillment of prophecies made by inspired prophets in ages past. In the very beginning of this dispensation we were plainly told in a revelation from the Lord that the time was nigh at hand when peace would be taken from the earth and the devil would have power over his own dominion. (See D&C 1:35.)

The prophets of our day also foretold that there should be wars and rumors of wars, and "the whole earth shall be in commotion, and men's hearts shall fail them, and they shall say that Christ delayeth his coming until the end of the earth. And the love of men shall wax cold, and iniquity shall abound." (D&C 45:26-27.)

When the disciples asked the Master, prior to His crucifixion, as to signs that should immediately precede His coming again to the earth, as He foretold, He answered by saying that—

> in those days, shall be great tribulation on the Jews, and upon the inhabitants of Jerusalem:
>
> . . . and except those days should be shortened, there should none of their flesh be saved.
>
> But for the elect's sake, according to the covenant, those days shall be shortened.
>
> For nation shall rise against nation, and kingdom against kingdom; there shall be famine and pestilence and earthquakes in divers places. (Inspired Version, Matthew 24:18-20, 30; see also Joseph Smith 1:18-20, 29.)

The Master undoubtedly spoke of times such as these when He foretold that a man would be "at variance against his father, and the daughter against her mother, and the daughter in law against her mother in law. And a man's foes shall be they of his own household." (Matthew 10:35-36.)

With all of this in mind, one may ask: To whom may those in distress and in great anxiety look for the answer and for "refuge from this storm" raging all about them?

Almighty God, through His Son, our Lord, has pointed the way and has given to all mankind a sure guide to safety when He declared that the Lord shall have power over His saints and would reign in their midst, when His mighty judgments would descend upon the world. (See D&C 1:36.)

He said to all men:

> Watch therefore: for ye know not what hour your Lord doth come.
>
> Therefore be ye also ready; for in such an hour as ye think not the Son of Man cometh. (Matthew 24:42, 44.)

He has counseled that His "disciples shall stand in holy places, and shall not be moved; but among the wicked, men shall lift up their voices and curse God and die." (D&C 45:32.)

From the incident of the *Apollo 13,* and having in mind the promises of the Lord to which I have made reference, I will now undertake to outline briefly the wondrously conceived plan upon obedience to which the salvation of every soul depends in his journey through mortality to his ultimate destiny—a return to that God who gave him life. This is that way by which the Lord will keep His promise to have power over His saints and to reign in their midst.

This plan is identified by name, and the overarching purpose is clearly set forth in an announcement to the Church in the beginning of this gospel dispensation.

More than a century ago the Lord declared:

> And even so I have sent mine everlasting covenant into the world, to be a light to the world, and to be a standard for my people, and for the Gentiles to seek to it, and to be a messenger before my face to prepare the way before me. (D&C 45:9.)

This plan, then, was to be as a covenant, which implied a contract to be participated in by more than one person. It was to be a standard for the Lord's elect and for all the world to benefit by it. Its purpose was to serve the needs of all men and to prepare the world for the second coming of the Lord.

The participants in the formulation of this plan in the

premortal world were all the spirit children of our Heavenly Father. Our oldest scriptures, from the writings of the ancient prophets Abraham and Jeremiah, affirm also that God, or Eloheim, was there; His Firstborn Son, Jehovah, Abraham, Jeremiah, and many others of great stature were there.

All the organized intelligences before the earth was formed, who had become spirits, were there, including many great and noble ones whose performance and conduct in that premortal sphere qualified them to become rulers and leaders in carrying out this eternal plan.

The Apostle Paul in his writings to the Corinthians taught that "there be gods many, and lords many," and then he added, "But to us there is but one God, the Father, *of whom* are all things, and we in him; and one Lord Jesus Christ, *by whom* are all things, and we by him." (1 Corinthians 8:5-6. Italics added.)

I would have you note particularly the use of the preposition "of," in reference to the Father, and the preposition "by," in reference to our Lord, Jesus Christ. In this statement is clearly defined the role of each, the Lord to do the bidding of the Father, in the execution of the whole plan of salvation for all mankind. (See Abraham 4.)

Understanding this principle in the plan of the government of God, we are given a glimpse of the council meeting of Gods, as briefly recorded in revelations to ancient prophets.

Under the Father's instruction and by Jehovah's direction, the earth and all pertaining thereto were organized and formed. They "ordered," they "watched over" and "prepared" the earth. They took "counsel among themselves" as to the bringing of all manner of life to the earth and all things, including man, and prepared it for the carrying out of the plan, which we could well liken to a blueprint, by which the children of God could be tutored and trained in all that was necessary for the divine purpose of bringing to pass, "to the glory of God," the opportunity of every soul to gain "immortality and eternal life." Eternal life means to have everlasting life in that celestial sphere where God and Christ dwell, by doing all things we are commanded. (See Abraham 3:25.)

The plan embodied three distinctive principles:

First, the privilege was to be given to every soul to choose for himself liberty and eternal life through obedience to the laws of God, or captivity and death as to spiritual things because of disobedience. (See 2 Nephi 2:27.)

Next to life itself, free agency is God's greatest gift to mankind, providing thereby the greatest opportunity for the children of God to advance in this second estate of mortality. A prophet-leader on this continent explained this to his son as recorded in an ancient scripture: that to bring about these, the Lord's eternal purposes, there must be opposites, an enticement by the good on the one hand and by the evil on the other, or to say it in the language of the scriptures, ". . . the forbidden fruit in opposition to the tree of life; the one being sweet and the other being bitter." This father further explained, "Wherefore, the Lord God gave unto man that he should act for himself. Wherefore, man could not act for himself save it should be that he was enticed by the one or the other." (2 Nephi 2:15-16.)

The second distinctive principle in this divine plan involved the necessity of providing a savior by whose atonement the most favored Son of God became our Savior, as a "Lamb slain from the foundation of the world" (Revelation 13:8), as revealed to John on the Isle of Patmos. Another prophet-teacher explained that the mission of the Son of God was to "make intercession for all the children of men; and they that believe in him shall be saved." (2 Nephi 2:9.)

We hear much from some persons of limited understanding about the possibility of one's being saved by grace alone. But it requires the explanation of another prophet to understand the true doctrine of grace as he explained in these meaningful words:

"For," said this prophet, "we labor diligently to write, to persuade our children, and also our brethren, to believe in Christ, and to be reconciled to God; for we know that it is by grace that we are saved, after all we can do." (2 Nephi 25:23.) Truly we are redeemed by the atoning blood of the Savior of the world, but only after each has done all he can to work out his own salvation.

The third great distinctive principle in the plan of salvation was the provision that "all mankind may be saved, by obedience to the laws and ordinances of the Gospel." (Article of Faith 3.) These fundamental laws and ordinances by which salvation comes are clearly set forth:

First, faith in the Lord Jesus Christ.

Second, repentance from sin, meaning the turning away from the sins of disobedience to God's laws and never returning again thereto. The Lord spoke plainly on this point. Said He: ". . . go your ways and sin no more; but unto that soul who sinneth [meaning, of course, returning again to the sins from which he has repented] shall the former sins return, saith the Lord your God." (D&C 82:7.)

Third, baptism by water and of the Spirit, by which ordinances only, as the Master taught Nicodemus, could one see or enter into the kingdom of God. (See John 3:4-5.)

This same teaching was forcibly impressed by the resurrected Savior to the saints on this continent, in what it appears likely was His final message to His disciples. The Master taught His faithful saints that—

no unclean thing can enter into his kingdom; therefore nothing entereth into his rest save it be those who have washed their garments in my blood, because of their faith, and the repentance of all their sins, and their faithfulness unto the end.

Now this is the commandment: Repent, all ye ends of the earth, and come unto me and be baptized in my name, that ye may be sanctified by the reception of the Holy Ghost, that ye may stand spotless before me at the last day.

Verily, verily, I say unto you, this is my gospel. . . . (3 Nephi 27:19-21.)

If the children of the Lord, which includes all who are upon this earth regardless of nationality, color, or creed, will heed the call of the true messenger of the gospel of Jesus Christ, as did the three astronauts on the "Aquarius" to the trained technicians at Mission Control in the hour of their peril, each may in time see the Lord and know that He is, as the Lord has promised, and then their calling and election will be made sure. They will "become the sons of Moses and of Aaron and the seed of Abraham, . . . and the elect of God." (D&C 84:34.)

This promise of the glory which awaits those who are faithful to the end was plainly portrayed in the Master's parable of the Prodigal Son. To the son who was faithful and did not squander his birthright, the father, who in the Master's lesson would be our Father and our God, promised this faithful son: "Son, thou art ever with me, and all that I have is thine." (Luke 15:31.)

In a revelation through a modern prophet, the Lord promises to the faithful and obedient today: ". . . all that my Father hath shall be given unto him." (D&C 84:38.)

Or will we be like those foolhardy ones on the river above the Niagara Falls who were approaching the dangerous rapids? Despite warnings of the river guards to go toward safety before it was too late, and in complete disregard of the warnings, they laughed, they danced, they drank, they mocked, and they perished.

So would have been the fate of the three astronauts on the "Aquarius" if they had refused to give heed to the minutest instruction from Houston Control. Their very lives depended upon obedience to the basic laws that govern and control the forces of the universe.

Jesus wept as He witnessed the world about Him in His day that had seemingly gone mad, and continually mocked His pleading that they come unto Him along "the strait and narrow way," so plainly marked out in God's eternal plan of salvation.

O that we could hear again His pleadings today as He then cried out:

> O Jerusalem, Jerusalem, thou that killest the prophets, and stonest them which are sent unto thee, how often would I have gathered thy children together, even as a hen gathereth her chickens under her wings, and ye would not! (Matthew 23:37.)

O that the world would see in another parable to John the Revelator the sacred figure of the Master calling to us today as He did to those of Jerusalem:

Said the Master:

> Behold, I stand at the door, and knock; if any man hear my voice, and open the door, I will come in to him, and will sup with him and he with me.
>
> To him that overcometh will I grant to sit with me in my throne, even as I also overcame, and am set down with my Father in his throne. (Revelation 3:20-21.)

Here, then, is the plan of salvation as taught by the true church, which is founded upon apostles and prophets, with Christ, the Lord, as the chief cornerstone (Ephesians 2:20), by which only can peace come—not as the world giveth, but as only the Lord can give to those who overcome the things of the world, as did the Master. "Neither is there salvation in any other: for there is none other name under heaven given among men, whereby we must be saved." (Acts 4:12.)

To all of this I bear my sincere witness in the name of our Lord Jesus Christ.

I once listened to a young girl's heartwarming testimony. Her father was afflicted with what the doctors had pronounced was an incurable malady. To his wife one morning this stricken father, after a night of pain and suffering, had said with great feeling, "I am so thankful today." "For what?" she asked. He replied, "For God's giving me the privilege of one more day with you."

I would desire with all my heart that all would likewise thank God for one more day! For what? For the opportunity to take care of some unfinished business; to repent; to right some wrongs; to influence for good some wayward child; to reach out to someone who cried for help—in short, thank God for one more day to prepare to meet God.

Don't try to live too many days ahead. Seek for strength to attend to the problems of today. In His Sermon on the Mount, the Master admonished, "Take therefore no thought for the morrow: for the morrow shall take thought for the things of itself. Sufficient unto the day is the evil thereof." (Matthew 6:34.)

Do all that you can do and leave the rest to God, the Father of us all. It is not enough to say I will do my best, but rather, I will do everything that is within my power; I will do all that is necessary.

In a plaque on the walls of the Radio City Music Hall in New York City are these profound words of wisdom: "Man's ultimate destiny depends, not upon whether he can learn new lessons or make new discoveries, and conquests, but upon his acceptance of the lessons taught."

My prayer is that the message of those words of wisdom may be translated into a determination on the part of all of us, to the end that our eyes will be so single to God, that our whole bodies shall be so filled with light, that there shall be no darkness in us, to the end that we may be able to comprehend all things. (See D&C 88:67.)

25

How to Receive a Blessing from God

THERE is a law, irrevocably decreed in heaven before the foundations of this world, upon which all blessings are predicated—

"And when we obtain any blessings from God, it is by obedience to that law upon which it is predicated." (D&C 130:21-22.)

This text is like many gospel texts: We must not think of it superficially; we must enlarge our understanding. Let us look at some of the deeper and more far-reaching rewards that come from the keeping of law.

The Lord has told us, "I, the Lord, am bound when ye do what I say; but when ye do not what I say, ye have no promise." (D&C 82:10.) In commenting about this, someone has said: "This is indisputable; the Lord is bound when we do what he says. If we want to live we must conform by obedience to the physical laws by which life is sustained. We must take nourishment, exercise, keep clean, etc. If we desire to become musicians, painters, authors, we must obey certain laws by which the respective talents are developed. In the same way, if we desire any spiritual blessings we must obey the laws upon which they also are predicated."

There are some laws that have to do with eternal life. Eternal life means life in the presence of the Eternal One, or life in the presence of the Father and the Son. The Lord tells us how we can prepare to enter back into His presence:

> Verily, thus saith the Lord: It shall come to pass that every soul who forsaketh his sins and cometh unto me, and calleth on my name, and obeyeth my voice, and keepeth my commandments, shall see my face and shall know that I am. (D&C 93:1.)

It is as simple as that. All we have to do in order to be prepared to enter the presence of the Lord is to forsake our sins, come unto Him, call on His name, obey His voice, and keep His commandments; then we shall be able to see His face and to know that He is. There is a postscript to this that I think is very important. The Lord said:

> For if you will that I give unto you a place in the celestial world, you must prepare yourselves by doing the things which I have commanded you and required of you. (D&C 78:7.)

The Lord does not say that we will get a place in the celestial world just by being good; He says we win our place by *doing* good.

A classic example in the Book of Mormon illustrates this point. The Lord gave to the brother of Jared, that great prophet, a blueprint of the ships that he was to construct, by which he was to take his people across large bodies of water to a promised land. As he surveyed these and began to build, he faced two problems: (1) no provision was made for ventilation and (2) there was no light. The ventilation problem was solved rather simply by having holes at proper places that could be opened and closed;

but the matter of light was one that he could not quite solve. So the brother of Jared cried to the Lord, saying,

> . . . behold, I have done even as thou hast commanded me; and I have prepared the vessels for my people, and behold there is no light in them. Behold, O Lord, wilt thou suffer that we shall cross this great water in darkness? (Ether 2:22.)

Notice how the Lord dealt with this question. He said to the brother of Jared, "What will ye that I should do that ye may have light in your vessels?" (Ether 2:23)—as much as to say, "Well, have you any good ideas? What would you suggest that we should do in order to have light?" And then the Lord said:

> For behold, ye cannot have windows, for they will be dashed in pieces; neither shall ye take fire with you, for ye shall not go by the light of fire.
>
> For behold, ye shall be as a whale in the midst of the sea; for the mountain waves shall dash upon you. Nevertheless, I will bring you up again out of the depths of the sea; for the winds have gone forth out of my mouth, and also the rains and the floods that I have sent forth. (Ether 2:23-24.)

Then the Lord went away and left him alone. It was as though the Lord were saying to him, "Look, I gave you a mind to think with, and I gave you agency to use it. Now you do all you can to help yourself with this problem; and then, after you've done all you can, I'll step in to help you."

The brother of Jared did some thinking. Then he gathered up sixteen stones, molten out of rock, and carried them in his hands to the top of the mount called Shelam, where he cried unto the Lord,

> O Lord, thou hast said that we must be encompassed by the floods. Now behold, O Lord, and do not be angry with thy servant because of his weakness before thee; for we know that thou are holy and dwellest in the heavens, and that we are unworthy before thee; because of the fall our natures have become evil continually; nevertheless, O Lord, thou hast given us a commandment that we must call upon thee, that from thee we may receive according to our desires. (Ether 3:2.)

Now, what is he doing? He is confessing his sins before he asks again. He has come to the conclusion that before he is worthy to seek a blessing, he must keep the basic laws upon which the blessings he seeks are predicated.

Then he says,

> Behold, O Lord, [I know that] thou hast smitten us because of our iniquity, and hast driven us forth, and for these many years we have been in the wilderness; nevertheless, thou hast been merciful unto us. O Lord, look upon me in pity, and turn away thine anger from this thy people. . . . (Ether 3:3.)

The brother of Jared is confessing the sins of the people, because the blessing he wants is not just for himself; it is for his whole people. Having done all that he knew how to do, he comes again with a specific request and says:

> And I know, O Lord, that thou hast all power, and can do whatever thou wilt for the benefit of man; therefore touch these stones, O Lord, with thy finger, and prepare them that they may shine forth in darkness; and they shall shine forth unto us in the vessels which we have prepared, that we may have light while we shall cross the sea.
>
> Behold, O Lord, thou canst do this. We know that thou art able to show forth great power, which looks small unto the understanding of men.
>
> And it came to pass that when the brother of Jared had said these words, behold, the Lord stretched forth his hand and touched the stones one by one with his finger. And the veil was taken from off the eyes of the brother of Jared, and he saw the finger of the Lord; and it was as the finger of a man, like unto flesh and blood; and the brother of Jared fell down before the Lord, for he was struck with fear. (Ether 3:4-6.)

This is the principle in action. If you want the blessing, don't just kneel down and pray about it. Prepare yourselves in every conceivable way you can in order to make yourselves worthy to receive the blessing you seek.

Brigham Young illustrated this when he said: "You may go to some people here, and ask what ails them, and they answer, 'I don't know but we feel a dreadful distress in the stomach and in the back; we feel all out of order, and we wish you to lay hands on us.'"

He said to these people, "Have you used any remedies?"—meaning herbs or whatever the pioneers had. "No," they said, "we wish the Elders to lay hands upon us, and we have faith that we shall be healed." President Young said:

> That is very inconsistent according to my faith. If we are sick, and ask the Lord to heal us, and to do all for us that is necessary to be done, according to my understanding of the Gospel of salvation, I might as well ask the Lord to cause my wheat and corn to grow without my plowing the ground and casting in the seed. It appears consistent to me to apply every remedy that comes within the range of my knowledge, and then ask my Father in Heaven, in the name of Jesus Christ, to sanctify that application to the healing of my body. . . .
>
> But supposing we were traveling in the mountains, and all we had or could get, in the shape of nourishment, was a little venison, and one or two were taken sick, without anything in the world in the shape of healing medicine within our reach, what should we do? According to my faith, ask the Lord Almighty to send an angel to heal the sick. This is our privilege. . . . (*Discourses of Brigham Young*, p. 163.)

When we are situated that we cannot get anything to help ourselves, then we may call upon the Lord and His servants who can do all. But it is our duty to do what we can within our own power.

That is a tremendous principle. In order to teach young people how to approach the Lord and how to prepare to receive what the Lord has promised for those who are faithful, we must teach them these fundamental steps. After Moroni had read this great experience of the brother of Jared, he added: ". . . wherefore, dispute not because ye see not, for ye receive no witness until after the trial of your faith." (Ether 12:6.)

The grandson of Lehi illustrates this principle also. Enos went out in the mountains to pray and to ask forgiveness for his sins. He closed his brief record about this experience by saying:

> And my soul hungered; and I kneeled down before my Maker, and I cried unto him in mighty prayer and supplication for mine own soul; and all the day long did I cry unto him; yea, and when the night came I did still raise my voice high that it reached the heavens. (Enos 4.)

I once read that scripture to a woman who laughed and said, "Imagine anybody praying all night and all day." I replied, "My dear sister, I hope you never have to come to a time where you have a problem so great that you have to so humble yourself. I have; I have prayed all day and all night and all the next day and all the next night, not always on my knees but praying constantly for a blessing that I needed most."

Enos continued:

> . . . while I was thus struggling in the spirit, behold, the voice of the Lord came into my mind again, saying: I will visit thy brethren according to their diligence in keeping my commandments. . . . (Enos 10.)

The Lord will bless us to the degree to which we keep His commandments. Nephi put this principle in a tremendous orbit when he said:

> For we labor diligently to write, to persuade our children, and also our brethren, to believe in Christ, and to be reconciled to God; for we know that it is by grace that we are saved, after all we can do. (2 Nephi 25:23.)

The Savior's blood, His atonement, will save us, but only after we have done all we can to save ourselves by keeping His commandments. All of the principles of the gospel are principles of promise by which the plans of the Almighty are unfolded to us.

It is important for us to understand God's laws and to teach them to our children. For the truth of this I bear you my humble witness: I know it is true, that "there is a law, irrevocably decreed in heaven before the foundations of this world, upon which all blessings are predicated—and when we obtain any blessing from God, it is by obedience to that law upon which it is predicated."

Section Six

THE PRIESTHOOD AND THE CHURCH

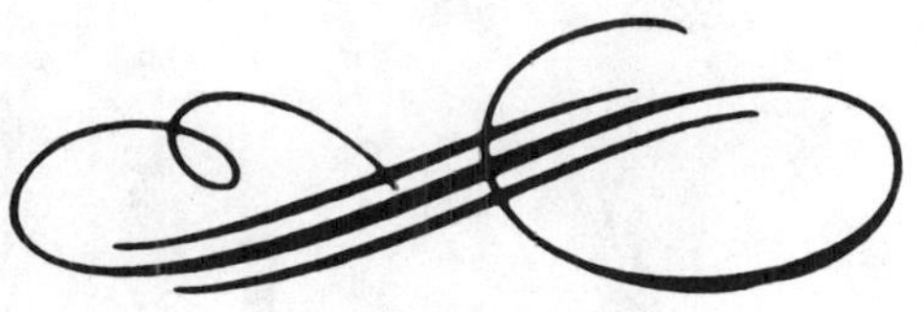

26

Magnify Your Priesthood

ON the west wall of the great Salt Lake Temple, underneath the center spires, is a symbolic representation of the constellation of stars known as "The Dipper" with the pointers pointing to the north star, which was said by the architect of the temple to represent the great truth that through the priesthood of God the lost may find their way.

In order to understand the import of that statement, I would divide my thoughts into three separate categories. The first requisite for the priesthood holder is to understand what priesthood is. The second, how priesthood should be exercised. And the third, how to magnify this priesthood.

There are two concepts that over the years have been expressed in defining the meaning of priesthood. One is that priesthood is the authority given by our Heavenly Father to man to authorize him to officiate in all matters pertaining to the salvation of mankind upon the earth. The other concept is expressed by another meaningful thought that priesthood is the power by which God works through man.

There is a difference between the holding of the priesthood by ordination, such as the office of elder, seventy, or high priest, and having the keys of the priesthood.

All elders of the Church, meaning all who hold the Melchizedek Priesthood, have all the priesthood necessary to preside in any calling in the Church, if they are called by those in authority, sustained by a vote of the people, and then ordained to the office and given the keys of that office by those in authority.

The Lord very clearly set this forth in a revelation in the early history of the Church:

> . . . it shall not be given to any one to go forth to preach my gospel, or to build up my church, except he be ordained by someone who has authority, and it is known to the church that he has authority, and has been regularly ordained by the heads of the church. (D&C 42:11.)

One of the most significant things about your priesthood is that by tracing the line of your authority through the one who ordained you back through the various steps, your priesthood authority can be traced back to the Savior himself.

A failure to understand this principle by which authority is given and received has led some astray, when some clever agent of some sect or splinter group, so-called, has claimed falsely to have priesthood authority. Occasionally, this misunderstanding is to be found among newly baptized converts who have as yet not fully understood the order of the presiding authority under which they are to serve.

Priesthood relationship to those who are in the body of a priesthood quorum and those who preside must be constantly taught and understood to avoid confusion, which would result in jealousy or contention. This frequently occurs when new members have not yet been fully indoctrinated with the teachings of the gospel and the disciplines of the Church. Failure to do so would in some instances result in apostasy.

Now to the second point, how priesthood is to be exercised.

In a great revelation we know as the 121st section of the Doctrine and Covenants, given through the inspiration of the Lord to the Prophet Joseph Smith, the Lord said some very significant things. He said the priesthood could only be controlled upon the principles of righteousness, and that if we were to use our priesthood office improperly "to cover our sins, or to gratify our pride, our vain ambition, or to exercise control or dominion or compulsion . . . the Spirit of the Lord is grieved." (See D&C 121:37.)

I was taught this by the late President J. Reuben Clark, Jr., who may be remembered by many of you as a former United States Ambassador to Mexico, when I made a remark in his presence that indicated that I had some lingering feelings because of some slight I had previously suffered. He said to me, very quietly, "Yes, you now have the authority, the whip hand, but you must not use it," for one holding a position of authority in the church and kingdom of God would surely bring the disfavor of our Lord, in whose service we must never forget we are, as holders of the priesthood.

The penalty if we do use our priesthood unrighteously is that the heavens withdraw themselves and the Spirit of the Lord is grieved. When we lose the Spirit, our priesthood authority is taken from us and we are left to ourselves "to kick against the pricks," when we are being irritated by the admonitions and instructions of our leaders. Then we begin to persecute the saints, which means criticize, and finally to fight against God, and the powers of darkness overtake us if we do not repent and turn from that evil course.

The qualities of acceptable priesthood leadership are also carefully defined in this revelation. One is to preside over the Church with patience and long-suffering, with gentleness and meekness, with love unfeigned. If one must discipline and reprove with sharpness, he must do it when moved upon by the Holy Ghost and then show forth afterwards an increase of love, lest the one whom he has reproved would think him to be an enemy. In all our priesthood callings we must never forget that the business of the church and kingdom of God is to save souls, and that all over whom we preside are our Father's children, and He will aid us in our endeavors to save every one.

There is a classic example of how our Lord would have us minister to those who need our aid. When Peter and John, as recorded in the book of the Acts of the Apostles, approached a man who had never walked and who was at the gates of the temple begging alms, instead of giving him money, the apostle Peter, you will remember, said to him, "Silver and gold have I none; but such as I have give I thee: In the name of Jesus Christ of Nazareth rise up and walk." (Acts 3:6.)

Then followed a significant statement in the record of that incident. Peter took him by the right hand and lifted him up. Remember that it wasn't enough for Peter to command him to walk; he then took him by the hand and lifted him up.

So must we, in dealing with our faltering saints, not be merely priesthood holders who criticize, scold, and condemn. We must like the apostle Peter: take them by the arm, encourage them, and give them a sense of security and respect for themselves until they can rise above their difficulties and can stand on their own feet.

That is the way the priesthood of God can bring salvation and fellowship to those who are weak, that they may become strong.

Now to the third point, how we should magnify our priesthood.

As a young boy of twelve years, Jesus, after having been found in the temple by Joseph and Mary, in response to their inquiry asked a significant question: "Wist ye not that I must be about my Father's business?" (Luke 2:49.) What did he mean by His Father's business?

In another revelation the Lord gave meaning to that young boy's question. To the elders of the Church assembled in Kirtland, Ohio, He impressed upon them their great responsibililies as holders of the sacred priesthood office of elder. "Wherefore," said he, "as ye are agents, ye are on the Lord's errand; and whatever ye do according to the will of the Lord is the Lord's business." (D&C 64:29.)

When one becomes a holder of the priesthood, he becomes an agent of the Lord. He should think of his calling as though he were on the Lord's errand. That is what it means to magnify the priesthood. Think of the Master asking each of you, as this young boy did of Joseph and Mary, Wist ye not that I must be about my Father's business? Whatever you do according to the will of the Lord is the Lord's business.

You must not think of your priesthood calling as just for Sunday. It is the will of the Lord that you keep the commandments of God. "Be ye clean that bear the vessels of the Lord." (D&C 38:42.) Remember always that the most important of the Lord's work you and I will ever do will be within the walls of our own homes. You must keep your family ties strong; never forget that profound declaration of President David O. McKay, which should always be in your minds: "No other success can compensate for failure in the home."

In your business life, in your social contacts, and in your public service, remember always to say to yourself as did the young British officer who was asked why he had shunned a drinking, riotous party at his officer's club. "Because," he replied, "I am a member of the Royal Household of England."

You who belong to God's holy priesthood must say to yourselves, "Neither can I stoop to engage in the wickedness of the world, because I (as the apostle Peter declared) am of the chosen generation, a royal priesthood, an holy nation, and of a peculiar people." (See 1 Peter 2:9.) Or to paraphrase the British officer's reply, "I cannot because I am a member of the Royal Household of God."

Remember those marvelous promises of the Lord to you if you would be full of charity to all men and

> let virtue garnish thy thoughts unceasingly; then shall thy confidence wax strong in the presence of God; and the doctrine of the priesthood shall distil upon thy soul as the dews from heaven.
>
> The Holy Ghost shall be thy constant companion, and thy scepter an unchanging scepter of righteousness and truth; and thy dominion shall be an everlasting dominion, and without compulsory means it shall flow unto thee forever and ever. (D&C 121:45-46.)

Those inspired words were from the Lord, and I repeat them as a reminder to each of you of your responsibilities as holders of the priesthood and the great blessings which will be yours if you magnify your callings as servants of the Most High God.

In my present calling as the president of the High Priesthood, or the Melchizedek Priesthood, in the Church today, I give you my blessing and link hands with you in that marvelous fellowship which is after the order of the Son of God.

May the work of salvation roll on under the guidance of your priesthood leadership, and may you be reminded again of the symbolism of the markings on the great Salt Lake Temple, that through the priesthood of God the lost may find their way.

27

Priesthood: The Strength of the Church

THE priesthood is the center, the core, the power by which all the activities of the Church are to be directed. What does it mean to be ordained to the priesthood? I suppose I have read the following two simple verses in section 36 of the Doctrine and Covenants a hundred times, and have never quite seen their significance until a short while ago. They constitute revelation given to Edward Partridge, the first bishop of the Church:

> Thus saith the Lord God, the Mighty One of Israel: Behold, I say unto you, my servant Edward, that you are blessed, and your sins are forgiven you, and you are called to preach my gospel as with the voice of a trump.
>
> And I will lay my hand upon you by the hand of my servant Sidney Rigdon, and you shall receive my Spirit, the Holy Ghost, even the Comforter, which shall teach you the peaceable things of the kingdom. (D&C 36:1-2.)

Do you get the significance of that? When one is ordained by authority, it is as though the Lord Himself is also laying His hand upon that person by the hand of His authorized servant, for the person being ordained to receive the gifts and the endowments of the Spirit that come under His jurisdiction and administration.

It was inspiration that came in the day of our present leader [President David O. McKay] to implement in the missions the plan that all priesthood members be organized into quorums.

Now we are suggesting to you that you develop that organization. If you have in the whole of your mission only sufficient for one quorum of elders, we ask you to organize them as one quorum with a presidency, even though they may have but a relationship carried on by correspondence, so that there will be a sense of feeling and belonging to a quorum in the brotherhood of the kingdom.

Frequently we find presidents who are urging that elders who have long been faithful in the Church be ordained high priests. We ask you to consider that more important than holding a specific office in the priesthood is the quorum relationship. If we have only one or two in a mission who are high priests, don't you see, in a sense we withdraw them from the fraternalism or brotherhood of a quorum, where they might have had far more priesthood association had they continued in the elders quorum. Now if there be a compelling reason to the contrary, the mission president would recommend to the First Presidency that a certain brother be ordained a high priest, explaining the reasons therefor, and the First Presidency will then take that recommendation under advisement. If they agree with your proposal, it may be referred to the General Authority who will next visit in your area. Then someone may be authorized to ordain the person.

The First Presidency are inclined, and we have been so instructed, to discourage the ordination of a man to a so-called higher office, when as a matter of fact it isn't a higher office. Unless he is called to a position that requires him to hold that priesthood, it would be better for him to remain as an elder, the greatest resevoir of the priesthood of the mission, so that brotherhood might be more fully realized.

> The foundation of the Church . . . is its authoritative priesthood. The organizations of the Church are but helps to the Priesthood. That places the Priesthood quorums in the position of leadership. They should be so ably conducted, so faithfully attended, so thoroughly serviceable, as to set an example to all other Church organizations. Necessarily, if a man must choose between loyalty to his Priesthood quorum and some other Church organization however good, his duty is to the quorum. (John A. Widtsoe, "The Priesthood Quorum Comes First," *Improvement Era,* December 1937, p. 760.)

That statement may need some explanation. In cases where brethren are called, for example, to supervise the Aaronic Priesthood, it is recommended that those brethren be free so they can attend their monthly priesthood meetings even though on other Sundays they may have to absent themselves from their priesthood groups.

Now the ultimate place to which quorums may take us is suggested by a statement from Joseph F. Smith. He said,

> We expect to see the day . . . when every council of the priesthood in the Church of Jesus Christ of Latter-day Saints will understand its duty; will assume its own responsibility, will magnify its calling, and fill its place in the Church, to the uttermost, according to the intelligence and ability possessed by it. When that day shall come, there shall not be so much necessity for work that is now being done by the auxiliary organizations because it will be done by the regular quorums of the Priesthood. . . . (*Gospel Doctrine,* p. 159.)

What is the purpose of a quorum of the priesthood? Let me read you two scriptures. In the 84th section the Lord said:

> Therefore, let every man stand in his own office, and labor in

> his own calling; and let not the head say unto the feet it hath no need of the feet; for without the feet how shall the body be able to stand?
>
> Also the body hath need of every member, that all may be edified together, that the system may be kept perfect. (D&C 84:109-110.)

And then the Lord said in another revelation:

> The above offices I have given unto you, and the keys thereof, for helps and for governments, for the work of the ministry and the perfecting of my saints.
>
> And a commandment I give unto you, that you should fill all these offices and approve of those names which I have mentioned, or else disapprove of them at my general conference. (D&C 124:143.)

One of the decisions that was made in October of 1922 was this:

> Those ordained to the priesthood, both to the Melchizedek and the Aaronic, are organized into quorums in order that both old and young may be taught and become familiar with the order of the priesthood which they hold, its keys and authorities; the field of endeavor occupied by each quorum, and its limitations. The method of conducting quorum meetings should always have this purpose in mind.

Now, brethren, I hope you can get the significance of what is being said. There may be occasions when you may feel inspired to ordain a man an elder who is only a few weeks old in the Church. Ordinarily we would not do that unless impelled by the Spirit, because if a man went through each grade, deacon, teacher, priest, then elder, he would be taught "so that both old and young may be taught and become familiar with the order of the priesthood which they hold, and its keys of authority, the field of endeavor occupied by each quorum and its limitations."

Now if for nothing else, it's a good thing to bring every man through every grade of priesthood, even if it be but a comparatively brief time, but you are to determine how fast you shall move him.

Elder Matthew Cowley of the Council of the Twelve used to tell us that every priesthood quorum in this church ought to be an "Alcoholics Anonymous," because we all have smokers and drinkers who have to have help before they can overcome their habits, and we ought not to be an organization that says to a man who is begging for help, "Well, join the Alcoholics Anonymous." We ought to say, "Now you come to priesthood quorum meetings and we will assign some man who used to have this habit to work with you, and we will give you the help with the power of the priesthood until you can overcome it."

Elder George Q. Morris and I were organizing a new stake in Boise, Idaho. We were told about a man who had done a wonderful work with the Aaronic Priesthood Adults, and we asked him how he had done it. He said, "It's just as simple as this. We discovered these inactive men didn't know any more about the gospel than if they had been born on some dark continent, and we decided if we were going to bring them into activity, we had to convert them. We had the mission president teach some special reactivation committee members the new missionary plan, just like the proselyting elders take out to the nonmembers, and then we sent them out two and two to hold cottage meetings with these inactive families, and did everything that you do with a nonmember, excepting to commit them to baptism."

President David O. Mckay, so frequently in the beginning of the welfare program, used to speak of it as a program of limitations that we only operated within a certain circle. If we were to get outside of that, then we were all wrong.

In the first place the welfare program needs leadership, and in the beginning, that had to be supplied by missionaries. It meant that many of our missionaries were largely hoeing peas and beans and corn rather than doing proselyting work. There was a danger when we put the welfare program too much forward that there were too many who wanted to join the Church for the "loaves and fishes," as the Master accused the people in his day. They didn't become members because of the gospel but because of the "loaves and the fishes." We found that happening in some cases. Also the scattered and sparse membership and the great distances make distribution unfeasible in many cases.

We have discouraged quorums of the priesthood—or for that matter, any Church unit—going into business ventures. In some of the distant stakes I have found some business activities that I didn't say no to because they were trying to raise funds for buildings that were now causing them great anxiety. I went to a mission years ago where they were setting up a commodity distribution program where the mission was to be the clearing house. The east part of the mission was in a producing area, and the west part of the mission was in a consuming area, and the mission president had the idea of using his office as the clearing house for commodities.

By the time I had asked half a dozen questions about public liability and insurance, about sales tax, and about union regulations and teamsters' dues and what not, the mission president said, "My goodness, I don't want anything to do with that," and so he threw the whole plan in the wastebasket as I had hoped he would, because it was not the place of the mission to be in that kind of business.

We have found burial fund plans where somebody has gotten the idea that quorum members ought to put a dollar a month into a fund and give it to the family of a deceased member of the quorum. Almost never have these fund plans worked out without a lot of difficulty. It means that the last survivors may not have anybody to pay for their burial, and when we divide and subdivide as we have, we can get into some of the worst quarrels and disagreements that you can imagine, and so we are telling you to stay out of the burial fund business, insurance, etc. Leave that to somebody else smarter than you are or less foolhardy.

Now there are things that we can do, and those things are suggested by what the Lord has told us. A visiting social welfare worker who headed up one of the government agencies in the early days of government relief asked me if I could give him the underlying principle behind the welfare program, and I quoted the 104th section of the Doctrine and Covenants:

> . . . the earth is full, and there is enough and to spare. . . .
>
> But it must needs be done in mine own way; and behold this is the way that I, the Lord, have decreed to provide for my saints, that the poor shall be exalted, in that the rich are made low.
>
> Therefore, if any man shall take of the abundance which I have made, and impart not his portion, according to the law of my gospel, unto the poor and the needy, he shall, with the wicked, lift up his eyes in hell, being in torment. (D&C 104:17, 16, 18.)

Two hours later we were still discussing that scripture, in which you can find every element of the welfare program described.

"To be lifted up to pride and joy to success" is the definition we followed. The rich being made low isn't communistic; it isn't socialistic. It means that those who have leadership, who have skills, who have means, who are willing to contribute, can be put to work with the one who is in need.

Here are some things that can be done. We can find employment for the unemployed and aid members in times of adversity. A member of the quorum falls ill. Who is going to milk his cows? Who is going to take care of his harvest? Who is going to do this, and who is going to do that?

A house burns down. The ideal is to teach your new priesthood members how to rally round rather than turn the whole job over to some public relief agency.

Encourage the putting aside for a rainy day in individual homes. That means teaching thrift, frugality, and avoidance of debt. Certainly that is a program that we ought to foster everywhere. We have already said that we ought not to have production projects nor bishops storehouses in missions for these reasons that I have shown you. When you get to be a stake we will determine at what point you are ready to take on the full welfare program—but not as growing districts with less than we think is sufficient for the full program.

I found, however, in one mission something that was ingenious. In one of these areas they had worked out a two weeks' suggested food list for an average-size family. They had two varieties in case the taste were different. They had an A variety for two weeks' supply and a B variety. Whenever the branch president would find a needy family, he would call upon the John Doe family to give up their two weeks' supply of the A variety and maybe the Bill Smith family to give up their two weeks' supply of the B variety and put them together, and there was provided a month's supply for the needy family. That was their contribution to the welfare program, and they of course replenished their own stock.

The next time the branch president had a needy family he called upon another family in the A group and another family in the B group, or maybe two in each, if the need was greater. Then they would replenish their supplies, and if there were still another need, he would go down the list until everybody in the branch had had the privilege of contributing from his own private stock. In a sense, don't you see, it was a home storage welfare distribution to needy families. Now again I am not instructing you, I am merely telling you what some of you have already done.

Why is it important to ordain men to the priesthood almost simultaneously with baptism?

These were answers that came to me as I thought about this question. Priesthood defined is the power of God given to man to act for Him in all things pertaining to the salvation of man—and I should add, within the limitations of each endowment of authority by the laying on of hands. Now, if to hold priesthood is to give men power of God to act for Him, and if we give that power to a newly baptized member, what does it do to the member?

Well, it increases his individual power over himself, over his natural powers to combat successfully the powers of the adversary, and all our new converts need that, don't they? It gives him power to maintain his place at the head of his own household in solving his family problems. It gives him power to influence friends and relatives to accept the gospel. It is difficult for us at this distance to see why a male convert over twelve years of age ought not to be given the first grade of priesthood, that of a deacon, almost simultaneously with baptism, and then as he earns it and merits it, he is moved up the ladder until finally he is worthy to go to the temple.

Now, just one more thought with reference to giving priesthood to men who belong to secret and fraternal orders. I was in a mission where there was an able man whose services were needed, but someone had the understanding that he could not be given the priesthood and used because he was a Mason. It was thought that there were some letters of instruction from the First Presidency, or President Joseph Fielding Smith, that gave them license to withhold priesthood or any activities from this man. When I asked them to show me the letters they referred to, we found that what they said in substance was: If there is such a man (and quite frequently you will find some of these leading men who turn up as members of some lodge—Mason, Eagle, Elks Club, etc.) the thing that you should always say is, "I am not concerned about what you have been. I am concerned about what you are going to be from now on."

If he understands and is truly converted, he will agree that his first allegiance will be to his priesthood and to the Church, and that he will cease his fraternal activities. Some of them argue that they should maintain their membership because of the insurance values of belonging. Whether they do that or not is their own business, but if they tell us that they are prepared to give their first allegiance to the Church, then we can give them the priesthood and full activity as merited by their worthiness.

President Heber J. Grant used to tell us about one such man who had been an active member in a Masonic Lodge, and when President Grant told this man he was being called to be the president of a stake, the man demurred, saying, "I am a 32nd Degree Mason." President Grant said the same thing to him: "I am not concerned with what you have been. It is what you are going to be from now on."

You cannot serve two masters, and so we say to you, use these men, and probably by their being used, you will gradually wean them from what you don't like to something that is better.

28

"And This Is My Gospel . . ."

A *MISSIONARY* once asked, "Since the restored Church claims that it is necessary to have the same organization that existed in the primitive church, particularly twelve apostles, how then can we claim that the kingdom of God and the gospel were upon the earth before the time of the Savior when they had no apostles?"

Before answering that question, let me refer to a statement from Napoleon I, while he was in exile in 1817: "I would believe in a religion if it existed from the beginning of time, but when I consider Socrates, Plato, and Mohammed, I no longer believe."

There are those who believe that the kingdom of God was not established until after the advent of the Savior and that the gospel of Jesus Christ was not upon the earth until the time of His advent.

As I have thought about that missionary's question about the organization of the Church, and about Napoleon's statement, three questions have formulated themselves in my thinking: The first, How old is the kingdom of God and the gospel upon the earth? The second, What are the essentials of a gospel dispensation in the world? And third, What officers are necessary in an organization to constitute the church and kingdom of God? I realize that to answer those questions fully would take much more time than is allotted to me, so I shall comment only briefly and make a few observations in answer to these questions.

In the Lord's revelation to Abraham, He spoke of the purpose in sending spirits upon the earth, to "prove them herewith, to see if they will do all things whatsoever the Lord their God shall command them" (Abraham 3:25), with a promise that if they would keep their second estate they should have glory added upon their heads forever and forever.

In the first chapter of the writings of John, the nature of that glory spoken of in the revelation to Abraham is implied. John said, "But as many as received him, to them gave he power to become the sons of God. . . ." (John 1:12.)

In a modern revelation that same statement is repeated with slight variation and then clarified, in these words:

> But to as many as received me, gave I power to become my sons; . . .
>
> And verily, verily, I say unto you, he that receiveth my gospel receiveth me; and he that receiveth not my gospel receiveth not me.

And then the Lord proceeds to define the fundamental principles of the gospel in these words:

> And this is my gospel—repentance and baptism by water, and then cometh the baptism of fire and the Holy Ghost, even the Comforter, which showeth all things, and teacheth the peaceable things of the kingdom. (D&C 39:4-6.)

The gospel plan, as these scriptures would indicate,

was laid in the heavens before the earth was organized and spirits were placed upon it.

That this gospel and the essentials of salvation have been upon the earth in every dispensation from the time of Adam, there can be no doubt. In an early revelation to Moses, which is found in the Pearl of Great Price, the Lord, speaking to Adam, said this:

> If thou wilt turn unto me, and hearken unto my voice, and believe, and repent of all thy transgressions, and be baptized, even in water, in the name of mine Only Begotten Son, who is full of grace and truth, which is Jesus Christ, the only name which shall be given under heaven, whereby salvation shall come unto the children of men, ye shall receive the gift of the Holy Ghost, asking all things in his name, and whatsoever ye shall ask, it shall be given you. (Moses 6:52.)

Then there follows an account of the baptism of Adam, and this declaration by a voice speaking out of heaven to Adam: "Behold, thou art one in me, a Son of God; and thus may all become my sons." (Moses 6:68.)

In writing to the Galatians, the Apostle Paul said, "And the scripture, foreseeing that God would justify the heathen through faith, preached before the gospel unto Abraham, saying, In thee shall all nations be blessed." (Galatians 3:8.)

He was speaking of the ordinance of baptism in Moses' day when he wrote these words to the Corinthians: ". . . how that all our fathers were under the cloud, and all passed through the sea; And were all baptized unto Moses. . . ." (1 Corinthians 10:1-2.)

And then of the children of Israel under the leadership of Moses, Paul again wrote to the Hebrews, and said, "For unto us was the gospel preached, as well as unto them: but the word preached did not profit them, not being mixed with faith in them that heard it." (Hebrews 4:2.)

All of these statements thus recorded in the Bible have been confirmed by modern revelation.

Just as in the dispensations of Adam, Abraham, and Moses were those fundamental teachings given and those fundamental ordinances of the gospel administered, so we hear the Savior speaking to Nicodemus, "Except a man be born of water and of the Spirit, he cannot enter into the kingdom of God." (John 3:5.)

To suppose that God would initiate ordinances on which salvation would be conditioned and then allow four thousand years to pass without any authority or any organization to administer those ordinances is untenable to the thinking man. A thinking man would have to conclude with Napoleon, "Unless a religion existed from the beginning, I cannot believe."

Now for just a moment, let's take a look at the Church organizations that have existed in each of these dispensations from the beginning. To Adam there was given "dominion . . . over every living thing that moveth upon the earth." (Genesis 1:28.) The government in his time was patriarchal and the priesthood ruled. Men holding the priesthood ruled by direct revelation and commandment.

In Enoch's time likewise, his government was patriarchal. Zion, the City of Holiness, was established, and Enoch gave a perfect economic law, known to us as the Order of Enoch. There was likewise a similar government from Noah to Abraham, as we are informed by modern revelation in these words:

> The order of this priesthood was confirmed to be handed down from father to son, and rightly belongs to the literal descendants of the chosen seed, to whom the promises were made. (D&C 107:40.)

From Moses to the prophet Samuel, Israel was governed by judges, who were chosen from among the people. And then you will recall, because they were "peculiar" in that type of government, the people sought for a king, to be like other peoples; a king to rule over them in secular matters, while a prophet would continue to guide in spiritual affairs. You will recall that Saul was then chosen, followed by David, and by Solomon, and then came the division of the children of Israel into the kingdom of Judah and the kingdom of Israel under Rehoboam and Jeroboam.

With the advent of Jesus, the Jews were in a state of apostasy, and you will recall He chose twelve men to be His special witnesses, and to one of these twelve, Peter, He gave the keys to the kingdom of God. The significance of that commission of the keys of the kingdom to Peter is better understood in the words of a revelation given to us by the Prophet Joseph Smith, when the Lord said this, speaking of the Prophet Joseph, "Unto whom I have given the keys of the kingdom, which belong always unto the Presidency of the High Priesthood." (D&C 81:2.)

In other words, Peter, holding the keys of the kingdom, was as much the president of the High Priesthood in his day as Joseph Smith and his successors, to whom also these "keys" were given in our day, are the presidents of the High Priesthood, and the earthly heads of the church and kingdom of God on the earth.

The Apostle Paul, describing the church organization in his day, said, "And God hath set some in the church, first apostles, secondarily prophets, . . . after that . . . helps, governments. . . ." (1 Corinthians 12:28.)

But in all of these church offices we are told again in the revelations, ". . . there is never but one on the earth at a time on whom this power and the keys of this priesthood are conferred. . . ." (D&C 132:7.)

We are living today in the dispensation of the fulness

of times, and we were given a statement, inspired by the Lord, to the Prophet Joseph Smith in these words, which make some explanation of what the dispensation of the fulness of times contemplated. He said:

> . . . for it is necessary in the ushering in of the dispensation of the fulness of times, which dispensation is now beginning to usher in, that a whole and complete and perfect union, and welding together of dispensations, and keys, and powers, and glories should . . . be revealed from the days of Adam even to the present time. And not only this, but those things which never have been revealed from the foundation of the world . . . shall be revealed . . . in this, the dispensation of the fulness of times. (D&C 128:18.)

The apostle Peter spoke of that, in referring to this same dispensation of the fulness of times, when he said there would be a "restitution of all things, which God hath spoken by the mouth of all his holy prophets since the world began." (Acts 3:21.)

It seems clear, then, that were the Church organization today to be devoid of that which Jesus gave in the way of organization, this dispensation would fail, by that same token, to be an established kingdom of God upon the earth in the dispensation of the fulness of times, in which were to be restored "all things." Undoubtedly the organization the Master gave was to be the pattern of organization more perfected than in the past dispensations. There is evidence of this in the fact that after He had left the people here following His resurrection, He went to the Nephites, and there again He chose twelve disciples, whom He set up to govern His church and that part of the kingdom here on this continent among the Nephites.

We might then ask, what is the kingdom of God? And again we are not left without an answer, for the Lord replied, "The keys of the kingdom of God are committed unto man on the earth. . . ." Where there are the keys to the kingdom, there is the Church of Jesus Christ, and it is the stone which was cut out of the mountain without hands, as told in Daniel's interpretation of the dream, which was to roll forth and smite the image and break it in pieces and to roll on until it should fill the whole earth. (See D&C 65.)

The Prophet Joseph Smith makes this definition of the kingdom of God:

> Some say that the kingdom of God was not set up upon the earth until the day of Pentecost, and that John did not preach the baptism of repentance for the remission of sins; but I say, in the name of the Lord, that the kingdom of God was set up upon the earth from the days of Adam to the present time. Whenever there has been a righteous man on the earth unto whom God revealed His word and gave power and authority to administer in His name, and where there is a priest of God . . . to administer in the ordinances of the gospel and officiate in the priesthood of God, there is the kingdom of God. . . . Where there is a prophet, a priest, or a righteous man unto whom God gives His oracles, there is the kingdom of God; and where the oracles of God are not, there the kingdom of God is not. (*Teachings of the Prophet Joseph Smith,* pp. 271-72.)

Just as the Master said in His day that the kingdom of God cometh not by observation, meaning that there would be no outward signs or political changes, so today it is now among us, as it has been in every dispensation of the gospel since the days of Adam.

Another statement was made by the prophets of the New Testament that to me has some significance. They are quoted as having said that "the kingdom of God is within you." (Luke 17:21.) A more correct translation probably would have said, "The kingdom of God is among you or in your midst," But as I thought of that other statement, "The kingdom of God is within you," I recalled an experience that we had with a group of students from Brigham Young University. They were gracious enough to come under the leadership of President Ernest L. Wilkinson to a little group over in the Lion House, and there sixteen, representing sixteen foreign countries, were asked to stand and tell how they came to know about the gospel and accept it, why they were attending Brigham Young University, and to bear their testimonies. It was a most intensely interesting evening. We heard from young men and women from Mexico, Argentina, Brazil, and Scandinavian countries, France, and England. Each story was the same. When they began to relate how they came to find the gospel, it was this: They were yearning for truth. They were seeking for light. They were not satisfied, and in the midst of their search, someone came to them with the truths of the gospel. They prayed about it and sought the Lord intensely, intently, with all their hearts, and came to receive a divine testimony by which they knew that this is the gospel of Jesus Christ.

One young woman said, "I had been studying the gospel, and this night I came to a meeting and I heard them sing 'Joseph Smith's First Prayer,' which gave in song the story of the first vision, and before they had finished that song, into my heart the Spirit bore testimony that this is the church and kingdom of God."

So within the heart of everyone, every honest seeker after truth, if he has the desire to know, and studies with real intent and faith in the Lord Jesus Christ, the kingdom of God may be within him, or in other words, the power to receive it is his.

I bear you my humble witness that this is the church and kingdom of God in the earth. This is the dispensation of the fulness of times. Except for the fact that it is but a continuation of the same gospel, the same fundamental principles, the same authority that has existed from the beginning of time, we would have to say with Napoleon, "Except you can prove to me that a religion has existed from the beginning, . . . I will not believe."

God help us to take this message to the world and convince them of the power of the gospel and the power which is within them to receive the kingdom of God while it is yet on the earth in its fulness.

29

The Lord's Plan for Times of Difficulty

FOR many years I have been deeply concerned with matters that pertain to the safety and welfare of this people. In my study of this subject and my attention to these matters, I have become impressed with the rich outpouring of Spirit that has dictated counsel, wisdom, and revelation sufficient for our needs. That the Lord is concerned about the welfare of this people there can be no question, as is evidenced by a revelation given early in the history of this church to the Prophet Joseph in these words: "And it is my purpose to provide for my saints, for all things are mine. But it must needs be done in mine own way. . . ." (D&C 104:15-16.)

I received some time ago a letter from a friend that suggests the concern of our Father and the way by which His concern will be manifest:

> For over a century men have been preaching the gospel of salvation but have never lifted their eyes beyond the old sectarian concept of a salvation men have to die to get. When we become conscious of

the fact that there is no time limit upon the saving principles and power of the gospel but that they may be drawn upon to meet the problems of today and tomorrow, as well as of the hereafter, we will then become the people who will be the light of the world.

The dispensation in which we live is intended to be a demonstration of the power and effectiveness of the gospel of Jesus Christ to meet these everyday problems here and now. The Lord declared in 1838:

> For thus shall my church be called in the last days, even The Church of Jesus Christ of Latter-day Saints.
>
> Verily I say unto you all: Arise and shine forth, that thy light may be a standard for the nations;
>
> And that the gathering together upon the land of Zion, and upon her stakes, may be for a defense, and for a refuge from the storm, and from wrath when it shall be poured out without mixture upon the whole earth. (D&C 115:4-6.)

The uncertainty of the leadership of men of the world in this day is evidenced by the fact that we have many changing programs that overnight and day by day seem to fluctuate between poles of the greatest of uncertainty. We hear much about "the abundant life" and "social security," and there are some, I fear, who are believers in the thought that these goals will come from working out the philosophies of men.

My purpose is to give you something of what the Lord has said pertaining to this day and what might be the expectations of the Latter-day Saints concerning the way by which the Lord would guide us to safe shores. Not only has the Lord given us the plan to follow, but He has given us through revelation one of the basic, if not the most basic, reasons for the ills that beset mankind. This is what the Lord said—and I suppose as you understand this you will recognize in it the reason for selfishness and for jealousies that develop into bitterness and hatred, and finally into war and bloodshed. Here is the simple statement of the Lord:

"But it is not given that one man should possess that which is above another, wherefore the world lieth in sin." (D&C 49:20.)

While the world today is groping for a solution (and some of our people, I am afraid, have the mistaken notion that they must look to some development of the philosophies of men in this nation or from nations abroad to solve present problems), the Latter-day Saints should never lose sight of the fact that for over one hundred years the Lord has given us the way and the plan by which might come the solution of all the economic problems of this day.

> For Zion must increase in beauty, and in holiness; her borders must be enlarged; her stakes must be strengthened; yea, verily I say unto you, Zion must arise and put on her beautiful garments.
>
> Therefore, I give unto you this commandment, that ye bind yourselves by this covenant, and it shall be done according to the laws of the Lord.
>
> Behold, here is wisdom also in me for your good.
>
> And you are to be equal, or in other words, you are to have equal claims on the properties, for the benefit of managing the concerns of your stewardships, every man according to his wants and his needs, inasmuch as his wants are just—
>
> And all this for the benefit of the church of the living God, that every man may improve upon his talent, that every man may gain other talents, yea, even an hundred fold, to be cast into the Lord's storehouse, to become the common property of the whole church—
>
> Every man seeking the interest of his neighbor, and doing all things with an eye single to the glory of God. (D&C 82:14-19.)

The Lord gave the details—the minutest of details—of the organization we have come to call the United Order. He told us how consecrations were to be made and received; He told us something about the establishment of stewardships and private ownerships, and how those within such an organization should act. This is not the first time that such an organization has been given to this people.

We read that shortly after the crucifixion of the Savior the followers of our Lord and Savior established an order where they had all things in common, and two hundred years after the Savior's coming we find a people on this continent of which it was said that they likewise were living in close bonds of fellowship and love, so much so that there was not to be found a happier people anywhere on the face of the earth.

Many years ago when I, under assignment from the First Presidency, accompanied Elder Melvin J. Ballard of the Council of the Twelve throughout the Church to make the initial announcement of the movement known as the Church Welfare Plan, he was asked everywhere: "Is this the beginning of the United Order?" And to all such questioners Brother Ballard's answer was the same: "No, it is not the beginning of the United Order, but it may be that in this movement the Lord may be giving His people an examination to see how far they have come toward a condition where they might live as one."

As I have thought about the question, and as I have thought about his answer, I have had difficulty understanding how a people who are not able to sacrifice to a point where they can pay a tenth of their interest annually and abstain from two meals on the first Sunday of the month and pay that as an offering for the care of the needy can believe that we are more than ten percent ready for the United Order.

Furthermore, I have difficulty understanding that they would be able to live in the United Order were it to be instituted in this day. I also have grave doubts that prosperous times will make possible that happy day spoken of. I fear we must yet see more difficult and trying times than any we have passed through before such a day can come.

There are some things of which I am sure, and that

is that contrary to the belief and mistaken ideas of some of our people, the United Order will not be a socialistic or communistic setup; it will be something distinctive, and yet it will be more capitalistic in its nature than either socialism or communism, in that private ownership and individual responsibility will be maintained. I am sure also that when it comes, it will come from the leaders of this church whom you sustain as prophets, seers, and revelators, and will not come from a man who does not occupy that position. It will not come as a political program, legislated by men not possessed of that authority. I am also convinced that the time is here when Zion must put on her beautiful garments preparatory for the second coming of the Savior, and I firmly believe that that preparation is in progress. I am likewise persuaded that the Church Welfare Plan is contributing mightily to that preparation.

It is more than just a coincidence that the First Presidency, in 1936, from the pulpit in the Salt Lake Tabernacle announced the beginning of the welfare movement and made this significant statement: "No pains must be spared to wipe out all feeling of diffidence, shame, or embarrassment on the part of those receiving relief. The ward must be one great family of equals."

I have seen from a humble beginning an organization grow to where now there have been produced throughout the Church great quantities of foodstuffs. I have seen a system of equitable distribution of those foodstuffs grow up under the guidance of our leaders, so much so that the storehouses we now have, or that are under construction, may each have an equitable supply of all these commodities and as great a variety as though the people lived here in the center part of the Church. I remember also that no bishop today who is faithful in bearing his responsibility may say that he cannot take care of faithful members of his ward because he has insufficient funds. I know that in these years we have been striving to a great end, and we have been led by the hand of our Father.

We have come to a day when the way of the Lord, as He described it, would be applied when the poor would be exalted, or in other words stimulated to success and pride, and uplifted because the rich have been made low—or in other words, because the rich have been made humble and willing to give of their substance, their time, their talents, their wisdom, and their example that the poor might be thus guided and directed. I have seen teamwork and cooperation grow, and I have seen the priesthood take its place in blessing this church temporally and spiritually in a most glorious way.

I am persuaded that the day of trial and tribulation, the time for testing the fidelity of the Latter-day Saints, is here as has been foretold. I am also convinced that you and I will not be prepared for living the celestial law in preparation for the Second Coming if we are not able to live the law of tithing, pay our fast offerings, and subscribe wholeheartedly to the workings of the welfare plan at the present time. In my mind there is grave doubt that any man can abide the day of the Second Coming who is not willing and able to follow the leadership of these men whom the Lord has appointed to counsel and guide us in this day.

I thank the Lord that we are not dependent alone upon the faith of those who lived centuries ago, or even a hundred years ago, for revelations that were given unto them in that day. In this day He has given us leaders who are possessed of the same spirit of revelation. This is what the Lord said, speaking to those who held apostleship:

> And this is the ensample unto them, that they shall speak as they are moved upon by the Holy Ghost.
>
> And whatsoever they shall speak when moved upon by the Holy Ghost shall be scripture, shall be the will of the Lord, shall be the mind of the Lord, shall be the word of the Lord, shall be the voice of the Lord, and the power of God unto salvation. (D&C 68:3-4.)

It should not be necessary today for us to expect new written revelation on every point when we have these men thus possessed of that same spirit of revelation. A brief review of the past instruction of our leaders should only serve to warn the disobedient to continue faithful. Today listen to the words of President Wilford Woodruff that he spoke many years ago:

> So far as temporal matters are concerned, we have got to go to work and provide for ourselves. The day will come when you will see the necessity for making your own shoes and clothing, raising your own food, and uniting together to carry out the purposes of the Lord. We will be preserved in the mountains of Israel in the day of God's judgment.

I therefore say to you, my brethren and sisters, prepare for that which is to come.

Have you made that preparation? Have you become a self-sustaining people? We were warned to be so by a man whom we sustained as the representative of our Heavenly Father here upon this earth. Today we are suffering from difficulties between capital and labor. Are you aware that a president of the Church in the last century told us something that, if we had heeded it, would have guided us safely past some of the ills of the present time? Lorenzo Snow spoke these words:

> Ye toiling millions who in the sweat of your faces earn your daily bread, the day of your redemption draweth nigh. Cease to waste your wages on that which helps to keep you in want. Regard not the wealth of your enemy and your employer as your oppressor. Seek for the union of capital and labor. Be provident when in prosperity. Do not become a prey to designing men who seek to stir up strife for their own selfish

ends. Strive for your rights by all lawful means, and desist from violence and destruction. Dissipation and vice are the chains that bind you to slavery.

Men and women of wealth, use your riches to give employment to the laborer; take the idle from the crowded centers of population, and place them on the untilled areas that await the hand of industry. Unlock your vaults, unloose your purses, and invest in enterprises that will give work to the unemployed and relieve the wretchedness that poisons the moral atmosphere around you. Make others happy and you will be happy yourself.

We have heard much said about keeping out of debt and avoiding speculation. From the inspired lips of the late President Anthony W. Ivins came these words (and they should be something of a condemnation to those who disregarded his words and should be something of a blessing to those who listened to and kept that counsel), referring to and warning against borrowing and going into debt:

I fear this, that under existing conditions we are gradually drifting toward a paternal government, a government which will so intrench itself that the people will become powerless to disrupt it, in which the lives and liberties of the people at large may be jeopardized. They are pouring millions of dollars in this time of need into sources for the benefit of the people and it is a great benefit and perhaps salvation, but it is going to result in this—I am going to make this statement—that if the present policy is continued it will not be long until the government will be in the banking business, it will be in the farming business, it will be in the cattle and sheep business, for many of these debts will never be paid. That will mean the appointment of innumerable agencies. The government now is overloaded with commissions and agencies, some of them administering the very laws that Congress itself has enacted. Someone else should be administering those laws. If you want to save yourself from the bondage of debt and political influences which are not of your own choosing, I ask you to think of what I have said. (*Conference Report*, October 1932, pp. 111-12.)

Now, my brethren and sisters, we have men today who have told us repeatedly and also warned against the evil and vice of liquor in our midst. We have been told that we must patronize and foster home industry, avoid speculation, and make savings in food and clothing for at least a year. We have had our leaders plead with us to pursue a course that would tend to keep us out of war. I admonish you in all sobriety and seriousness to listen and heed before it is too late.

Oh, may we not be those of whom the Lord complained: "In the day of their peace they esteemed lightly my counsel; but, in the day of their trouble, of necessity they feel after me." (D&C 101:8.) Remember that the Lord said: "For if you will that I give unto you a place in the celestial world, you must prepare yourselves by doing the things which I have commanded you and required of you." (D&C 78:7.)

Today we are here because our ancestors listened to the counsel of President Brigham Young and turned deaf ears to the pleadings of men like James J. Strang, Sidney Rigdon, and others who would have led us from the path of truth and right. I bear you my witness in all humility that if your children and my children, our grandchildren, and our great-grandchildren remain faithful to this church, it will be because you and I remained steadfast in the testimony that these men are the prophets of the living God and that we must follow their counsel if we would be saved in the days of peril. Therefore, "stand ye in holy places and be not moved," that we might abide the day of the coming of the Son of Man and be caught up in the clouds of heaven to meet our Redeemer when He comes on earth to reign, and reign with Him a thousand years with our children and the redeemed of our Father's house.

30

"By Their Fruits Ye Shall Know Them"

THE Master said:

> Beware of false prophets, which come to you in sheep's clothing, but inwardly they are ravening wolves.
>
> Ye shall know them by their fruits. Do men gather grapes of thorns, or figs of thistles?
>
> Even so every good tree bringeth forth good fruit; but a corrupt tree bringeth forth evil fruit.
>
> A good tree cannot bring forth evil fruit, neither can a corrupt tree bring forth good fruit.
>
> Every tree that bringeth not forth good fruit is hewn down, and cast into the fire.
>
> Wherefore by their fruits ye shall know them. (Matthew 7:15-20.)

Sometimes those who have discoursed upon this text have interpreted this parable, or figure of speech, as you may call it, as the fruits by which a people or a person might be judged, applied primarily to temporal growth or to material gain. This concept is well illustrated by an article about the Church which appeared in a national magazine known as the *Christian Century*. This is what the article said:

> Looking at the phenomenal growth of the Church of Jesus Christ of Latter-day Saints (Mormon) in recent years, other churches which view many Mormon beliefs and some Mormon practices as unbiblical and bizarre ask, "What does it have that we don't?" (January 23, 1963, p. 102.)

Then the article went on to enumerate the membership growth, the number of missionaries, the number of missions, the new congregations, the number of hospitals, the educational programs, church members occupying high posts in government. Then it went on to explain that while the author proclaimed disbelief in many teachings and disciplines, he suggested a reappraisal of methods and programs such as house-to-house evangelism, relief programs for the poor, education, recreation, employment for those who cannot provide for themselves, the requiring of two years of missionary service without compensation, and the extensive use of laymen to keep to a minimum the number of professional church leaders, as possible explanations of the growth of the Church.

The article then concluded with this very significant statement from a book written by Frank S. Meads entitled *Handbook of Denominations in the United States;* he declared that the Mormons' "missionary experience strengthens both them and their church, and offers a model of church service and zeal equalled in very few of the other larger churches in America." (New York: Abingdon Press, 1956, p. 126.)

This last comment suggests the true fruits by which the Church and its disciples may best be judged. It also brings to mind something that was written by Dr. J. L. von Mosheim in his *Ecclesiastical History* relative to the mark of true disciples in the period following the crucifixion of the Savior. He said, "Historians testify that even after the Master's death, he was still their omnipotent protector and their benevolent guide." Dr. Mosheim spoke of the fulfilment of the Master's promise that He would send to them the gift of the Holy Ghost, the Comforter, who would "teach them all things, bring all things to their remembrance and show them things to come. He would guide them into all truth and would testify of him." (See John 14:26; 15:26; 16:13.)

Then the doctor explained that this fulfilment came on the day of Pentecost. He recorded a remarkable change noticeable in the disciples after this great event in these words:

> The consequences of this grand event were surprising and glorious, infinitely honourable to the Christian religion, and the divine mission of its triumphant author. For no sooner had the apostles received this precious gift, this celestial guide, than their ignorance was turned into light, their doubts into certainty, their fears into a firm and invincible fortitude, and their former backwardness into an ardent and inextinguishable zeal, which led them to undertake their sacred office with the utmost intrepidity and alacrity of mind. This marvellous event was attended with a variety of gifts; particularly the gift of tongues, so indispensably necessary to qualify the apostles to preach the gospel to the different nations. These holy apostles were also filled with a perfect persuasion, founded on Christ's express promise, that the divine presence would perpetually accompany them, and show itself by miraculous interpositions, as often as the success of their ministry should render this necessary. And, indeed, there were undoubted marks of a celestial power perpetually attending their ministry. There was in their very language an incredible energy, and amazing power of sending light into the understanding, and conviction into the heart. (J. L. von Mosheim, *Ecclesiastical History*, pp. 61, 67.)

Today it might well be said that the greatest miracles we see are not the healings of sick bodies, but the miraculous changes that come into the lives of those who become members of the Church, as all missionaries will testify. The greatest strength of the Church is not the number of units we have, not the amount of tithing that is paid, nor the congregations; but the greatest strength is the united and fervent testimonies that are in the hearts of church members. And by that same token, we might say that the greatest weapon against all untruth, whether it be in science, so-called, or in the philosophies of the world, or in communism, or what not—the greatest weapon is the truth of the gospel of Jesus Christ, which preached in power will be a bulwark against these false ideas in the world today.

The Master made some applications of the meaning of these spiritual gifts as "fruit" or "fruits." He said,

> I am the vine, ye are the branches: He that abideth in me, and I in him, the same bringeth forth much fruit: for without me ye can do nothing.
>
> Ye have not chosen me, but I have chosen you, and ordained you, that ye should go and bring forth fruit, and that your fruit should remain that whatsoever ye shall ask of the Father in my name, he may give it you. (John 15:5, 16.)

Speaking of these same gifts, the prophet Alma says:

> Yea, after having been such a highly favored people of the Lord; yea, after having been favored above every other nation, . . .
>
> Having been visited by the Spirit of God; having conversed with angels, and having been spoken unto by the voice of the Lord; and having the spirit of prophecy, and the spirit of revelation, and also many gifts, the gift of speaking with tongues, and the gift of preaching, and the gift of the Holy Ghost, and the gift of translation. . . . (Alma 9:20-21.)

From the beginning, our prophet-leaders have declared, as did the Apostle Paul, "that your body is the temple of the Holy Ghost which is in you" (1 Corinthians 6:19), and then he said, "If any man defile the temple of God, him shall God destroy; for the temple of God is holy, which temple ye are" (1 Corinthians 3:17).

And again in a revelation in our day, the Lord said,

"For if you keep my commandments you shall receive of his fulness, and be glorified in me as I am in the Father; therefore, I say unto you, you shall receive grace." (D&C 93:20.)

In other words, these scriptures are repeating what the Master had declared: If we would have the good fruits of these spiritual gifts, we must make sure that we keep the tree good.

An interesting distinction between those who bring forth good fruit and those who do not is well illustrated in the parable of the sower, as you recall, where the Master described the three categories of presumably church members—those who brought forth fruit: "some hundredfold," He said, "some sixtyfold, some thirtyfold." (Matthew 13:8.)

And in the interpretation of Lehi's dream in the Book of Mormon, he has four categories: those who partook of the fruit and remained steadfast; those who partook and then were blinded by mists of darkness which arose from the river, and lost their way; those who went so far as to taste the fruit and then fell away because they were ridiculed by those living in spacious dwellings, representing the riches of the world; and finally those who refused to partake of the delicious fruit of the tree. (See 1 Nephi 8.)

We were back East once and a good bishop made an interesting comment about what he called the saddest words that he knows of a man in high station. He read from the words in the days of the Apostle Paul when Paul before King Agrippa had borne his powerful testimony of his conversion. King Agrippa's reply was, "Almost thou persuadest me to be a Christian." (Acts 26:28.) Then the bishop said, "The king knew the truth but he lacked the courage to do that which would be required; and he could only say then, 'Almost thou persuadest,' almost persuaded under certain circumstances to do the thing the Lord would want him to do."

And then he characterized some things that he discovered in his own ward in a short but powerful sermon:

> In response to the Master, "Come . . . follow me" (Mark 10:21), some members almost, but not quite, say, "thou persuadest me almost to be honest but I need extra help to pass a test."
>
> Almost thou persuadest me to keep the Sabbath day holy, but it's fun to play ball on Sunday.
>
> Almost thou persuadest me to love my neighbor, but he is a rascal; to be tolerant of others' views, but they are dead wrong; to be kind to sister, but she hit me first; to go home teaching, but it's too cold and damp outside tonight; to pay tithes and offerings, but we do need a new color TV set; to find the owner of a lost watch, but no one returned the watch I lost; to pass the sacrament, but I've graduated from the deacons now; almost thou persuadest me to be reverent, but I had to tell my pal about my date last night; almost thou persuadest me to attend stake leadership meeting, but I know more than the leader on that subject, so why should I go? Thou persuadest me almost to go to sacrament meeting, but there is going to be such an uninteresting speaker tonight. Almost! Almost! Almost! but not quite, not able quite to reach.

There are incidents which illustrate how good fruit can be developed by proper cultivation of the seeds of faith through keeping fully the commandments, and I want to cite just two very briefly, even though at first the quality of the fruits of the Spirit was not so.

I received a letter from a mother of four who had gone through illness, pain that was alleviated by what were discovered later to be habit-forming pills, and then came the fight to overcome these devastating drugs until she almost despaired of life. Then she went to visit a friend, and to her surprise she found that her friend was paralyzed by some cancerous affliction and the severe medical treatments that had followed. After visiting this faithful, devoted friend, she went home. She said, "I had a long talk with the Lord, and I started to count my blessings instead of thinking that the Lord was persecuting me personally. Now I go to Relief Society. I am visiting the sick, and I am taking something that I have cooked when I visit. I am taking church books to friends from whom I had previously been estranged."

Then she wrote, "I have now climbed from the dark depths to the brink where I can now see the sun. I am trying to follow the counsel, 'Keep your eyes fixed on the stars.'"

Elder Franklin D. Richards, Assistant to the Council of the Twelve, and I were asked one night by a fine young bishop and his stake leaders if we would participate in administering to him. He was facing the possibility of an operation for a fatal malady. They had in obedience to the Lord's command sought in the Lord's way for help. He was giving all the service he could as a bishop. He and his wife had been married in the temple, and with his wife they had been faithful in having a little family; and now he had come asking the Lord for help. We heard no more about it until this last week there came a letter from his wife that said this:

"They operated and while they found masses of what had appeared by X ray to be malignant tumors in the chest cavity, amazingly they were all found to be benign. As for my husband and me, one word describes our feelings now—rededication—to each other, to the Lord, and to our part in building up His kingdom upon this earth. My husband asked me to mention in this letter to you that the bishop who returns to the people of his ward is a more humble, compassionate, and dedicated servant than ever before. It has taken this experience, though frightening as it has been, to bring me to the full realization of how precious life itself is and how glorious is the gospel which unites a love like ours for all time and eternity."

Through their surmounting sickness, heartaches, and disappointments, they had had experiences that had resulted in better fruit. They had proved their fruit by their works. By their fruits, the Lord had proved them. Life and service have taken on altogether different meaning.

Some words of President David O. McKay seem appropriate to what I am talking about:

> Man's earthly existence is but a test as to whether he will concentrate his efforts, his mind, his soul, upon things that will contribute to the comfort and gratification of his physical nature, or whether he will make as his life's pursuit the acquisition of spiritual qualities.

In short, he said that the development of one's spiritual qualities will determine whether or not his has been a good tree, and it will be determined only by the quality of the fruit, or the spiritual gifts which come therefrom.

A young mother went through the trying experience of having a little child killed in an accident, and she came seeking a blessing for comfort. She asked through her tears, "Must there always be pain in this life?"

I thought a few minutes, and then said, "The Apostle Paul said of the Master, the Lord and the Savior, 'Though he were a Son, yet learned he obedience by the things which he suffered.' (Hebrews 5:8.) I suppose that the answer is yes; there must always be pain in this life of travail and sorrow, and there is a purpose in it all."

God help us to understand how we shall develop sometimes through heartache, sorrow, and tears those spiritual qualities except for which none of us can achieve to the place of kinship to Him who suffered more than any of us may understand, and this I pray and bear you my solemn witness in the name of the Lord Jesus Christ.

31

Meeting the Needs of a Growing Church

IN 1961 the First Presidency of the Church launched a great movement that is now known as the Church correlation program. A letter was sent to the General Church Priesthood Committee that stated the following:

> We of the First Presidency have over the years felt the need of a correlation between and among the courses of study put out by the General Priesthood Committee and by the responsible heads of other Committees of the General Authorities for the instruction of the Priesthood of the Church.
>
> We have also felt the very urgent need of a correlation of studies among the Auxiliaries of the Church. We have noted what seemed to be a tendency toward a fundamental, guiding concept, particularly among certain of the Auxiliary organizations, that there must be every year a new course of study for each of the Auxiliary organizations so moving. We questioned whether the composite of all of them might not tend away from the development of a given line of study or activity having the ultimate and desired objective of building up a knowledge of the gospel, a power to promulgate the same, a promotion of the growth, faith, and stronger testimony of the principles of the Gospel among the members of the Church. . . .

We think that the contemplated study by the Committee now set up should have the foregoing matters in mind. We feel assured that if the whole Church curricula were viewed from the vantage point of what we might term the total purpose of each and all of these organizations, it would bring about such a collation and limitation of subjects and subject matters elaborated in the various Auxiliary courses as would tend to the building of efficiency in the Auxiliaries themselves in the matter of carrying out the purposes lying behind their creation and function.

We would therefore commend to you Brethren of the General Priesthood Committee the beginning of an exhaustive, prayerful study and consideration of this entire subject, with the cooperative assistance of the Auxiliaries themselves so that the Church might reap the maximum harvest from the devotion of the faith, intelligence, skill, and knowledge of our various Auxiliary Organizations and Priesthood Committees.

This is your authority to employ such necessary technical help as you might need to bring this about. We shall await your report.

Faithfully your brethren,
David O. McKay
J. Reuben Clark, Jr.
Henry D. Moyle
THE FIRST PRESIDENCY

In that same letter they called attention to the fact that the membership of the Church might be divided into three groups: the children's group, under twelve years of age; the youth group, from twelve to the twenties; and the adults from the youth group on through life.

That is what set us to a study of this whole plan that we now speak of as correlation. In our study we came across another prophetic statement. At the April conference in 1906, President Joseph F. Smith made this statement:

We expect to see the day, if we live long enough (and if some of us do not live long enough to see it, there are others who will), when every council of the Priesthood in the Church of Jesus Christ of Latter-day Saints will understand its duty; will assume its own responsibility, will magnify its calling, and fill its place in the Church, to the uttermost, according to the intelligence and ability possessed by it. When that day shall come, there will not be so much necessity for work that is now being done by the auxiliary organizations, because it will be done by the regular quorums of the Priesthood. The Lord designed and comprehended it from the beginning, and he had made provision in the Church whereby every need may be met and satisfied through the regular organizations of the Priesthood. It has truly been said that the Church is perfectly organized. The only trouble is that these organizations are not fully alive to the obligations that rest upon them. When they become thoroughly awakened to the requirements made of them, they will fulfil their duties more faithfully, and the work of the Lord will be all the stronger and more powerful and influential in the world. (*Conference Report*, April 1906, p. 3.)

An organization was set up under the direction of the First Presidency following that assignment, and seven members of the Twelve and the Presiding Bishop were named as the Correlation Executive Committee. It should be understood when we say executive committee that the Correlation Committee in total includes the First Presidency and the Council of the Twelve Apostles. We then considered ourselves a task committee to bring for final approval all our work to that body whom we represented.

Three correlation committees were set up; the children's correlation committee; the youth correlation committee; and the adult correlation committee, with aides or editorial boards for curriculum study and lessons for family home teaching. Also appointed were managing directors for four phases of priesthood activity: home teaching, missionary, welfare, and genealogy. These directors were three Assistants to the Twelve and one of the presidents of the First Council of the Seventy, with one of the members of the executive committee as the chairman of the group working with these managing directors.

We then called to our aid professionally trained men to be our general secretaries. These men, trained in educational work, preferred not to be paid employees. They asked to make this contribution to the Church on their own time and without cost, and to continue their teaching roles at the universities where they were employed. There are also others of our secretarial staff whose work relates to correlation.

We therefore set ourselves, under the direction of and with the help of these aides, to the monumental task of correlating all the curricula in all Church organizations and to a continuing study of correlation problems for action of the First Presidency and the Twelve.

Some developments have been outwardly observed by the membership of the Church. I call these to your attention so that you will have them in mind.

The first step that was made was to place the priesthood in the place where the Lord had placed it: to watch over the Church.

In the Doctrine and Covenants, section 20, the Lord said:

> The teacher's duty is to watch over the church always, and be with and strengthen them;
>
> And see that there is no iniquity in the church, neither hardness with each other, neither lying, backbiting, nor evil speaking.
>
> And see that the church meet together often, and also see that all the members do their duty. (D&C 20:53-55.)

This, you will note by careful reading of this great revelation in its entirety, was to apply to the whole priesthood of the Church.

The name of home teaching was given to this movement, to distinguish it from ward teaching. When this was discussed with President David O. McKay, some suggested we should call them watchmen—"priesthood watchmen"—but the President wisely counseled that we had better not let the membership of the Church think of the priesthood as detectives, that it would be better to call them the priesthood home teachers.

The genealogical representatives called our attention to the fact that home teachers was the title they gave to their genealogical visitors to the homes in each ward.

Home teaching, in essence, means that we consider separately each individual member of the family who consitutes the entire home personnel. Home teaching, as distinguished from ward teaching, is to help the parents with home problems in their efforts to teach their families the fundamentals of parental responsibility, as contracted with merely bringing a message, a gospel message, to the entire family. Quorum leaders were given the responsibility of selecting, training, and supervising quorum members in visiting with and teaching assigned families of their own quorum members.

Presidents or group leaders of each Melchizedek Priesthood quorum and general secretaries of Aaronic Priesthood—Adult and Youth were then brought together in what were called "priesthood executive committees." Once a week this committee, bringing together representatives of every priesthood group, has been meeting with the bishopric, and there have been correlated and discussed all problems pertaining to the priesthood. Here is a teaching opportunity for the bishop to train the leaders of each priesthood group in his ward.

Greater emphasis on the teaching of the children in the home by the parents was brought forth in what we call the family home evening program. This was not new. More than fifty years ago it was given emphasis; and as we went back into history, we found that in the last epistle written to the Church by President Brigham Young and his counselors, it was urged that parents bring their children together and teach them the gospel in the home frequently. So family home evening has been urged ever since the Church was established in this dispensation. Hundreds of thousands of family home evening manuals with lessons for each week have been prepared and placed in the hands of every parent throughout the Church. Each year's theme of the home evening lessons has been correlated with the Melchizedek Priesthood and the Relief Society lessons, and the Sunday School general board has instituted a special class each week for parents to aid in their weekly family home evening and to help prepare the parents to be better teachers of their children.

Plans were laid early in this dispensation to meet the challenge of anticipated growth as indicated by the scriptures and by prophetic utterances of presidents of the Church. President McKay gave us the key to our search for what we should do in these matters. In discussing a matter pertaining to the missions, he said this: "Now in changing our policy here, let us keep as near as we can to the revelations of the Lord, and we will never be wrong if we do that." That sounds like good logic, doesn't it?

That injunction from the President took us into a study of all that the Lord has said about the place of the priesthood and how it should operate in the kingdom. We found what the Lord said about the work of the Twelve:

> The Twelve are a Traveling Presiding High Council, to officiate in the name of the Lord, under the direction of the Presidency of the Church, agreeable to the institution of heaven; to build up the church, and regulate all the affairs of the same in all nations, first unto the Gentiles, and secondly unto the Jews. (D&C 10:33.)

About the seventy the Lord said:

> It is the duty of the traveling high council to call upon the Seventy, when they need assistance, to fill the several calls for preaching and administering the gospel, instead of any others. (D&C 107:38.)

I think you will see in what has gone forward in the last few years that now, as never before in our recollection, the seventies have been given a major role in the missionary work of the Church. Perhaps the door has opened as widely as it has ever been for the work of the seventies, and we thank the Lord for the work of our leaders in the seventies quorums.

Now to support what the First Presidency's message has already said about others who would be called as leaders:

> Whereas other officers of the church, who belong not unto the Twelve, neither to the Seventy, are not under the responsibility to travel among all nations, but are to travel as their circumstances shall allow, notwithstanding they may hold as high and responsible offices in the church. (D&C 107:98.)

That would allow, besides those mentioned, a place for the Assistants to the Twelve.

Then we found another scripture that had significance. It has always been there, but we had never read this scripture as we saw it now. The Lord said in the 84th section of the Doctrine and Covenants (this is to the Twelve):

> Therefore, go ye into all the world; and unto whatsoever place ye cannot go ye shall send, that the testimony may go from you into all the world unto every creature.
>
> And as I said unto mine apostles, even so I say unto you, for you are mine apostles, even God's high priests; ye are they whom my Father hath given me; ye are my friends. (D&C 84:62-63.)

Where we couldn't go, then, the Lord has said, "Send," that the testimony, your testimony, might by those you send be brought to every creature throughout the world.

Soon after the death of President Brigham Young, President John Taylor and the Twelve took over the presiding authority of the Church for approximately three years before President Taylor was sustained as the president of the Church. In a message to the Church at that time, two or three things were said to which I would like to call your attention:

> . . . the keys of the kingdom are still right here with the Church. . . . the holy Priesthood and Apostleship, which He restored to the earth, still remain to guide and govern, and to administer ordinances to the Church which He has established. Our beloved brother Brigham Young has gone from us, to join the Prophet Joseph and the host of the holy and the pure who are behind the vail; but we do not therefore lose the benefit of his labors. He is now in a position to do more for that work which he loved so well, and for which he labored so ardently, than he could possibly do in the flesh; and that work will roll onward with increased power and accelerated speed. (*Messages of the First Presidency,* James R. Clark, ed., Bookcraft Inc., 1965, vol. 2, p. 299.)

And then they quoted from the Prophet Joseph Smith's instructions the following:

> The Twelve are not subject to any other than the First Presidency, viz: myself, Sidney Rigdon, and Frederick G. Williams, who are now my counselors (and where I am not there is no First Presidency over the Twelve).

After the death of the Prophet Joseph, President Young, in speaking to the Saints, said:

> . . . Here are the Twelve, appointed by the finger of God, who hold the keys of the Priesthood, and the authority to set in order and regulate the Church in all the world. (Ibid.)

Then there followed a statement which indicated that there was some tendency to look back to the previous administration and think what the Prophet Joseph might have done had he been there. President Brigham Young and his counselors wrote this in their closing epistle to the Church:

> Here is Elder Amasa Lyman and Elder Sidney Rigdon; they were counselors in the First Presidency, and they are counselors to the Twelve still if they keep their places; but if either wishes to act as

"spokesman" for the prophet Joseph, he must go behind the vail where Joseph is. (Ibid.)

Now that was a rather interesting observation.

May I now say this: Those keys of the kingdom are still here with the Church today. As President Taylor declared,

. . . the holy Priesthood and Apostleship, which He restored to the earth, still remain to guide and govern, and to administer ordinances to the Church which He has established. (Ibid.)

Then President John Taylor added this final statement, which indicates something in which you will be interested:

That there may be a correct understanding among all the Stakes of Zion respecting the time for holding the quarterly Conferences in the different Stakes, and the Presidents be enabled to make preparations therefor, we have deemed it best to make the following appointments for the conference during the next half year. [This was in 1877.] It will be seen that in most instances they will be held in two Stakes upon the same days. This is unavoidable, in consequence of the great number of Stakes. (*Messages of the First Presidency* 2:301.)

And then I counted the "great" number of stakes: Salt Lake, Davis and Utah, Weber and Juab, Tooele and Box Elder, Wasatch and Cache, Summit and Bear Lake, Morgan and Sanpete, Sevier and Millard, Panguitch and Beaver, Kanab and Iron [Parowan], and St. George—twenty stakes, a great number of stakes. There were nine missions—nine organized missions—at that time. Well, as we think about that now, and as they closed that epistle after making that profound statement about the great number of stakes, the Twelve then added:

And now, brethren and sisters, we exhort you to arouse yourselves and seek unto the Lord in fervent faith and prayer. We know that our Father in heaven is a God of Revelation. He is ready and willing to pour out His blessings and gifts upon those who seek unto Him

> for them. We need them as individuals and as a people to qualify us for the duties which devolve upon us. We should remember and carry into practical effect the counsels and instructions we have so liberally received from our departed President. He has gone from us; but the flock is not left without a shepherd. Latter-day Saints should so live that they will know the voice of the True Shepherd, and not be deceived by pretenders. . . . the Latter-day Saint who does not live so as to have the revelations of Jesus constantly with him, stands in great danger of being deceived and falling away. . . . All the signs which the Lord promised to send in the last days are making their appearance. They show that the day of the Lord is near. A great work has to be done, and there is but little time in which to accomplish it; great diligence is, therefore, required. . . . Let us not slacken our diligence, or give way to doubt, unbelief or hardness of heart; but be strong in the Lord, and cry unto Him unceasingly to give us the power to build up His Zion on the earth, and to help establish a reign of righteousness, peace, and truth. (*Messages of the First Presidency* 2:302-303.)

And so ended that remarkable epistle to the Church.

Now to point up our challenge of the present growth and to prepare for the fulfillment of the hastening of the Lord's work, which He promised He would do in His own time: If one were to paint a picture in broad strokes of just a few features of the future, here are some things that will challenge the Church in the years that lie ahead:

When I came into the Council of the Twelve we had thirty-five missions. I helped to organize, along with President Joseph Fielding Smith, the 138th stake. We now have over 600 stakes.

During the seventy years from 1830 to 1900, the Church grew by 258,000 members. Today, a quarter of a million expansion in membership takes not seventy years; but in only two or three years, we expand by a quarter of a million.

Our Church membership is increasing at about three times the growth rate of the population of the United States. But, just as significantly, the regional distribution of Church membership is also following some clear trends that we must recognize, not only intellectually, but also administratively.

In 1910, Utah and Idaho contained approximately 75 percent of all Church membership. Today, only 40 percent of the Church's members live in these two states. Utah once held two-thirds of all members. Today, even though the number of members in Utah has now risen from 224,000 in 1910 to 714,000, only one-third of all members now live in Utah. Brazil now has 23,000 Latter-day Saints; Australia, 21,000; and Mexico, 50,000.

During the last ten years, membership in the southern states has risen from 72,000 to 170,000; in South America from 6,000 to 67,000; and in Asia from 1,500 to 21,000.

We have no choice but to think regionally.

Research has been done by the department of statistics at the Brigham Young University by Dr. Howard Nielsen, and he estimates the Church membership by 1985 will total from 5,700,000 to 7,700,000, depending on the rate of conversions.

By the year A.D. 2000 we could have a total membership of over ten million people.

In 1985 there will be more than one million members in Utah, but they will represent only 21 percent of all Church membership. California will have almost a million members by then, and the southern states one-half million. Canada will host 160,000 members, with more than 200,000 in the British Isles, and over one-quarter million in Central and South America. By 1985, depending on our effectiveness and external events, we should have 1,000 stakes and nearly 10,000 wards.

In the calendar year 1985, about 200 new stake presidents will be appointed to new or existing stakes, and General Authorities will need to direct five stake reorganizations each week. The brethren will then need to clear between fifty and sixty names for the office of bishop each week.

Well, you begin to see something about the growth, and so we could go on with auxiliary organizations.

Now just a word about the missions: It is estimated that in the missions within that period, we could have as many as 185 missions by then, with probably as many as 30,000 missionaries.

Perhaps this is enough, then, to indicate the great challenge that demands an extended authoritative supervisory ministry.

When the first five Assistants to the Twelve were called in 1941, the Presidency said:

> The rapid growth of the Church in recent times, the constantly increasing establishment of new wards and stakes, . . . all have built up an apostolic service of the greatest magnitude.
>
> The First Presidency and Twelve feel that to meet adequately their great responsibilities and to carry on efficiently this service for the Lord, they should have some help. (*Improvement Era,* May 1941, p. 269.)

That was said when we had 137 stakes. Now, when we have so many more stakes and missions, you begin to see what we are talking about. All of this is sobering to think about, even superficially. It is awesome to contemplate, at any length. How can we best provide the necessary leadership with enough worthy, able leaders in the right places at the right time? How can we best finance a kingdom of this scope and dimension? How can we best absorb, fellowship, and teach this many souls?

While sacrament meeting attendance rose from 21 percent in 1921 to 36 percent in 1965, we appear to have hit a plateau. We are not advancing much from that 36 percent. Effective teaching of the gospel and showing how it relates directly to the lives of people today are partial but needed answers to this challenge.

The next step has been the appointment of Regional Representatives of the Twelve. This was the official announcement from the First Presidency:

As many of you will remember, in 1941, it became necessary for the First Presidency and the Twelve to provide for additional brethren to help with the work of overseeing and setting in order an ever-growing, worldwide Church. Thus in the General Conference of April, 1941, Assistants to the Twelve were named and sustained, "to be increased or otherwise from time to time as the necessity of carrying on the Lord's work seems to dictate."

Since then the world-wide demands of the Church have increased in ever greater degree, and it is felt by the First Presidency and the Twelve that a further provision for guidance and direction is now needed.

What, therefore, is now proposed is the calling of as many brethren as may be necessary to be known as Regional Representatives of the Twelve, each, as assigned, to be responsible in some aspects of the work to carry counsel to and to conduct instructional meetings in groups of stakes or regions as may be designated from time to time.

These Regional Representatives of the Twelve will not be "General" Authorities, as such, but will serve somewhat as do stake presidents, giving full Church service for greater or lesser periods of service as circumstances may suggest.

Fuller details will be in evidence as this plan proceeds under the guidance of the First Presidency and the Twelve. (*Improvement Era*, January 1968, pp. 30-31.)

Almost all of those who have been called to be Regional Representatives of the Twelve have served in stake presidencies or as mission presidents or both. Areas of the Church where clusters of stakes can be brought together are assigned to the Regional Representatives, and so far as possible these men are assigned to areas as near to their homes as possible. Others are assigned to distant areas and to areas outside the continental United States, particularly those countries that need men with special language aptitudes to teach effectively the leaders in these foreign language stakes.

As the Church has grown, the General Authorities have not had adequate time, at stake conferences, to sit down and do an adequate job of teaching and training new stake officers. So, in stake quarterly conferences now, the General Authorities are the only official visitors to attend stake conferences except in those single stakes that are not aligned with regions. In those stakes the Regional Representative of the Twelve goes to conferences when no General Authority is to be in attendance; and with auxiliary representatives, they hold regional meetings semiannually throughout the Church.

The General Authorities go to stake quarterly conferences on Saturday afternoon and there conduct a leadership session in the afternoon with the stake presidency, the high council, and the bishoprics; with all the priesthood leaders in the evening; and on Sunday morning, with the stake presidency. And then we are endeavoring to get all the families to come to conference. In order to provide a place for the small children, we suggest that in every stake the stake Sunday School presidency arrange for a Junior Sunday School, perhaps in a separate building, if one can be found nearby, or in another area of the stake conference center; and there, with a suggested program that we will give, the children will be taken care of during the two-hour period, which will perhaps be broken down into periods, with some diversion for the children.

Now there is only one general session of conference in each stake; in the afternoon, when the General Authority is in attendance, we can take time to give instruction that we haven't had time to give in the past.

As we read the revelations we found something significant about stake conferences, as the Lord designed them. Let me point out what the Lord said, as recorded in section 20 of the Doctrine and Covenants, about stake conferences:

> The several elders composing this church of Christ are to meet in conference once in three months, or from time to time as said conferences shall direct or appoint. . . .
>
> It shall be the duty of the several churches, composing the church of Christ, to send one or more of their teachers to attend the several conferences held by the elders of the church. (D&C 20:61, 81.)

That was a stake conference. If we understand that instruction correctly, we should understand that the prime purpose of a stake conference is to instruct the leaders of the stakes; and that is what we are now intending to do more than we have done in the past.

It is expected that every ward in the stake will return home and have a sacrament meeting in the evening, where the greater number of the membership of the Church can be brought into some worshiping assembly on the day of a stake quarterly conference.

At the conferences where no General Authority is in attendance, we ask our stake presidents not to have an imported speaker to take the place of a General Authority or to expect their Regional Representative to come. He will only go there as he may indicate he would desire for some special purpose or may be assigned by the First Presidency or the Twelve. This is the opportunity for the stake president with his staff, meaning his auxiliary and priesthood leaders, to instruct his people as the leaders have been instructed in their previous regional meetings. And so our quarterly conferences are more intensive training by General Authorities, and we are gearing ourselves to do a better job than we have been doing in the past.

Now, then, I conclude with just one or two observations. Again and again has been repeated the statement that the home is the basis of a righteous life. With new and badly needed emphasis on the "how," we must not lose sight of the "why" we are so engaged. The priesthood programs operate in support of the home; the auxiliary programs render valuable assistance. Wise regional leadership can help us to do our share in attaining God's overarching purpose, "to bring to pass the immortality and eternal life of man." (Moses 1:39.) Both the revelations of God and the learning of men tell us how crucial the home is in shaping the individual's total life experience. Running through all this is the urgency of impressing the importance of better teaching and greater parental responsibility in the home. Much of what we do organizationally, then, is scaffolding, as we seek to build the individual, and we must not mistake the scaffolding for the soul.

Now may I just say this: I was with one of the brethren who formerly presided over the Sweden Mission. He told me about being on a ship that was going out among the various islands into the open sea. As the ship was being steered near one particularly unimpressive island, he wondered why it wasn't steered past another island. Finally he noticed ahead what appeared to be broomsticks sticking up; these sticks were attached to buoys, to guide the ship through safe channels. Engineers had discovered the safe places.

God's engineers have charted the course ahead of us. Now our critics (and we expect we have some; usually they are those without knowledge or with little or no vision) will wonder why we didn't take some other course to meet the problem. This reminds me of the saying: "A man is usually down on what he ain't up on." We suppose we will have more and more of that.

The Lord's chosen leaders have signaled us now to

move forward. When Moses went to lead the children of Israel out into the desert, it was not the Moses who had climbed the mount with fear; but it was the Moses endowed by the power of Almighty God. When he lifted his staff and signaled, the whole company moved forward. We must not lose ourselves in the mechanics of leadership and neglect the spiritual." . . . if your eye be single to my glory," the Lord said, "your whole bodies shall be filled with light, and there shall be no darkness in you. . . ." (D&C 88:67.)

Evidence of improved leadership will bring more consistent study of the scriptures, greater concern of the holders of the priesthood in watching over the Church, more devotion to family duties, more of our young people married worthily in the temple, greater faith and righteous exercise of the priesthood, and so on.

The Prophet Joseph Smith said as he wrote from Liberty Jail:

> Let no man count them as small things; for there is much which lieth in futurity, pertaining to the saints, which depends upon these things.
>
> You know, brethren, that a very large ship is benefited very much by a very small helm in the time of a storm, by being kept workways with the wind and the waves.
>
> Therefore, dearly beloved brethren, let us cheerfully do all things that lie in our power; and then may we stand still, with the utmost assurance, to see the salvation of God, and for his arm to be revealed. (D&C 123:15-17.)

To this I bear humble testimony, in the name of the Lord Jesus Christ.

32

Signs of the True Church

A *FATHER* and his teenage daughter, not members of the Church, attended a missionary conference we held in the state of South Dakota while I was touring a mission. They waited after the meeting to talk with me about their frustrations in their sincere search for the truth.

They explained that they were receiving lessons from our missionaries and were very much impressed by the teachings, but before committing themselves for baptism, these investigators asked the one question all honest souls must ask: How can I be certain that this is the true church and the true gospel of Jesus Christ? The father in his young manhood had joined a sectarian church but shortly left it to join another because the first he had joined did not baptize him by immersion, which, from his study of the scriptures, he was convinced was the only proper mode of baptism.

Later an uncle induced him to affiliate with a sect that militantly declared all others to be of the devil. His spiritual wanderings led him into association with a friend who proselyted him for the "Universal Church," as he called it, which knew no creed and had no organization. It had only a simplified and nebulous formula: "Believe and be saved!"

The dilemma of the family had recently been intensified when the oldest daughter, at the conclusion of a Bible class of a few weeks' duration, began asking the minister who had conducted the class some questions raised by the teachings of our missionaries. Confused and unable to answer, the minister had impatiently rebuked her by saying that if she had studied her Bible lessons as she should, she wouldn't be asking such foolish questions. Now the father wanted to know just how he could be certain that this was the true church so he wouldn't make another mistake.

He had progressed to a point in his studies where he knew that there were many forms of religion in the world, the teachers in each claiming to be right. In each form of religion he had found some truth, but he was baffled when he encountered teachings in each which contradicted the scriptures. He knew that the Savior had taught only one form of religion which could be called the gospel of Jesus Christ.

I pointed out that the true gospel of Jesus Christ must embrace all truth and contain nothing but the truth. The Apostle Paul taught plainly that "there is one body, and one Spirit, even as ye are called in one hope of your calling; One Lord, one faith, one baptism, One God and Father of all, who is above all, and through all, and in you all." (Ephesians 4:4.)

To his disciples, the Master had emphasized: "I am the way, the truth, and the life: no man cometh unto the Father, but by me." (John 14:6.) Just as Peter has declared: ". . . there is none other name under heaven given among men, whereby we must be saved" (Acts 4:12), so it seems perfectly clear that the true church must make Jesus, our Savior, the center and core of its doctrines and that through obedience of the ordinances as initiated by Him and His disciples and from His teachings learn the way to salvation and eternal life.

The early apostles, in no uncertain language, vigorously rejected all teachings, contrary to those of the Master and His chosen disciples: "But though we, or an angel from heaven, preach any other gospel unto you than that which we have preached unto you, let him be accursed." (Galatians 1:8.) But this echoed the Master's warning: ". . . in vain they do worship me, teaching for doctrines the commandments of men." (Matthew 15:9.) And as John had bluntly put it: "He that saith, I know him, and keepeth not his commandments, is a liar, and the truth is not in him." (1 John 2:4.)

There are certain outward marks of the true church which one must observe. First one must apply the simple test of the Master: "Beware of false prophets. . . . Ye shall know them by their fruits. . . ." (Matthew 7:15-16.) False teachers teach falsehood and their works are evil. True teachers teach and live righteously and will not teach doctrines contradicting the teachings of the Lord given directly by Him, to us, or by revelation through His prophets.

Certain signs will always be found following the true believers:

> In my name shall they cast out devils: they shall speak with new tongues;
>
> They shall take up serpents; and if they drink any deadly thing, it shall not hurt them; they shall lay hands on the sick, and they shall recover. (Mark 16:17-18.)

We in the church of Jesus Christ today, as did the disciples of that other day, believe in the gift of tongues, prophecy, revelation, visions, healings, and interpretation of tongues, etc.

To His followers, the "other sheep," as He referred to them, on this western continent, to whom He came after His death and resurrection, He gave another sure way by which we could distinguish His true church from the false. Said the Master:

> And how be it my church save it be called in my name? For if a church be called in Moses' name then it be Moses' church; or if it be called in the name of a man then it be the church of a man; but if it be called in my name then it is my church, if it so be that they are built upon my gospel. (3 Nephi 27:8.)

Now mark carefully that last statement. Not only must His church be called by His name, but it must also be built upon His gospel. Call the roll, my friends, of all the churches you know. How many are called by His name, and of those who have His name in the titles, how many teach His gospel in its fulness? Remember, this is The Church of Jesus Christ of Latter-day Saints, as were the members of those former days called saints! The simple record from which we have quoted above declared: "And they who were baptized in the name of Jesus were called the church of Christ." (3 Nephi 26:21.) So it must be in every dispensation if it be His true church.

The Master's church was an orderly, organized body "built upon the foundation of the apostles and prophets, Jesus Christ himself being the chief corner stone." (Ephesians 2:20.) This organization with teachers, helps, and a complete government (see 1 Corinthians 12:28) was "for the perfecting of the saints, for the work of the ministry, for the edifying of the body of Christ." (Ephesians 4:12.) The officers in the true church had to have divine authority from authorized ordinances and not just "assumed" authority. The Lord told His apostles: "Ye have not chosen me, but I have chosen you, and ordained you, that ye should go and bring forth fruit. . . ." (John 15:16.) and to the chiefest of the apostles He gave the "keys" of the kingdom of God, or in other words, the keys of authority to the Church of Jesus Christ, that whatsoever would be bound in earth should be bound in heaven.

This authority was known as the holy priesthood, of which the Apostle Paul declared: "And no man taketh this honour unto himself, but he that is called of God, as was Aaron." (Hebrews 5:4.) The meaning of that statement is made plain by another prophet of our day: "We believe that a man must be called of God, by prophecy, and by the laying on of hands, by those who are in authority to preach the Gospel and administer in the ordinances thereof." (Article of Faith 5.)

There is yet another strangely significant mark of the true church to which the Master referred when He said: "If ye were of the world, the world would love his own: but because ye are not of the world, but I have chosen you out of the world, therefore the world hateth you." (John 15:19.) Sad but true, the true followers of Jesus Christ have always been a persecuted people by those of the world who know not Christ nor His teachings. By contrast the Master warned: "Woe unto you, when all men shall speak well of you! for so did their fathers to the false prophets." (Luke 6:26.) Search the history of the Church of Jesus Christ in this day and you will find clearly a parallel for that of which Jesus spoke.

The scriptures, particularly, after one's prayerful and diligent study, will serve as the safest guide in the discovery of the true church, for the gospel the Savior taught has not changed. It is the same today as it was when He dwelt upon the earth.

Faith, the scriptures affirm, is the first principle of the

true church. "For God so loved the world, that he gave his only begotten Son, that whosoever believeth in him should not perish, but have everlasting life." (John 3:16.) And again, "He that believeth on me, the works that I do shall he do also" for "If a man love me, he will keep my words. . . . " (John 14:12, 23.) Thus in plainness did our Lord teach this first principle.

The Master's first recorded utterances were "Repent: for the kingdom of heaven is at hand "(Matthew 4:17), and "Whosoever shall not receive the kingdom of God as a little child shall in no wise enter therein" (Luke 18:17). Repentance from all their sins prepared the true believers for the first ordinance of the gospel, which is baptism by immersion for the remission of sins.

The Savior Himself was baptized by John the Baptist, as He said, "to fulfil all righteousness." (Matthew 3:15.) If it be so with Him, what about ourselves? Nicodemus was told: "Except a man be born of the water and the Spirit, he cannot enter into the kingdom of God." (John 3:5.) The Master left no doubt as to the why of the baptism which He taught.

> And no unclean thing can enter into his kingdom; therefore nothing entereth into his rest save it be those who have washed their garments in my blood, because of their faith, and the repentance of all their sins, and their faithfulness unto the end. (3 Nephi 27:19.)

That was why Peter admonished his hearers, "Repent, and be baptized every one of you in the name of Jesus Christ for the remission of sins, and ye shall receive the gift of the Holy Ghost." (Acts 2:38.) For through baptism by one having authority, the recipient may indeed figuratively wash his garments in the blood of the Son of God, who atoned for the sins of all who receive Him and come in at the door of the sheepfold, by baptism. "But if they would not repent," the Savior declared in plainness, "they must suffer even as I." (D&C 19:17.)

The Holy Ghost is one of the Godhead, the Comforter promised by the Master, through whom spiritual gifts are given to those who obey the gospel. The Holy Ghost would testify of the Savior. ". . . he will guide you into all truth," "bring all things to your remembrance," and even "shew you things to come." (John 16:13; 14:26; 16:13.)

In this last great gift through one of the Godhead, even the Holy Ghost, is to be found the way to the certain knowledge, after one's study of the scriptures, as I have briefly explained, have convinced him that this, The Church of Jesus Christ of Latter-day Saints, has all the marks of the true church of Jesus Christ.

A prophet of another day gave to investigators and truth seekers that unfailing test of truth in these words:

> And when ye shall receive these things, I would exhort you that ye would ask God, in the name of Christ, if these things are not true; and if ye shall ask with a sincere heart, with real intent, having faith in Christ, he will manifest the truth of it unto you, by the power of the Holy Ghost. And by the power of the Holy Ghost ye may know the truth of all things. (Moroni 10:4-5.)

A young missionary met me at the train and sought an interview because of his failure during the first months of his mission to get a testimony of the truth of that which he was teaching.

His attention was called to what the Apostle Paul had said, that your body is "the temple of God, and that the Spirit of God dwelleth in you," and that "if any man defile the temple of God, him shall God destroy." (1 Corinthians 3:16-17.) The first essential, therefore, in gaining a testimony is to make certain that one's personal spiritual "housekeeping" is in proper order. His mind and body must be clean if he would enjoy the in-dwelling gift of the Holy

Ghost by which he could know the certainty of spiritual things.

The Master took His hearers to one more important step in gaining a testimony when, in answer to the question as to how they were to know whether or not His was true doctrine, He said: "If any man will do his will, he shall know of the doctrine, whether it be of God, or whether I speak of myself." (John 7:17.) Thus if you would seek a blessing, you must keep the commandments upon which the blessings you seek are predicated.

We concluded our conversation as I pointed out to our young missionary the final necessary step to gain sure knowledge. The Lord revealed that way to John when He said: "Behold, I stand at the door, and knock: if any man hear my voice, and open the door, I will come in to him, and will sup with him, and he with me." (Revelation 3:20.)

When we qualify by righteous living, we place ourselves in tune with the infinite or, as Peter puts it, we become "partakers of the divine nature, having escaped the corruption that is in the world through lust." (2 Peter 1:4.)

In this condition, the sincere prayer of the righteous heart opens to any individual the door to divine wisdom and strength in that for which he righteously seeks.

I was at the stake conference where my young missionary companion of the Chicago railroad incident was called to report his mission. He related the conversation, as I have sketched it, and then declared to the congregation that as a result of his obedience to the counsel he had been given, there came to him an experience, to use his own words, "that really humbled me and triggered a witness of the Spirit. I felt a quiet excitement within myself that bore witness to certain parts of the gospel which I had questioned. This feeling grew within me until now I can say that I know this is the true church of Jesus Christ, that Joseph Smith is a prophet of God, and that the Holy Ghost does live and bear witness of the truth.

As that young missionary came to know, so may everyone who prepares himself, as I have explained, come to know with a certainty which defies all doubt.

May I remind you to ponder the marvelous promise of the Lord to all who are faithful:

> And if your eye be single to my glory, your whole bodies shall be filled with light, and there shall be no darkness in you; and that the body which is filled with light comprehendeth all things. (D&C 88:67.)

That each one who seeks thus may earnestly gain for himself that unshakable testimony which will place his feet firmly on the pathway which leads surely toward the glorious goal of immortality and eternal life is my humble prayer.

33

The Sixth Article of Faith

"WE believe in the same organization that existed in the Primitive Church, viz., apostles, prophets, pastors, teachers, evangelists, etc." (Article of Faith 6.)

By the term "primitive church," reference is made to that which is ancient or old and dating back to earlier times. "The church" as it is used frequently, but loosely, with reference to professors of various beliefs has two different meanings. It may mean the whole body of Christian worshippers everywhere, or it may refer to any specific religious society or body.

"The church" as spoken of in the scriptures had a more significant meaning. The "primitive church" has reference to the organization of the followers of the Master who had submitted to the ordinances of the gospel by which they became members, which ordinances were administered by men vested with divine authority and power from on high. As to other terms referring to this organization, the Lord has give us a revelation as follows:

. . . be prepared for the days to come, in the which the Son of Man shall come. . . . to meet the kingdom of God which is set up on the earth. Wherefore, may the kingdom of God go forth, that the kingdom of heaven may come. . . . (D&C 65:5-6.)

Here the Church of Jesus Christ is made synonymous with the kingdom of God, which parallels a similar organization in heaven.

Now there are a number of questions raised by this declaration of our faith with reference to church organization: (1) Was the gospel upon the earth and an organization of His people before the Savior's time? (2) If His "kingdom" as above defined was upon the earth before the meridian of time, what sort of organization was it? (3) What officers and authority are necessary in the kingdom of God?

From the earliest scriptural records, we find declared the fundamental teachings of the gospel and that the essential ordinances were performed by which all of our Father's children might gain eternal life and become the "sons and daughters" of God by adoption unto His kingdom, which is to gain eternal life.

But besides the gospel from the beginning, there must needs be some organization having authority to administer these gospel ordinances and to teach these principles. The Prophet Joseph Smith has given us a clear-cut declaration with reference to this matter:

Where there is no kingdom of God there is no salvation. What constitutes the kingdom of God? Where there is a prophet, a priest, or a righteous man unto whom God gives His oracles, there is the kingdom of God. . . . (*DHC* 5:257.)

Down through the various gospel dispensations since Adam, there have been always the essentials prescribed by Joseph Smith for the kingdom of God on earth. In the beginning, that government was patriarchal; then in the days of the prophet Samuel, the children of Israel were governed by judges, and followed thereafter by kings chosen and authorized by divine appointment. The organization set up by the Master was apparently more complete than formerly and undoubtedly was the pattern of organization to be followed thereafter, as evidenced by the fact that He set up a similar organization among the Nephites on the western continent.

In the dispensation in which we live, the dispensation of the fulness of time, there was to be, as Peter declared: "a restitution of all things," which unquestionably implies the essentials of organization and authority in all former dispensations as well as teachings and ordinances.

The Lord declared that in this last dispensation there shall be "a whole and complete and perfect union, and welding together of dispensations, and keys, and powers, and glories . . . from the days of Adam. . . ." (D&C 128:18.)

In Elder James L. Barker's scholarly writings on the apostasy, *The Divine Church*, he uses a unique illustration to demonstrate the strength and weakness of the ancient scriptures and the importance of modern revelation:

> . . . if a scientist were in possession of fragments only of a scientific instrument, with many parts altogether lacking, he would be unable to reconstruct the instrument. However, if after having studied the fragments, he were given a complete instrument in perfect condition, he would be able to identify each fragment with the corresponding part of the perfect instrument. (Vol. 1, p. 76.)

So it is with the fragmentary record in the Bible concerning the organization which existed in the primitive church. We are able by reading the Bible to identify every priesthood office existing in the restored church of Jesus Christ, but modern revelation, giving us the complete organization, is necessary in order to understand how the organization functioned and the relationship of church officers to each other.

One of the errors into which men, unguided by revelation, have fallen today is to confuse terms used in the Bible describing the duties and nature of various callings in the Church with the proper titles by which priesthood offices were designated. Hence such words as pastor, evangelist, minister, overseer, father of the flock (a term applied to bishops and applied in apostate churches with titles which mean father) were often used in reference to duties rather than to designate an office of the priesthood. We are grateful for the "perfect model," to use Elder Barker's illustration, by which we know how the Church was to be organized and how it was to function.

Our sixth Article of Faith as to the nature of the organization in the Church of Jesus Christ is but another testimony of the divinity of this latter-day work.

Section Seven

PUT ON THE WHOLE ARMOR OF GOD

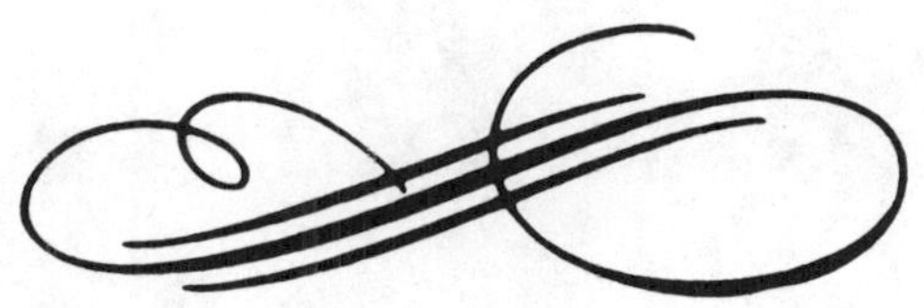

34

Your Coat of Armor

PERHAPS you have listened, as I have, to speakers who in their sermons have spoken repeatedly of our existence here in mortality as "the battle of life." Have you ever tried to think through that suggested analogy of life likened to a "battle"? To have a battle as we understand it, there must first have been an issue or principle over which opposing forces contend, each force under the generalship of a master strategist called the commanding officer. To be successful, each such army must train its soldier in the science of war, in rigid discipline, and have each fighting man properly outfitted with the equipment and the weapons of war. As a prelude to the actual clash of arms, spies and fifth columnists have been at work behind the lines of the enemy forces to do two things: first, to discover the strength and the weaknesses of the enemy, and second, to spread propaganda among the enemy in an attempt to demoralize and to spread confusion. The measure of success in each engagement is the number of casualties inflicted upon the enemy—in prisoners taken, in killed, and in wounded.

Preachers of other dispensations, not unlike the preachers of our day, saw and spoke of life as a continuing conflict between opposing forces. The prophet Isaiah tells of a "grievous" vision that came to him in which the Lord directed him to set a watchman to report what he could see from his watchtower. As the watchman in the vision obediently reported hour after hour the coming of horsemen, chariots, lions, etc., the voice of the Lord came again to Isaiah, saying, "Watchman, what of the night? Watchman, what of the night"? (Isaiah 21:11.) Thus, the suggestion that even more to be feared than the enemies we can see are the "enemies of the night" not perceived by physical sight.

In full accord with the prophet Isaiah's vision was the declaration of the Master Himself.

> . . . fear not them which kill the body, but are not able to kill the soul: but rather fear him which is able to destroy both soul and body in hell. (Matthew 10:28.)

That there is a force of evil in the world is as certain as that there is being directed a work of righteousness, and that between these two forces there is an eternal conflict with the price of the human soul as the stake. The scriptures declare it to be so.

> And there was war in heaven. . . . And the great dragon was cast out, that old serpent, called the Devil, and Satan, which deceiveth the whole world: he was cast out into the earth, and his angels were cast out with him. (Revelation 12:7-9.)

Likewise the scriptures explain the reason.

> Wherefore, because that Satan rebelled against me, and sought to destroy the agency of man, which I, the Lord God, had given him, and also, that I should give unto him mine own power . . . I caused that he should be cast down;
>
> And he became Satan, yea, even the devil, the father of all lies, to deceive and to blind men, and to lead them captive at his will, even as many as would not hearken unto my voice. (Moses 4:3-4.)

Now you are able to see clearly the analogy of our earthly existence as "the battle of life."

Satan commands a mighty force comprising one-third of all God's spirit children who were cast out with him—tangible and real although not always discernible by sight, and under whose masterful direction there goes forward constantly propaganda of lying and deceit. One of the most potent of his lies is described by a prophet:

> And behold, others he flattereth away, and telleth them there is no hell; and he saith unto them: I am no devil, for there is none—and thus he whispereth in their ears, until he grasps them with his awful chains, from whence there is no deliverance. (2 Nephi 28:22.)

Jesus Christ is the captain of Israel's host and employs even mightier forces, both visible and invisible. His mightiest propaganda is truth, the complete embodiment of which is found in the fulness of the gospel of Jesus Christ.

So the poet wrote:

Once to every man and nation comes a moment to decide,
In the strife of Truth with Falsehood, for the good or evil side;
Some great cause, God's new Messiah, offering each the bloom or blight,
Parts the goats upon the left hand and the sheep upon the right;
And the choice goes by forever twixt that darkness and that light.

—JAMES RUSSELL LOWELL
"The Present Crisis"

The great missionary to the gentiles, Paul the apostle, declares the reality of this individual spiritual warfare and urges us to arm for the conflict. Here are his words:

> . . . be strong in the Lord, and in the power of his might.
>
> Put on the whole armour of God, that ye may be able to stand against the wiles of the devil.
>
> For we wrestle not against flesh and blood, but against principalities, against the rulers of the darkness of this world, against spiritual wickedness in high places.

Wherefore take unto you the whole armour of God, that ye may be able to withstand in the evil day, and having done all, to stand. (Ephesians 6:10-13.)

Note carefully that the Apostle Paul's declaration implies that our most deadly contest in life is not with human enemies which may come with guns, with army tanks, or bombing planes to destroy us, but that our eternal struggle is with enemies which strike out of darkness and may not be perceived by human senses.

The Apostle Paul demonstrates his great ability as an inspired teacher as he pictures each of us as a warrior being clothed with the essential armor to protect the four parts of the human body which apparently Satan and his hosts, by their vigilant spy system, have found to be the most vulnerable parts through which the enemies of righteousness might make their "landing," as it were, and invade the human soul. Here are his inspired teachings:

Stand therefore, having your loins girt about with truth, and having on the breastplate of righteousness;

And your feet shod with the preparation of the gospel of peace.

And take the helmet of salvation. . . . (Ephesians 6:14-15, 17.)

Did you note carefully the four main parts of your bodies to be guarded:

1. A girdle about your loins.
2. A breastplate over your heart.
3. Your feet shod.
4. A helmet on your head.

These instructions take on full significance when it is remembered the loins are those portions of the body between the lower ribs and the hips in which are located the vital generative organs, and also that in the scriptures and other inspired writings the loins symbolize virtue or moral purity and vital strength. The heart suggests our daily conduct in life, for as the Master taught:

> . . . out of the abundance of the heart the mouth speaketh. A good man . . . bringeth forth good things: and an evil man . . . bringeth forth evil things. (Matthew 12:34-35.)

The feet typify the course you chart in the journey of life. The head, of course, represents your intellect.

But now pay careful heed to the fabric from which the various parts of your armor are to be fashioned.

Truth is to be the substance of which the girdle about your loins is to be formed if your virtue and vital strength are to be safeguarded. How can truth protect you from one of the deadliest of all evils, unchastity? First, for a definition of truth: Truth is knowledge, so the Lord tells us, "knowledge of things as they are, and as they were, and as they are to come." (D&C 93:24.) Now consider for a few moments the essential knowledge which will put to flight immorality, the ever-present enemy of youth:

Man and woman are the offspring of God and created after His own image and likeness as mortal beings. One of the first commandments given to our first mortal parents, "to multiply and to replenish the earth," has been repeated as a sacred instruction to every faithful and true Latter-day Saint young man and young woman married in holy wedlock. To the end that this sacred purpose of parenthood be realized, our Creator has placed within the breast of every true man and woman a strong mutual attraction for each other, which acquaintance ripens in friendship, thence through the romance of courtship, and finally matures into happy marriage. But now mark you, *never once has God issued such a command to unmarried persons!* Indeed, to the contrary; he has written high on the decalogue of crime and second only to murder the divine injunction, "Thou shalt not commit adultery" (which is unquestionably interpreted to mean all unlawful sexual association, inasmuch as the Master used interchangeably the words *adultery* and *fornication* in defining sexual impurity, and it has been severely condemned in every dispensation by authorized church leaders).

Those who make themselves worthy and enter into the new and everlasting covenant of marriage in the temple for time and all eternity will be laying the first cornerstone for an eternal family home in the celestial kingdom that will last forever. Their reward is to have "glory added upon their heads forever and forever." These eternal truths, if you believe them with all your soul, will be as a girdle of armor about your loins to safeguard your virtue as you would protect your life.

But now again may I put you on guard as to Satan's methods used in an attempt to destroy you. The Lord, after giving us the definition of truth quoted above, said this: "And whatsoever is more or less than this is the spirit of that wicked one who was a liar from the beginning." (D&C 93:25.)

When you are prompted to immodesty in dress or to unclean or obscene speech or brazen conduct in your courtship, you are playing Satan's game and are becoming the victim of his lying tongue. Just so, if you allow the vain theories of men to cause you to doubt your relationship to God, the divine purpose of marriage, and your future prospects for eternity, you are being victimized by the master of lies, because all such is contrary to truth, which saves you from these perils.

Now, what about the breastplate which will safeguard your heart or your conduct in life? The Apostle Paul says that breastplate shall be made of a stuff called righteousness. The righteous man, although far superior to his fellows who are not, is humble and does not parade his righteousness to be seen of men but conceals his virtues as he would modestly conceal his nudity. The righteous man strives for self-improvement knowing that he has daily need of repentance for his misdeeds or his neglect. He is not so much concerned about what he can get but more about how much he can give to others, knowing that along that course only can he find true happiness. He endeavors to make each day his masterpiece so that at night's close he can witness in his soul and to his God that whatever has come to his hand that day, he has done to the best of his ability. His body is not dissipated and weakened by the burdens imposed by the demands of riotous living; his judgment is not rendered faulty by the follies of youth; he is clear of vision, keen of intellect, and strong of body. The breastplate of righteousness has given him "the strength of ten—because his heart is clean."

But to continue with your coat of armor. Your feet, which are to represent your goals or objectives in life, are to be shod. Shod with what? "With the preparation of the gospel of peace." The apostle who wrote that phrase certainly knew life from actual experience—"preparation of the gospel of peace"! He knew that preparedness is the way to victory and that "eternal vigilance is the price of safety." Fear is the penalty of unpreparedness and aimless dawdling with opportunity. Whether in speech or in song, whether in physical or moral combat, the tide of victory rests with him who is prepared.

The old philosophers understood the importance of having this preparation begin in the formative period of life, for we are admonished to "train up a child in the way he should go: and when he is old, he will not depart from it." (Proverbs 22:6.) To point out this same truth, one old adage declared: "If you follow the river you will reach the sea," and another suggests a warning: "Following the course of least resistance makes men and rivers crooked."

Embodied in the gospel of Jesus Christ are the straightforward negative injunctions divinely given to the great lawgiver of Israel, Moses—"Thou shalt not . . . !"—to be followed later by the positive declarations in the Sermon on the Mount, which outline a veritable blueprint for your course through life. The gospel plan enjoins us to the observance of prayer, to walk uprightly, to honor our parentage, to keep the Sabbath Day holy, and to refrain from idleness. Happy is that one whose feet are shod with the preparation of these teachings from his youth to withstand the evil day. He has found the way to peace by "overcoming the world." He has built his house upon a rock, and when the storms come, the winds blow, and the rains do beat upon the house, it will not fall because it is founded upon a rock. (See Matthew 7:24-25.) Such a one is not afraid; he will not be overcome by a surprise attack, for he is ready for any emergency: he is prepared!

And now finally to the last piece of the prophet-teacher's armored dress. We will put a helmet upon the head. Our head or our intellect is the controlling member of our body. It must be well protected against the enemy, for "as a man thinketh in his heart, so is he." (Proverbs 23:7.) But now in order for this helmet to be effective, it must be of an exquisite design. It must be of a supermaterial to be effective in our eternal conflict with the invisible enemy of all righteousness. Our is to be the "helmet of salvation." Salvation means the attainment of the eternal right to live in the presence of God the Father and the Son as a reward for a good life in mortality.

With the goal of salvation ever in our mind's eye as the ultimate to be achieved, our thinking and our decisions which determine action will always challenge all that would jeopardize that glorious future state. Lost indeed is that soul who is intellectually without the "helmet of salvation" which tells him that death is the end and that the grave is a victory over life, and brings to defeat the hopes, the aspirations, and the accomplishments of life. Such a one might well conclude that he may as well "eat, drink, and be merry, for tomorrow we die."

The conclusion reached by a committee of eminent divines appointed to investigate the cause of the wave of "student suicides" which swept over the country a few years ago was very significant. The summary of their findings declared: "The philosophy of the students who took their lives was such that they had never given religion serious thought, and when a test came they had nothing to hold fast to."

In contrast to the tragic picture, the one who confidently looks forward to an eternal reward for his efforts in mortality is constantly sustained through his deepest trials; when his bank fails, he does not commit suicide; when his loved ones die, he does not despair; when war and destruction dissipate his fortune, he does not falter. He lives above his world and never loses sight of the goal of his salvation.

Our intellects, so protected, must always measure learning by the gospel criteria: Is it true? Is it uplifting? Will it benefit mankind? In the choices of life—our friends, our education, our vocation, our companion in marriage—all these and more must be made with an eye single to eternal life. Our thoughts must "smell of the sunshine" if our association would be inspiring and uplifting. If we would refrain from murder, we must learn not to become angry; if we would free ourselves from sexual sin, we must control immoral thought; if we would avoid the penalty of imprisonment for theft, we must learn not to covet. So taught Jesus, the Master Teacher and our Savior. (See Matthew 5:21-28.)

> O that cunning plan of the evil one! O the vainness, and the frailties, and the foolishness of men! When they are learned they think they are wise, and they hearken not unto the counsel of God, for they set it aside, supposing they know of themselves, wherefore, their wisdom is foolishness and it profiteth them not. And they shall perish. (2 Nephi 9:28.)

Children of the covenant who have upon their heads the helmet of salvation are not as these. The thrill of victory is within their grasp.

But now may I call your attention to one significant fact concerning the armor with which you now have been clothed. You have no armor whatsoever to protect you from the rear. Does this suggest yet another quality essential to this eternal conflict with "spiritual wickedness in high places"? Evidently no one can win this battle running *from* the enemy. The contest must be face to face. There must be no retreat. So came the clear-ringing counsel of the First Presidency to our boys during the last World War: "Boys, keep yourselves clean! Better die clean than to come home unclean." Courage and determination and continual aggressiveness to the right are the essential qualities for the battle of life, else all the armor in the world suggested for our protection would be of no avail. Thus equipped within and without, we are now ready.

But wait a moment! Are we to have no weapons with which to fight? Are we to be mere targets for the enemy to attack? Let's read now what Paul, the great apostle-teacher, said about our weapons:

> Above all, taking the shield of faith, wherewith ye shall be able to quench all the fiery darts of the wicked.
>
> And take . . . the sword of the Spirit, which is the word of God. (Ephesians 6:16-17.)

May I attempt to describe briefly that shield of faith? Faith is a gift from God, and blessed is the man who possesses it. "He who carries the lamp will not despair," wrote one of the great industrial leaders with reference to a business crisis, "no matter how dark the night. That lamp I call faith." Suppose we examine a few of life's problems to see just how effective the shield of faith can be.

In what we might liken unto a great "pincer movement" of enemy forces to encircle us, we are being surfeited with the doctrine that we can get "something for nothing." When the smoke of the present frenzied social conflict has cleared away and the carnage resulting therefrom carefully counted, we shall have had proved again that we cannot get something for nothing and continue to prosper, and that the habit of giving instead of getting is the way to happiness. Then our faith in those tried and trusted virtues of thrift, self-sacrifice, and frugality will have triumphed over the vices of reckless spending, selfishness, and a disregard for decent standards of common civic virtue and morality.

It was the faith of our pioneer fathers that prompted them, as they pitched camp to begin a new settlement, to devoutly invoke the blessings of Almighty God upon their efforts. They prayed for the rains to come, for the fertility of the soil, for protection against destructive forces to the end that their crops would grow and that a harvest would be gathered. When a bounteous harvest came, they thanked God; for the protection of loved ones, they gave recognition to an Omnipotent Power; in death and sorrow, in floods and in storm, they saw the workings of a Divine Will. Out of such faith there was born in them, and can be likewise in you, a conviction that "a man and the Lord are a big majority in any test."

If we have faith in our kinship to a Great Creator, we

recognize by that same token our relationship to man. Such faith banishes hate in time of war and supplants therefore a sympathy for our enemy; the envies and jealousies of human society become, in the white light of faith, merely the growing pains of a family of children growing up to maturity and to a better understanding of how, as grown-ups, they should act. By faith we surmount daily obstacles and disappointments, and our defeats we thus interpret as necessary for our experience and development; we realize that to be thrown upon one's own resources is to be cast into the lap of fortune where our faculties undergo an unexpected development. With faith we become pioneers for the generations yet unborn and find ourselves becoming joyous in the contemplation of service we may render to our fellowmen even though the reward be but a martyr's crown.

Note now how the "shield of faith" and the "sword of the spirit which is the word of God" work together, perfectly coordinated as weapons in the hands of one who has upon him the "armor of righteousness." The scriptures declare, "faith cometh by hearing, and hearing by the word of God." (Romans 10:17.) Just as one in hand-to-hand combat with only a shield and without a sword would soon be overcome, just so without the word of God from the scriptures and by revelation, our faith becomes weak in the face of modern destructionists who call themselves "liberals." Shielded by faith, the commandments known as the Decalogue from Mount Sinai are transformed from mere platitudes of a philosopher to the thundering voice of authority from on high, and the teachings of the scriptures become the revealed word of God to guide us to our celestial home. Obedience to civil law would become a moral and a religious obligation, as well as a civic duty, if we believed that "the powers that be are ordained of God.

Whosoever therefore resisteth the power, resisteth the ordinance of God. . . ." (Romans 13:1-2.)

Armed with the word of God, the shattered dreams of youth and the frustrations which result from the stresses of war and the vigors of life do not embitter us or stifle our ambitions or prompt us in our despondency to cry out in despair, "Oh, what's the use?" Guided by faith taught by the word of God, we view life as a great process of soul-training. Under the ever-watchful eye of a loving Father, we learn by "the things which we suffer," we gain strength by overcoming obstacles, and we conquer fear by triumphant victory in places where danger lurks. By faith, as the word of God teaches, we understand that whatever contributes in life to the lofty standard of Jesus—"Be ye therefore perfect, even as your Father which is in heaven is perfect" (Matthew 5:48)—is for our good and for our eternal benefit even though into that molding may go the severe chastening of an all-wise God, "For whom the Lord loveth he chasteneth, and scourgeth every son whom he receiveth." (Hebrews 12:6.)

Thus schooled and drilled for the contest with the powers of darkness and with spiritual wickedness, we may be "troubled on every side, yet not distressed; we are perplexed, but not in despair; Persecuted, but not forsaken; cast down, but not destroyed." (2 Corinthians 4:8-9.)

> The night is far spent, the day is at hand; let us therefore cast off the works of darkness, and let us put on the armour of light.
>
> Let us walk honestly, as in the day; not in rioting and drunkenness, not in chambering and wantonness, not in strife and envying. (Romans 13:12-13.)

Youth of Zion, put on the whole armor of God!

35

The Constitution for a Perfect Life

"WHO is the greatest in the kingdom of heaven?" (Matthew 18:1.) The answer to that question had been the subject of controversy among the chosen Twelve as they sat in council in the home of Peter at Capernaum. Perhaps the question had more particularly reference to Peter, James, and John, who had so recently come from the experience on the Mount of Transfiguration, as to which of these three would be the first in the church next to the Master Himself. It is more likely that they were merely trying to determine those qualifications in a man that fitted him for the highest place in the kingdom. At any rate, as Jesus entered the council room, He discerned the question at issue as though it had been asked. He called a little child to Him, probably one of Peter's children, and set the child in the midst of them and then took it in His arms and said:

> Verily I say unto you, Except ye be converted, and become as little children, ye shall not enter into the kingdom of heaven.

Whosoever therefore shall humble himself as this little child, the same is greatest in the kingdom of heaven. (Matthew 18:3-4.)

I think similar feelings to those of the Twelve on that occasion were in the minds of a group of young women who wrote this question: "What are the steps a young man or woman should take to really live a full life?" Perhaps the Master would suggest a similar reply to the answer He gave to the Twelve, for to really live a full life is to strive with one's full heart to be greatest in God's kingdom, for of such, as little children, is the kingdom of heaven. To humble one's self as a little child, therefore, is to live to the highest of the Master's expectations concerning us.

Those who constitute the membership of the kingdom have been referred to as "saints." Moses called the children of Israel "saints." (See Deuteronomy 33:2.) Daniel in a great vision saw that the "saints" would possess the kingdom. (Daniel 7:22.) Both the apostles John and Paul in their writings referred to members of the Church as "saints." In our own day that name has been incorporated into the name of the Church by revelation. (D&C 115:3.) What is its significance? A great prophet in the land of Zarahemla on the American continent, in delivering the last sermon of his life, has given us a statement that throws light upon its meaning and also gives additional explanation of the statement of the Savior to the Twelve. King Benjamin declared that to become a saint, one

. . . putteth off the natural man and becometh a saint through the atonement of Christ the Lord, and becometh as a child, submissive, meek, humble, patient, full of love, willing to submit to all things which the Lord seeth fit to inflict upon him, even as a child doth submit to his father. (Mosiah 3:19.)

But then, you want to know the "steps" by which one can have his life patterned to that fulness which makes him a worthy citizen or "saint" in God's kingdom. The best answer may be found by a study of the life of Jesus in the scriptures, for it has been said that "our gospels are not merely the record of oral teachings; they are the potraits of a living man." (Dean Inge.) Christ came not only into the world to make an atonement for the sins of mankind, but to set an example before the world of the standard of perfection of God's law and of obedience to the Father. In His Sermon on the Mount the Master has given us somewhat of a revelation of His own character, which was perfect, or what might be said to be "an autobiography, every syllable of which He had written down in deeds," and in so doing has given us a blueprint for our own lives. Anyone clearly understanding the true import of His words comes to the realization that an unworthy member of the Church, although he might be in the kingdom of God, yet would not be of the kingdom because of his unworthiness.

You may know you are living a full, rich life when you have the real joy of living, for "men are, that they might have joy." (2 Nephi 2:25.) What is it, then, that gives you that high emotional ecstasy called joy? Does it come from the unusual or does it come from common things? He who is moved thus only by the unusual is as one who must flag a failing appetite with strong spices and flavorings that destroy the true sense of taste. You are making a serious error if you mistake an emotional thrill that passes with the moment for the upsurge of deep feelings that is the joy of living. If one feels strong surges of happiness and desire from the quiet of a happy home, from the unfolding of a beautiful life, from the revelation of divine wisdom, or from a love for the beautiful, the true and good, he is having a taste of the fulness of the joy that the living of a rich, full life only can bring.

In that matchless Sermon on the Mount, Jesus has given us eight distinct ways by which we might receive this kind of joy. Each of His declarations is begun by the word "blessed." Blessedness is defined as being higher than happiness. "Happiness comes from without and is dependent on circumstances; blessedness is an inward fountain of joy in the soul itself, which no outward circumstances can seriously affect." (Dummelow's *Commentary.*) These declarations of the Master are known in the literature of the Christian world as the Beatitudes and have been referred to by Bible commentators as the preparation necessary for entrance into the kingdom of heaven. For the purposes of this discussion may I speak of them as something more than that as they are applied to you and me. They embody, in fact, the constitution for a perfect life.

Let us consider them for a few moments. Four of them have to do with our individual selves, the living of our own inner, personal lives, if we would be perfect and find the blessedness of that inward joy.

> Blessed are the poor in spirit.
> Blessed are they that mourn.
> Blessed are they that hunger and thirst after righteousness.
> Blessed are the pure in heart.

To be poor in spirit is to feel yourselves as the spiritually needy, even dependent upon the Lord for your clothes, your food, the air you breathe, your health, your life; realizing that no day should pass without fervent prayer of thanksgiving, for guidance and forgiveness and strength sufficient for each day's need. If a youth realizes his spiritual need, when in dangerous places where his very life is at stake, he may be drawn close to the fountain of truth and be prompted by the Spirit of the Lord in his hour of greatest trial. It is indeed a sad thing for one, because of his wealth or learning or worldly position, to think himself independent of this spiritual need. It is the opposite of pride or self-conceit. To the worldly rich it is that "he must possess his wealth as if he possessed it not" and be willing to say without regret, if he were suddenly to meet financial disaster, as did Job, "the Lord gave, and the Lord hath taken away; blessed be the name of the Lord." (Job 1:21.) Thus, if in your humility you sense your spiritual need, you are made ready for adoption into the "church of the Firstborn," and to become "the elect of God."

To mourn, as the Master's lesson here would teach, one must show that "godly sorrow that worketh repentance" (2 Corinthians 7:10) and wins for the penitent a forgiveness of sins and forbids a return to the deeds of which he mourns. It is to see, as did the Apostle Paul, "glory in tribulations. . . knowing that tribulation worketh patience; And patience, experience; and experience, hope." (Romans 5:3-4.) You must be willing "to bear one another's burdens, that they may be light." (Mosiah 18:8.) You must be willing to mourn with those that mourn, and comfort those that stand in need of comfort. (Mosiah 18:9.) When a mother mourns in her loneliness for the return of a wayward daughter, you with compassion must forbid the casting of the first stone. It is the kind of mourning portrayed in the deep feelings of the marine on Saipan who wrote to us during World War II when his buddy was killed, "As I lay in my foxhole that night I wept bitterly." Your mourning with the aged, the widow, and the orphan should lead you to bring the succor they require. In a word, you must be as the publican and not as the Pharisee. "God be merciful to me a sinner." (Luke 18:13.) Your reward for so doing is the blessedness of comfort for your own soul through a forgiveness of your own sins.

Did you ever hunger for food or thirst for water when just a crust of stale bread or a sip of tepid water to ease the pangs that distressed you would seem to be the most prized of all possessions? If you have so hungered, then you may begin to understand how the Master meant we should hunger and thirst after righteousness. It's that hungering and thirsting that leads Latter-day Saints away from home to seek the fellowship with Saints in sacrament services and that induces worship on the Lord's day. It is that which prompts fervent prayers and leads our feet to holy temples and bids us be reverent therein. One who keeps the Sabbath Day will be filled with a lasting joy far more to be desired than the fleeting pleasures derived from activities indulged in contrary to God's commandments. If you ask with "a sincere heart, with real intent, having faith in Christ, he will manifest . . . truth . . . unto you, by the power of the Holy Ghost," and by its power you "may know the truth of all things." (Moroni 10:4-5.) Build "each new temple nobler than the last . . . till thou at length are free," then "your whole bodies shall be filled with light, and there shall be no darkness in you. . . ." (D&C 88:67.)

If you would see God, you must be pure. There is in Jewish writings the story of a man who saw an object in the distance, an object that he thought was a beast. As it drew nearer he could perceive it was a man; as it came still closer he saw it was his friend. You can see only that which you have eyes to see. Some of the associates of Jesus saw Him only as a son of Joseph the carpenter. Others thought Him to be a winebibber or a drunkard because of His words. Still others thought He was possessed of devils. Only the righteous saw Him as the Son of God. Only if you are the pure in heart will you see God, and also in a lesser degree will you be able to see the "God" or good in man and love him because of the goodness you see in him. Mark well that person who criticizes and maligns the man of God or the Lord's anointed leaders in His Church. Such a one speaks from an impure heart.

But in order to gain entrance into the kingdom of heaven we must not only be good, but we are also required to do good and be good for something. So if you would walk daily toward that goal of perfection and fulness of life, you must be schooled by the remaining four articles in the Master's constitution for a perfect life. These beatitudes have to do with man's social relations with others:

Blessed are the meek.
Blessed are the merciful.
Blessed are the peacemakers.
Blessed are they which are persecuted.

A meek man is defined as one who is not easily provoked or irritated and is forbearing under injury or annoyance. The meek man is the strong, the mighty, the man of complete self-mastery. He is the one who has the courage of his moral convictions, despite the pressure of the gang or the club. In controversy his judgment is the court of last resort and his sobered counsel quells the rashness of the mob. He is humble-minded; he does not bluster. "He that is slow to anger is better than the mighty. . . ." (Proverbs 16:32.) He is a natural leader and is the chosen of army and navy, business and church, to lead where other men follow. He is the "salt" of the earth and shall inherit it.

Our salvation rests upon the mercy we show to others. Unkind and cruel words, or wanton acts of cruelty toward man or beast, even though in seeming retaliation, disqualify the perpetrator in his claims for mercy when he has need of mercy in the day of judgment before earthly or heavenly tribunals. Is there one who has never been wounded by the slander of another whom he thought to be his friend? Do you remember the struggle you had to refrain from retribution? Blessed are all you who are merciful, for you shall obtain mercy!

Peacemakers shall be called the children of God. The trouble-maker, the striker against law and order, the leader of the mob, the law-breaker are prompted by motives of evil; and unless they desist, they will be known as the children of Satan rather than God. Withhold yourselves from him who would cause disquieting doubts by making light of sacred things, for he seeks not for peace but to spread confusion. That one who is quarrelsome or contentious, and whose arguments are for other purposes than to resolve the truth, is violating a fundamental principle laid down by the Master as an essential in the building of a full rich life. "Peace and goodwill to men on earth" was the angel song that heralded the birth of the Prince of Peace.

To be persecuted for righteousness' sake in a great cause where truth and virtue and honor are at stake is God-like. Always there have been martyrs to every great cause. The great harm that may come from persecution is not from the persecution itself but from the possible effect it may have upon the persecuted who may thereby be deterred in their zeal for the righteousness of their cause. Much of that persecution comes from lack of understanding, for men are prone to oppose that which they do not comprehend. Some of it comes from men intent upon evil. But from whatever cause, persecution seems to be so universal against those engaged in a righteous cause that the Master warns us, "Woe unto you, when all men shall speak well of you! for so did their fathers to the false prophets." (Luke 6:26.)

May youth everywhere remember that warning when you are hissed and scoffed at because you refuse to compromise your standards of abstinence, honesty, and morality in order to win the applause of the crowd. If you stand firmly for the right, despite the jeers of the crowd or even physical violence, you shall be crowned with the blessedness of eternal joy. Who knows but that again in our day some of the saints or even apostles, as in former days, may be required to give their lives in defense of the truth. If that time should come, God grant they will not fail.

Gradually as we ponder prayerfully all these teachings, we will make what may be to some the startling discovery that after all, God's measure of our worth in His kingdom will not be the high positions we have held here among man, nor in His church, nor the honors we have won, but rather the lives we have led and the good we have done, according to the "constitution for a perfect life" revealed in the life of the Son of God.

May you make the Beatitudes the constitution of your own lives and thus receive the blessedness promised therein.

36

The Iron Rod

SOME time ago there appeared in the *Wall Street Journal* a thought-provoking article, written by an eminent theologian at Columbia University, under the subject heading "An Antidote for Aimlessness," which you recognize as a condition that is prevalent in the world today. I quote from this article by Rabbi Arthur Herlzterg:

> What people come to religion for, is an ultimate metaphysical hunger, and when that hunger is not satisfied, religion declines . . . the moment that clerics become more worldly, the world goes to hades the faster.
>
> . . . Religion represents the accumulation of man's insight over thousands of years into such questions as the nature of man, the meaning of life, the individual's place in the universe. That is, precisely, the question at the root of man's restlessness.
>
> Man seeks something to end his state of confusion and emptiness . . . in the latest parlance, an antidote for aimlessness. We do not know if the truths of religious tradition can be interpreted to satisfy this need, but we are sure that here, not in political activism, is religion's path to relevance.

As an answer to those who may be wandering aimlessly, searching for something to satisfy their need and to end their state of confusion and emptiness, I would like to introduce a few thoughts by relating a remarkable vision which came to an ancient prophet by the name of Lehi—600 years before Christ. To the faithful members of the Church this will be an oft-related incident recorded in the Book of Mormon. To those not of our faith this may, if they will ponder seriously, be very significant in the light of many trends in our modern society.

In this vision, the prophet Lehi was led by a heavenly messenger through a dark and dreary waste to a tree laden with delicious fruit, which proved to be very satisfying to his soul. He beheld a river of water nearby along which was a straight and narrow path leading to the tree laden with delicious fruit. Between the river bank and the path was a rod of iron, presumably to safeguard the travelers from falling off the narrow path into the river.

As he looked, he saw large groups of people crowding forward to gain access to the spacious field where the tree with fruit was located. As they pressed forward along the path, a great mist of darkness arose, so dense that many who started lost their way and wandered off and were drowned in the murky water or were lost from view as they wandered into strange paths. There were others, however, likewise in danger of being lost because of the blinding mist, who caught hold of the iron rod and, by so doing, held their course so that they too could partake of the delicacies which had beckoned them to come, despite the hazardous journey. Across, on the opposite side of the river, were multitudes of people pointing fingers of scorn at those who made the journey safely.

As with many other ancient prophets in biblical history, dreams or visions of this nature were effective means by which the Lord communicated with his people through prophet-leaders. Just so, this dream had great significance, as the Lord revealed to the prophet Lehi. The tree laden with fruit was a representation of the love of God, which He sheds forth among all the children of men. The Master Himself, later in His earthly ministry, explained to Nicodemus how that great love was manifested. Said He: "For God so loved the world, that he gave his only begotten Son, that whosoever believeth in him should not perish, but have everlasting life"; and then the Master added: "For God sent not his Son into the world to condemn the world; but that the world through him might be saved." (John 3:16-17.)

The rod of iron as seen in the vision interpreted was the word of God, or the gospel of Jesus Christ, which led to the tree of life that the Master explained to the woman at the well in Samaria was as "a well of [living] water springing up into everlasting life." (John 4:14.)

As seen in the vision, those who were across the river pointing fingers of scorn represented the multitudes of the earth which are gathered together to fight against the apostles of the Lamb of God. The scorners, so the Lord revealed, represented the so-called wisdom of the world, and the building itself in which they were gathered was the "pride of the world." (See 1 Nephi 11 and 12.)

If there is any one thing most needed in this time of tumult and frustration, when men and women and youth and young adults are desperately seeking for answers to the problems which afflict mankind, it is an "iron rod" as a safe guide along the straight path on the way to eternal life, amidst the strange and devious roadways that would eventually lead to destruction and to the ruin of all that is "virtuous, lovely, or of good report."

These conditions as they would be found in the earth when these scriptures, now called the Book of Mormon, were to be brought forth were foreseen by the prophets. As I read some of these predictions, I would have you think of conditions with which we are surrounded today:

> And I know that ye do walk in the pride of your hearts; and there are none save a few only who do not lift themselves up in the pride of their hearts; unto . . . envying, and strifes, and malice, and persecutions, and all manner of iniquities . . . because of the pride of your hearts.
>
> . . . behold, ye do love money, and your substance, and your fine apparel, and the adorning of your churches, more than ye love the poor and the needy, the sick and the afflicted. (Mormon 8:36-37.)

The Apostle Paul also spoke of a time of peril when

> men [would] be lovers of their own selves, covetous, boasters, proud, blasphemers, disobedient to parents, unthankful, unholy,
>
> Without natural affection, trucebreakers, false accusers, incontinent, fierce, despisers of those things that are good,
>
> Traitors, heady, highminded, lovers of pleasures more than lovers of God;
>
> Having a form of godliness, but denying the power thereof. . . . (2 Timothy 3:2-5.)

There are many who profess to be religious and speak of themselves as Christians, and, according to one such, "as accepting the scriptures only as sources of inspiration and moral truth," and then ask in their smugness: "Do the revelations of God give us a handrail to the kingdom of God, as the Lord's messenger told Lehi, or merely a compass?"

Unfortunately, some are among us who claim to be Church members but are somewhat like the scoffers in Lehi's vision—standing aloof and seemingly inclined to hold in derision the faithful who choose to accept Church authorities as God's special witnesses of the gospel and His agents in directing the affairs of the Church.

There are those in the Church who speak of themselves as liberals who, as one of our former presidents has said, "read by the lamp of their own conceit." (Joseph F. Smith, *Gospel Doctrine* [Deseret Book Co., 1939], p. 373.) One time I asked one of our Church educational leaders how he would define a liberal in the Church. He answered in one sentence: "A liberal in the Church is merely one who does not have a testimony."

The late Dr. John A. Widtsoe of the Council of the Twelve, an eminent educator, make a statement relative to this word *liberal* as it applied to those in the Church. This is what he said:

> The self-called liberal [in the Church] is usually one who has broken with the fundamental principles or guiding philosophy of the group to which he belongs. . . . He claims membership in an organization but does not believe in its basic concepts; and sets out to reform it by changing its foundations. . . .
>
> It is folly to speak of a liberal religion, if that religion claims that it rests upon unchanging truth.

And then Dr. Widtsoe concludes his statement with this:

> It is well to beware of people who go about proclaiming that they are or their churches are liberal. The probabilities are that the structure of their faith is built on sand and will not withstand the storms of truth. ("Evidences and Reconciliations," *Improvement Era* 44:609.)

Wouldn't it be wonderful if, when there are questions which are unanswered because the Lord hasn't seen fit to reveal the answers as yet, all such could say, as Abraham Lincoln is alleged to have said, "I accept all I read in the Bible that I can understand, and accept the rest on faith."

How comforting it would be to those who are the restless in the intellectual world, when such questions arise as to how the earth was formed and how man came to be, if they could answer as did an eminent scientist and devoted Church member. A sister had asked: "Why didn't the

Lord tell us plainly about these things?" The scientist answered: "It is likely we would not understand if he did. It might be like trying to explain the theory of atomic energy to an eight-year-old."

Wouldn't it be a great thing if all who are well schooled in secular learning could hold fast to the "iron rod," or the word of God, which could lead them, through faith, to an understanding, rather than to have them stray away into strange paths of man-made theories and be plunged into the murky waters of disbelief and apostasy?

I heard one of our own eminent scientists say something to the effect that he believed some professors have taken themselves out of the Church by their trying to philosophize or intellectualize the fall of Adam and the subsequent atonement of the Savior. This was because they would rather accept the philosophies of men than what the Lord has revealed until they, and we, are able to understand the "mysteries of godliness" as explained to the prophets of the Lord and more fully revealed in sacred places.

There were evidently similar questions and controversies in the Master's time. In one terse answer, He gave the essential ingredients to safety amidst the maze of uncertainty. To settle an apparent controversy among His disciples as to who would be the greatest in the kingdom of God, He said: ". . . except ye be converted, and become as little children, ye shall not enter into the kingdom of [God]." (Matthew 18:3.)

To become converted, according to the scriptures, means having a change of heart and the moral character of a person turned from the controlled power of sin into a righteous life. It means to "wait patiently on the Lord" until one's prayers can be answered and until his heart, as Cyprian, a defender of the faith in the Apostolic Period, testified: "In my heart, purified of all sin, there entered a light which came from on high, and then suddenly and in a marvelous manner, I saw certainty succeed doubt."

Conversion must mean more than just being a "card carrying" member of the Church with a tithing receipt, a membership card, a temple recommend, etc. It means to overcome the tendencies to criticize and to strive continually to improve inward weaknessess and not merely the outward appearances.

The Lord issued a warning to those who would seek to destroy the faith of an individual or lead him away from the word of God or cause him to lose his grasp on the "iron rod," wherein was safety by faith in a Divine Redeemer and His purposes concerning this earth and its peoples.

The Master warned: "But whoso shall offend one of these little ones which believe in me, it were better. . . . that a millstone were hanged about his neck, and that he were drowned in the depth of the sea." (Matthew 18:6.)

The Master was impressing the fact that rather than ruin the soul of a true believer, it would be better for a person to suffer an earthly death than to incur the penalty of jeopardizing his own eternal destiny.

The Apostle Paul impressed also the danger of false teachings by bad example. Said he:

> But take heed lest by any means this liberty of yours become a stumbling block to them that are weak. . . .
>
> And through thy knowledge shall the weak . . . perish, for whom Christ died?
>
> But when ye sin so against the brethren, and would their weak conscience, ye sin against Christ. (1 Corinthians 8:9, 11-12.)

Speaking to the learned and highly sophisticated generation in his time, the prophet Jacob said something which seems to be so often needed to be repeated today:

> . . . When they are learned they think they are wise, and they

hearken not unto the counsel of God, for they set it aside, supposing they know of themselves, wherefore, their wisdom is foolishness and it profiteth them not. . . .

But to be learned is good if they hearken to the counsels of God. (2 Nephi 9:28-29.)

We fervently thank the Lord for the faithfulness and devotion of many in and out of the Church who are in high places in business, in governmental circles, in the legal profession, doctors, trained social workers, nurses, and those in the fields of the sciences and the arts. Particularly are we grateful for those who accept positions of leadership in the Church, who serve as home teachers or class leaders in the priesthood or in the auxiliaries, who make themselves available for volunteer service in helping to care for the unfortunate in all lands and among minorities within and without the Church, and in giving particular attention to the needs of the widows and the orphans.

I say to all such, as did Jesus to Zacchaeus: "This day is salvation come to [their] house." (Luke 19:9.) These are they who are holding fast to the "iron rod" which can lead us all, in safety, to the tree of life.

I once read a column in the *Washington Post*, by George Moore, who styled himself as the "hermit of Mount Vernon." (Mount Vernon, of course, was the ancestral home of George Washington.) In this article he said, "I have spent the last twenty years of my life at Mount Vernon reducing my ignorance." He claimed that a person never learns anything until he realizes how little he knows. In this article he makes this most illuminating observation about George Washington: "Washington never went to school. That's why he was an educated man, he never quit learning."

What George Moore said of himself I suppose could be said of many of you and of myself: "I have spent more than three score years of my life reducing my ignorance."

Therein, it is my conviction, is the challenge to all who achieve distinction in any field. Some quit learning when they graduate from a school; some quit learning about the gospel when they have completed a mission for the Church; some quit learning when they become an executive or have a prominent position in or out of the Church.

Remember, as George Moore said of Washington, "We can become educated persons, regardless of our stations in life, if we never quit learning."

The late President Dwight D. Eisenhower wrote this:

> Any man who does his work well, who is justifiably self-confident and not unduly disturbed by the jeers of the cynics and the shirkers, any man who stays true to decent motives and is considerate of others is, in essence, a leader. Whether or not he is ever singled out for prominence, he is bound to achieve great inner satisfaction in turning out superior work.
>
> And that, by the way, is what the good Lord put us on this earth for. ("What Is Leadership?" *Reader's Digest,* June 1965, p. 54.)

With the restoration of the true gospel of Jesus Christ and the establishment of the Church in the dispensation of the fulness of times, we were given instructions by revelation, the magnitude of which, as the late President Brigham H. Roberts explained, was "not merely as to whether baptism should be by immersion or for the forgiveness of sins, but the rubbish of accumulated ages was swept aside, the rocks made bare, and the foundations of the Kingdom of God were relaid."

It may seem preposterous to many to declare that within the teachings of The Church of Jesus Christ of Latter-day Saints may be found a bulwark to safeguard against the pitfalls, the frustrations, and the wickedness in the world. The plan of salvation formed in the heavens points clearly to the straight and narrow path that leads to eternal life, even though there are many who refuse to follow that way.

In a great revelation, the Lord gave instruction by commandment to the leaders of the Church of that early day that they should be seekers after truth in many fields.

First, of course, He commanded that they should "teach one another the doctrine of the kingdom . . . in all things that pertain [to] the kingdom of God. . . ." (D&C 88:77-78.) Then He counsels as to the wide sweep of learning about which we should seek. His church was not to be an ignorant ministry in various fields of secular learning. And then the Lord addressed His revelation to all others who may not have faith: ". . . seek learning, even by study and also by faith." (D&C 88:118.)

One might well ask: How does one get "learning by faith"? One prophet explains the process: First, one must arouse his faculties and experiment on the words of the Lord and desire to believe. Let this desire work in you until you believe in a manner that you can give place even to a portion of the word of the Lord. Then, like a planted seed, it must be cultivated and not resist the Spirit of the Lord, which is that which lighteneth everyone born into the world. You can then begin to feel within yourselves that it must be good, for it enlarges your soul and enlightens your understanding and, like the fruit of the tree in Lehi's vision, it becomes delicious to the taste. (See Alma 32.)

It was an English novelist who was quoted as saying: "He who seeks God has already found Him."

Let no one think that "learning by faith" contemplates an easy or lazy way to gain knowledge and ripen it into wisdom.

From heavenly instructions and added to which are the experiences of almost anyone who has sought diligently for heavenly guidance, one may readily understand that learning by faith requires the bending of the whole soul through worthy living to become attuned to the Holy Spirit of the Lord, the calling up from the depths of one's own mental searching, and the linking of our own efforts to receive the true witness of the Spirit.

The mission of this church is to bear witness of the truths of the gospel and put to flight the false teachings on every side that are causing the restlessness and the aimlessness that threaten all who have not found the straight path and that which could be an anchor to their souls.

37

"After All We Can Do"

SOME time ago my attention was attracted to a picture in one of the local newspapers. The picture showed two men with a shovel setting a highway sign. Within the block "U," which is the official designation of the Utah State Highway Department, was the figure 187, and then a sign underneath the block "U," which read: "The shortest designated highway in the state." Then I read the cutline underneath and the accompanying article, which described this short highway as being only one-quarter of a mile in length. It curved gracefully off to the right of the main highway 91 going south and led down over the brow of the hill, seemingly to invite anyone who wanted to travel that pleasant way. Then I looked more closely to see what the picture was. One of the men was the warden of the Utah State Penitentiary, and the other was a member of the state prison board. The highway marked U-187 led to a building that I could distinguish at the foot of the hill. With somewhat of a shock I recognized this building as the

Utah State Penitentiary. The shortest designated highway in the state was a wide paved road from the mainly traveled road to the state prison!

I would like to draw something of a parallel to this "shortest designated highway" with another highway. This other highway in life is also broad. It is a way to destruction, as the Master explained to His disciples when He said, in a very significant statement, ". . . for wide is the gate, and broad is the way, that leadeth to destruction, and many there be which go in thereat." (Matthew 7:13.)

I remember a remark the late President Charles A. Callis made to me one day. We were talking about some of these matters, and he remarked, "You know, I think that probably the most important thing we as General Authorities ought to be preaching is not only repentance from sin, but even more important than that, to teach the young people particularly, and the entire Church generally, the awfulness of sin and the terror that follows him who has so indulged."

Years of experience since that time, and interviews with those who have unfortunately taken that short, broad highway, have convinced me that because of their suffering, those who have or are living lives of unrepented sinning would have given all that they possessed if someone could have warned them and could have told them of the awfulness of the sins from which they now suffer.

Nephi predicted and spoke of the sad state of those who habitually sinned and would not repent when he said:

> For the Spirit of the Lord will not always strive with man. And when the Spirit ceaseth to strive with man then cometh speedy destruction, and this grieveth my soul. (2 Nephi 26:11.)

Mormon described some people, his people, from whom the Spirit of the Lord had departed, and when I read that and then read what I shall now read to you, it seems clear to me that what he was talking about was not merely the inability to have the companionship of or the gift of the Holy Ghost, but he was talking of that light of truth to which every one born into the world is entitled and which will never cease to strive with the individual unless he loses it through his own sinning. This is what Mormon said:

> For behold, the Spirit of the Lord hath already ceased to strive with their fathers; and they are without Christ and God in the world; and they are driven about as chaff before the wind.
>
> . . . behold, they are led about by Satan, even as chaff is driven before the wind, or as a vessel is tossed about upon the waves, without sail or anchor, or without anything wherewith to steer her; and even as she is, so are they. (Mormon 5:16, 18.)

A story is told of the late President Calvin Coolidge, who was a master of few words in his expressions. He came home from his church meeting one morning, and his wife asked, "What did the preacher talk about this morning?" His reply was, "Sin." She again asked, "What did the minister say about it?" His reply was, "The minister was agin' it." And so are all preachers of righteousness; they are against this thing called sin.

What is sin? The apostle John described it or defined it as the transgression of the law. "Whosoever committeth sin transgresseth also the law: for sin is the transgression of the law." (I John 3:4.)

Brigham Young made that definition still more meaningful when he said that "sin consists in doing wrong when we know and can do better, and it will be punished with a just retribution, in the due time of the Lord." (*Journal of Discourses* 2:133.)

The source of sin is a subject oft debated and theorized by philosophers and others as to how it originates and whence it comes, but we with the sacred scriptures are left with a certainty that removes all question as to the author and the beginning of sin. The record tells us that Satan came among the children of Adam and Eve and said unto them:

> I am also a son of God; and he commanded them, saying: Believe it not; and they believed it not, and they loved Satan more than God. And men began from that time forth to be carnal, sensual, and devilish. (Moses 5:13.)

And then King Benjamin taught:

> . . . neither will ye suffer that they transgress the laws of God, and fight and quarrel one with another, and serve the devil, who is the master of sin, or who is the evil spirit which hath been spoken of by our fathers, he being an enemy to all righteousness. (Mosiah 4:14.)

The Master understood how powerful was this master of sin when He spoke of him as the "Prince of this world," and He taught his disciples to pray that they might not be led into temptation.

This, like that other highway to the Utah State Prison, is also a very short highway down the road of sin. You will remember the Lord's warning to Cain when He said, "If thou doest well, shalt thou not be accepted? and if thou doest not well, sin lieth at the door. . . ." (Genesis 4:7.)

It is just that short to the way of sin—right at our very doors.

Now the scriptures have told us about the identity of those who are going to inhabit that prison which lies at the end of that short highway:

> These are they who are liars, and sorcerers, and adulterers, and whoremongers, and whosoever loves and makes a lie.
>
> These are they who suffer the wrath of God on earth.
>
> These are they who suffer the vengeance of eternal fire.
>
> These are they who are cast down to hell [and that is the name of

the prison] and suffer the wrath of Almighty God, until the fulness of times, when Christ shall have subdued all enemies under his feet, and shall have perfected his work. (D&C 76:103-106.)

And again, the nature of the punishment which shall be received in that prison is clearly explained by the prophet Amulek:

> For behold, if ye have procrastinated the day of your repentance even until death, behold, ye have become subjected to the spirit of the devil, and he doth seal you his; therefore, the Spirit of the Lord hath withdrawn from you, and hath no place in you, and the devil hath all power over you; and this is the final state of the wicked. (Alma 34:35.)

Now as to the location of that place, reference is made to it in these words: "And the end thereof, neither the place thereof, nor their torment, no man knows." (D&C 76:45.)

Like all broad highways of life which beckon to that prison, there are allurements that we are ofttimes encouraged to follow. As Father Lehi explained to his son Jacob:

> . . . it must needs be that there was an opposition; even the forbidden fruit in opposition to the tree of life; the one being sweet and the other bitter. (2 Nephi 2:15.)

In other words, he set the tree of the knowledge of good and evil in opposition to the tree of life. The fruit of the one which was "bitter" was the tree of life, and the forbidden fruit was the one which was "sweet to the taste."

James Russell Lowell caught this great truth in his poem, "The Present Crisis:"

Careless seems the great Avenger; history's
pages but record
One death-grapple in the darkness 'twixt old
systems and the Word;
Truth forever on the scaffold, Wrong forever
on the throne,—
Yet that scaffold sways the future, and, be-
hind the dim unknown,
Standeth God within the shadow, keeping
watch above his own.

We see some of the signs which, like the signs to the state penitentiary, we know lead us downward. Some are called taverns; some are called lounges; and some are called roadhouses. They have bright, neon-lighted signs outside with catch-phrase names. They are dimly lighted inside; they have sensuous music. These are the unmistakable trademarks of the hell holes of Satan.

Nephi spoke of some teachings against which we must be on guard lest we follow that road, when he said that in a day to come, which we realize now is our day, there would be those who would teach us to become angry against that which is good to lull us away into carnal security, and to flatter us by telling us there is no devil, there is no hell. (See 2 Nephi 28:20-22.)

Dr. J. M. Sjodahl has made this rather interesting comment:

> Some have asserted that the story of the fall is but a myth, or an allegory, but it is given in the Scriptures as part of the history of the human family, and must be either accepted as such, or rejected as fiction. The fall was as necessary for the development of the race as was the creation.

Now mark you this statement: "The story of the first fall is, moreover, the story of every sin." (*Doctrine and Covenants Commentary*, 1965 edition, p. 160.)

Now consider, for illustration, the various sins—the breaking of the Word of Wisdom, unchastity, dishonesty, etc.—and then think of what is said here:

> Temptation begins with doubt as to the truth of the prohibition. "Has God said * * * ?" [is always the question of him who doubts and is tempted to sin.] It is continued by a contemplation of the pleasure that may be derived from doing that which has been prohibited. It ends with a sense of shame and degradation and dread of the presence of God. Such is the beginning and development of every transgression. (Ibid.)

Now the way to eternal life has fortunately been marked out just as plainly. I know a young woman who was about to fail in her faith because of a sudden sorrow that she was not quite prepared to bridge over after having been a convert of a few years. She had a dream in which she saw herself going back to the church of her previous acquaintance. As she drove along in her car, she came to a road that she took only to find that it was a road under construction, and after ten tortuous miles returning she found to her amazement that there were plain warning signs all along the way which, if she had observed, would have guided her along a safe detour road and past the shoals of difficulty.

Well the Master said it:

> Enter ye in at the strait gate: . . .
>
> Because strait is the gate, and narrow is the way, which leadeth unto life, and few there be that find it. (Matthew 7:13-14.)

As Jesus was teaching in the cities and villages toward Jerusalem as to what the kingdom of heaven was like, one asked Him, "Are there few that be saved?" That question reminded me of the remark of a good friend of mine who had heard one of the brethren talk about the requirements in order to attain the celestial kingdom. This friend said to me somewhat wearily after he had heard the sermon, "He has made it so difficult that I don't think anyone could qualify for the celestial kingdom."

Contrary to that, the Master said,

> Take my yoke upon you, and learn of me; for I am meek and lowly in heart: and ye shall find rest unto your souls.
>
> For my yoke is easy, and my burden is light. (Matthew 11:29-30.)

When you think about it, there is so much promised in the gospel for so little required on our part. For example, the ordinance of baptism is given us for the remission of sins, for entrance into the kingdom—a new birth; the gift of the Holy Ghost gives us the right to companionship with one of the Godhead; administration to the sick qualifies the individual with faith for a special blessing; by paying our tithing, the windows of heaven may be opened unto us; by fasting and by paying our fast offerings, we are told that then we might call on the Lord and He will hear our cry and our call; celestial marriage promises us that family life will exist beyond the grave. But all of these blessings are ours on one condition, and this is spoken of by Nephi, when he said:

> For we labor diligently to write, to persuade our children, and also our brethren, to believe in Christ, and to be reconciled to God; for we know that it is by grace that we are saved, [but mark you this condition] *after all we can do*. (2 Nephi 25:23. Italics added.)

The Master did not directly answer that question, "Are there few that be saved?" But He answered, "Strive to enter in at the strait gate." Strive means to struggle in opposition or contention, to contend, to battle for or against a person or a thing opposed, to strive against temptation, and to strive for truth.

Well, in all that striving, remember Temple Bailey's parable for mothers. "The young mother said to the guide at the beginning of her way, 'Is the way long?' And the guide replied, 'Yes, and the way is hard, and you will be tired before you reach the end of it. But the end will be better than the beginning.'"

Oh, that we might think of these warnings and remember the prayer of the Prophet Joseph in the midst of his persecutions, when he cried out, asking why the Lord would not see and alleviate the sufferings of the Saints, and then heard the Lord answer:

> My son, peace be unto thy soul; thine adversity and thine afflictions shall be but a small moment;

> And then, if thou endure it well, God shall exalt thee on high; thou shalt triumph over all thy foes. (D&C 121:7-8.)

Oh, may we pray the prayer of the Alcoholics Anonymous, those men who are striving to come back: "O Lord," they pray, "give me the humility to accept the things I cannot change, and the courage to change the things I can change, and then the wisdom to tell the difference."

38

As a Man Thinketh

WHY is it wrong to steal?

That question, asked of an unbeliever by a young missionary whose claims of the restored gospel had been challenged, brought forth a discussion of the importance of the Ten Commandments in establishing the fundamental principles as guides in making laws. Likewise all morality must have a religious base, for without the declarations contained in the word of the Lord, mankind would lack the essentials that must enter into a determination of right and wrong. Any man or any nation that has discarded God and a belief in doctrines revealed through His prophets soon begins to give evidence of moral instability and eventually disintegration.

It remained for the Master Teacher to carry still further the teachings of the decalogue when He declared:

> Ye have heard that it was said by them of old time, Thou shalt not kill; and whosoever shall kill shall be in danger of the judgment:

> But I say unto you, That whosoever is angry with his brother without a cause shall be in danger of the judgment. . . .
>
> Ye have heard that it was said by them of old time, Thou shalt not commit adultery:
>
> But I say unto you, That whosoever looketh on a woman to lust after her hath committed adultery with her already in his heart. (Matthew 5:21-22, 27-28.)

The great truth taught herein is clear: thought is the father of an act. No man ever committed murder who did not first become angry. No one ever committed adultery without a preceding immoral thought. The thief did not steal except he first coveted that which was his neighbor's.

A wise Heavenly Father, to provide opportunity for the growth of human souls, has given unto every man the right to act for himself. To enable man to do that, the Lord has permitted opposition to the tree of life. So great is the power of evil in the world that it has been declared "that man is as prone to do evil as sparks are to fly upward."

Not unmindful of the power of this opposition, our Father has in every dispensation given to us, His children, the holy scriptures by His inspiration to make us wise in overcoming temptation through faith in Him. These scriptures are "profitable for doctrine, for reproof, for correction, for instruction in righteousness: That the man of God may be perfect, throughly furnished unto all good works." (2 Timothy 3:16-17.) So important in the Father's plan of salvation are the scriptures that incidents are recorded wherein God commanded the taking of life to obtain possession of precious writings without which His children would stumble and be blinded by the darkness of the world, but with which "they could be likened to the people of the scriptures for their profit and learning."

Upon the parents in the home and upon the Church there is placed a great responsibility to so teach the truths of the gospel that an anchor will be provided for each soul.

Without such an anchor, man would be as the "waves of the sea driven by the winds and tossed," driven by every wind of doctrine of uncertain origin that would muddle his thinking as to that which is wrong in the sight of God. We should be the best-educated people on the face of the earth if we heed the injunctions of the Lord.

If our youth are thus fortified, they will not be disturbed in their religious faith when they come in contact with false educational ideas that contradict the truths of the gospel. They are armed against the poison darts of slander and hypocrisy.

Young men of the armed services, if guided in their thinking by "rock bottom" truth, will not yield in an unguarded moment of weakness to a temptation that would be a moral blight throughout their lives. They will sense the fact that they are a part of eternity today, and that whether the end of their mortal lives shall be soon or late, the all-important question is, How did they die and why?

Young sweethearts approaching marriage, if guided by thoughts conveyed by gospel truth, would sanctify themselves by keeping the law of celestial marriage to gain eternal happiness. Political philosophies strange to the free agency of man as taught by the prophets would be vigorously opposed. Old age would approach the grave with the calm assurance and unafraid.

"Mark the perfect man, and behold the upright: for the end of that man is peace." (Psalm 37:37.)

"For as [a man] thinketh in his heart, so is he. . . ." (Proverbs 23:7.)

39

Concept of the Christlike Life

A YOUNG Latter-day Saint youth at Fort Lewis, Washington, asked, "What is your concept of the Christlike life? Please explain in detail the qualifications necessary for one to gain an exaltation in the kingdom of heaven."

I am intrigued by that question; and if the Spirit of the Lord is willing, I will address my response directly to that young man, because I believe that his question is the question that is being asked by many serious-minded Latter-day Saint youths today.

Young man, your question is not unique. It is not different. It is the same question that has been asked by the honest in heart ever since the world began. It is the question that was in the mind of Nicodemus, the master in Israel, when he came to the Savior by night and the Master, discerning the purpose of his coming, explained to him what was necessary for him to enter or even to see the kingdom of God.

It was the same question asked by the zealous Saul of Tarsus on that memorable occasion while on his way to Damascus when he was blinded by the light; he heard a voice speak out of heaven and was humbled as only one can be humbled in the presence of a great spiritual experience. In answer to the Lord's rebuke, the humble Saul asked, "Lord, what wilt thou have me to do?" (Acts 9:6.)

It was the cry of the sinful David who, amidst his pleadings and his sufferings, gained the knowledge of the course which he must pursue, in order that his soul would not be left in hell. It was the same thing the Jews asked on the day of Pentecost: "What must we do to be saved?" (Acts 2:37.)

To answer your question fully, and that of these others to which I have made reference, would require a full explanation of the plan of salvation given in the gospel of Jesus Christ. While yet in your youth, you have done well to ask that question, young man, to seek counsel as to your course in life, for every soul who lives has the possibility, as you have, of an exaltation in the celestial kingdom.

Let us turn first to some of our beliefs. In our first Article of Faith, we state: "We believe in God, the Eternal Father, and in His Son, Jesus Christ, and in the Holy Ghost." Our thirteenth Article of Faith states: "We believe in being honest, true, chaste, benevolent, virtuous, and in doing good to all men. . . ."

But I would have you now think of another of the Articles of Faith, because it has particular significance in the answer to your question: "We believe that through the Atonement of Christ, all mankind may be saved, by obedience to the laws and ordinances of the Gospel." (Article of Faith 3.)

A great philosopher has said the same thing in other

words when he declared: "Every one of us with help of God and within the limitations of human capability, himself makes his own disposition, his character, and his permanent condition." (Emil Souvestre.)

May I give you in answer to your question the example of two youths who, faced with the stern temptations of life, met those tests and came through nobly and victoriously, despite the odds against them. I give you these examples in order that you may learn and recognize three of the great dangers that confront youth today.

The first, an example of a young girl whom I met when I was asked to address a group of young girls a few years ago at the Lion House, where they were being shepherded under the direction of the great Young Women's Mutual Improvement Association. At the close of our meeting this lovely girl took me aside, and from her purse she unfolded a picture of a handsome young soldier. Underneath the picture was something about love, and his name signed. I asked, "Well, what does this mean?"

Tears were swimming in her eyes. She replied, "I met that young man here in an army camp. He was not a member of the Church. He was clean and fine, and he had the ideals I had longed for in a companion, all except one thing—he was not a member of the Church. And when he proposed marriage to me, I said, 'Only will I be married when I can be married in the house of the Lord, because love means something more than just a thing that pertains to this life. It is an eternal thing, and I want to be married in the temple.'"

Well, he reasoned with her, he pleaded with her, he scolded, and then he became angry; and finally, after repeated efforts to break down her religious objection to a marriage out of the temple, he left her. It was now time to go overseas, and she cried her heart out the night he left, thinking that maybe she had made a mistake because her heart had gone out to this fine young man.

During a long ocean voyage over to Australia, where he was to be stationed and from where he was to go into combat, he began to think about this young woman. He began to think that he had been a little hasty in his judgment about her religious convictions. Perhaps it was her religion that had made her the fine girl that she was. With that on his mind, he began to seek companionship with our Latter-day Saint men. He finally met a Latter-day Saint chaplain there and became associated with the Latter-day Saint boys of the camp and to study the gospel. On her birthday he had sent her this picture, and behind the picture was a slip of paper which proved to be a certificate evidencing the fact that he had been baptized a member of The Church of Jesus Christ of Latter-day Saints. In the letter that accompanied the picture, he had said, "I am preparing now to live worthy so that when I come home, I can be ordained an elder and together we can be married in the house of the Lord."

There, young man, is the first thing that you must think of if you would have an exaltation in the celestial kingdom. Marriage is eternal, and there was a young woman who realized the foundation on which she must build if she were to have a fulness of eternal happiness.

The second example is that of an impetuous young man. One morning he was confronted by his mother with a rather startling statement. His mother said to him, "Son, last night I had a premonition. I had a feeling that you are going to be faced with a grave temptation by a certain woman who is setting her cap for you. I warn you to be on guard."

This youth brushed it aside in his characteristic way, "Oh, Mother, you are silly; nothing is farther from the fact. She is a fine woman." And the mother replied, "Well, be careful, my son." Within thirty days from the time of his mother's warning, that youth stood face to face with the temptation about which his mother had been warned.

Youth, if you want to be guided by wisdom, stay close to your parents. Listen to the counsel of your father and your mother and lean heavily upon the experience of their lives, because they are entitled to inspiration in the rearing of their family. Young man, may I plead with you to keep yourself morally clean? Revere womanhood. May I remind you of what our youth repeated some years ago as a slogan in the MIA. It was a quotation from a portion of a message of the First Presidency particularly to servicemen in military service during some of these strenuous, difficult times through which you and others like you have lived. This is what the First Presidency wrote:

> How glorious and near to the angels is youth that is clean. This youth has joy unspeakable here and eternal happiness hereafter. Sexual purity is youth's most precious possession. It is the foundation of all righteousness. Better dead clean, than alive unclean.

Honor your name, young man. You have come of an illustrious family. Not to maintain the high standards which the Presidency have suggested would not only be a blight upon you, but a blight upon that great family name you bear, and a blight upon the Church for which your forefathers and ancestors sacrificed their lives to establish.

In the prayer at the dedication of the Idaho Falls Temple, the First Presidency said something of great importance to the girls about the purity of life. This is what the Presidency wrote in that inspired prayer:

> We pray for the daughters of Zion. May they be preserved in virtue, chastity, and purity of life, be blessed with vigorous bodies and minds, and with great faith. May they develop into true womanhood and receive choice companions under the new and everlasting covenant

for time and for all eternity in thy temples provided for this priceless privilege and purpose. (*Improvement Era,* October 1945, p. 563.)

Young man, should you find companionship with a beautiful young girl, will you remember that quotation, and will you take occasion during your courtship to read to her that most vital message from the prophets of the living God in our day to warn her also against one of the besetting sins of this world in which we live?

Young man, I would warn you, along with the others of your age, to be forewarned of the threats to your faith. I warn you against the man-made philosophies and the doctrines that would destroy that faith in God basic to exaltation in the celestial kingdom.

If you remember those examples, young man, and live worthy of your name, the marvelous rewards of our Heavenly Father will be yours. Listen to what the Lord promised:

> Verily, thus saith the Lord: It shall come to pass that every soul that forsaketh his sins and cometh unto me, and calleth on my name, and obeyeth my voice, and keepeth my commandments, shall see my face and shall know that I am. (D&C 93:1.)

And after you begin to understand that, then, young man, go to the 76th section of the Doctrine and Covenants, which in some respects is one of the most glorious visions that has ever been given to mortal man. Read from the 50th to the 70th verses of that great vision, and you will have understanding in better words that I can give you today.

My son, go and have your patriarchal blessing, for there under inspiration your patriarch will give you, as someone has said, "paragraphs from the book of your own possibilities."

And now after this brief conversation with you, my

young brother, may I close it by a little quotation from a great thinker who said this:

> The highest of all arts is the art of living well. Beyond the beauty of sculpture and painting, of poetry or music, is the beauty of a well-spent life. Here all can be artists. Every man can be a hero.
>
> Obedience to that Divine command, "Be ye therefore perfect, even as your Father which is in heaven is perfect" (Matthew 5:48), will ally man with God and will make of earth a paradise.

God bless you, my young friend. Keep on thinking the serious thoughts and asking those serious question, and in time, as you keep your eyes fixed upon the stars to guide you on and on and upward, you will reach your objective—an exaltation in the celestial kingdom of our Heavenly Father, which I pray for you and all youth of Zion, and all the world if that were possible, in the name of the Lord Jesus Christ.

40

Follow the Counsel of the Brethren

We pray for our Saints everywhere, pray that they will hold steadfast. But, some of the greatest of our enemies are those within our own ranks. It was the lament of the Master, as He witnessed one of those chosen men, whom under inspiration He chose as one of the Twelve, betray Him with a kiss and for a few paltry pieces of silver turn Him over to His enemies. Judas then stood by and, realizing the enormity of what he had done, took the only escape out to sacrifice himself. And Jesus could only explain that of the Twelve, meaning Judas, he had a devil.

When we see some of our own today doing similar things, some who have been recognized and honored in the past as teachers and leaders who later fall by the wayside, our hearts are made sore and tender. But sometimes we have to say just like the Master said, "The devil must have entered into them."

I always remember the word of the Lord when I hear

things said by those who are trying to tear down His work. The Lord has said:

> Wherefore, confound your enemies; call upon them to meet you both in public and in private; . . ."
>
> Wherefore, let them bring forth their strong reasons against the Lord.
>
> Verily, thus saith the Lord unto you—there is no weapon that is formed against you, shall prosper;
>
> And if any man lift his voice against you he shall be confounded in mine own due time.
>
> Wherefore, keep my commandments. . . . (D&C 71:7-11.)

What he is trying to have us understand is that he will take care of our enemies if we continue to keep the commandments. So, you Saints of the Most High God, when these things come, and they will come—this has been prophesied—you just say, "No weapon formed against the work of the Lord will ever prosper, but all glory and majesty of this work that the Lord gave will long be remembered after those who have tried to befoul their names and the name of the Church will be forgotten, and their works will follow after them."

We feel sorry for them when we see these things happen.

I am sure that many people come to conference with many questions on their minds, seeking to know the answers to some of the troublesome things about them, wanting to know what to do in this case or in that case, how to act under these circumstances. As we have listened to their questions, we have remembered what the Lord said here in the preface to the revelations. He said:

> And the arm of the Lord shall be revealed; and the day cometh that they who will not hear the voice of the Lord, neither the voice of his servants, neither give heed to the words of the prophets and apostles, shall be cut off from among the people.

What I the Lord have spoken, I have spoken, and I excuse not myself; and though the heavens and the earth pass away, my work shall not pass away, but shall all be fulfilled, whether by mine own voice or by the voice of my servants, it is the same. (D&C 1:14, 38.)

In another great revelation He explained something else that we would have the Saints remember. Where are you going to go to hear and find out what the Lord wants you to do today? The Lord declared again:

And this is the ensample unto them [he is talking now to those who are leaders of the Church], that they shall speak as they are moved upon by the Holy Ghost.

And whatsoever they shall speak when moved upon by the Holy Ghost shall be scripture, shall be the will of the Lord, shall be the mind of the Lord, shall be the voice of the Lord, and the power of God unto salvation. (D&C 68:3-4.)

To the Twelve shortly after the organization of the Church, He said something else that I would like you to remember before I draw one or two conclusions from what the Lord has told us. The Lord here is talking about the revelations that had been compiled up to that time in the Doctrine and Covenants.

First may I quote something that the Prophet Joseph Smith said about the Book of Mormon: "I told the brethren that the Book of Mormon was the most correct book on earth, and the keystone of our religion, and a man would get nearer to God by abiding by its precepts, than by any other book." (*Documentary History of the Church* 4:461.) And then he added, "If we didn't have the Book of Mormon and the revelations of God, we would have nothing." (*DHC* 2:52.)

It is that foundation upon which the church and kingdom of God is built in our day; and so with respect to these revelations the Lord said this, as may be found in the eighteenth section of the Doctrine and Covenants:

> And now I speak unto you, the Twelve—Behold my grace is sufficient for you; you must walk uprightly before me and sin not.
>
> And I, Jesus Christ, your Lord and your God, have spoken it.
>
> These words [meaning the revelations] are not of men nor of man, but of me; wherefore, you shall testify they are of me and not of man;
>
> For it is my voice which speaketh them unto you; for they are given by my Spirit unto you, and by my power you can read them one to another; and save it were by my power you could not have them. (D&C 18:31, 33-35.)

And then He added this: "Wherefore, you can testify [meaning that one stands in the pulpit and reads from these revelations] that you have heard my voice, and know my words." (D&C 18:36.) For, He said, ". . . whether by mine own voice or by the voice of my servants, it is the same." (D&C 1:38.)

In the eighty-eighth section of the Doctrine and Covenants, the Lord said:

> The earth rolls upon her wings, and the sun giveth his light by day, and the moon giveth her light by night and the stars also give their light, as they roll upon their wings in their glory, in the midst of the power of God.
>
> Unto what shall I liken these kingdoms, that ye may understand?
>
> Behold, all these are kingdoms, and any man who hath seen any of the least of these hath seen God moving in his majesty and power. (D&C 88:45-47.)

Likewise I say to you, as I stand with you and see the moving hand of the Lord in the affairs of the nations of the world today, we are seeing the signs of our times as foretold by the prophets and by the Master Himself, and we see what is happening and the things transpiring before us in our day. In the Church, we have been witnessing some of the most dramatic things, and I can testify that you are seeing what the Lord is revealing for the needs of this people today.

May I paraphrase what the Lord has said in this great revelation from which I have quoted: any man who has seen any of the least of these happenings among us today, has seen God today moving in His majesty and in His power. Let us make no mistake about that.

Where else can you go for guidance? Where is there safety in the world today? Safety can't be won by tanks and guns and the airplanes and atomic bombs. There is only one place of safety and that is within the realm of the power of Almighty God that He gives to those who keep His commandments and listen to His voice, as He speaks through the channels that He has ordained for that purpose.

In the answer that He gave to His disciples, when He told them that He was coming again, He explained some important things to them. The disciples asked Him, ". . . Tell us, when shall these things be and the end of the world or the destruction of the wicked, which is the end of the world?" (See Matthew 24:3.) In their question, you have the definition of what it means to say "the end of the world."

And then He gave to His disciples what we read in the twenty-fourth chapter of the Book of Matthew, what may be better understood from the Inspired Version, which is found in the Pearl of Great Price. He said, when the fig tree "begins to put forth leaves, you know that summer is nigh at hand." (Joseph Smith 1:39.)

He gave them certain signs by which they might know that His coming was nigh, even at their very doors. There will be great tribulation upon the Jews and upon the inhabitants of Jerusalem, "such as was not before sent upon Israel, of God, since the beginning of their kingdom until this time; no, nor ever shall be sent again upon Israel." (Joseph Smith 1:18.)

And except those days should be shortened, there should none of their flesh be saved; but for the elect's sake, according to the covenant, those days shall be shortened.

Behold, these things I have spoken unto you concerning the Jews; and again, after the tribulations of those days which shall come upon Jerusalem, if any man shall say unto you, Lo, here is Christ, or there, believe him not;

For in those days there shall also arise false Christs, and false prophets, and shall show great signs and wonders, insomuch, that, if possible, they shall deceive the very elect, who are the elect according to the covenant. [That means the members of this Church.]

Wherefore, if they shall say unto you: Behold, he is in the desert; go not forth; Behold, he is in the secret chambers; believe it not;

For as the light of the morning cometh out of the east and shineth even unto the west, . . . so shall also the coming of the Son of Man be. (Joseph Smith 1:20-22, 25-26.)

Then He speaks of the wars that shall come:

. . . for nations shall rise against nation, and kingdom against kingdom; there shall be famines, and pestilences, and earthquakes, in divers places.

And again, because iniquity shall abound, the love of many shall wax cold; but he that shall not be overcome, the same shall be saved.

And, again, this Gospel of the Kingdom shall be preached in all the world, for a witness unto all nations, and then shall the end come, or the destruction of the wicked.

And immediately after the tribulation of those days, the sun shall be darkened, and the moon shall not give her light, and the stars shall fall from heaven, and the powers of heaven shall be shaken.

Verily, I say unto you, this generation, in which these things shall be shown forth, shall not pass away until all I have told you shall be fulfilled.

But of that day, and hour, no one knoweth; no, not the angels of God in heaven, but my Father only.

But as it was in the days of Noah, so it shall be also at the coming of the Son of Man;

For it shall be with them, as it was in the days which were before the flood; for until the day that Noah entered into the ark they were eating and drinking, marrying and giving in marriage;

And knew not until the flood came, and took them all away; so shall also the coming of the Son of Man be.

Then shall be fulfilled that which is written, that in the last days, two shall be in the field, the one shall be taken, and the other left;

Two shall be grinding at the mill, the one shall be taken, and the other left;

And what I say unto one, I say unto all men; watch, therefore, for you know not at what hour your Lord doth come.

Therefore be ye also ready, for in such an hour as ye think not, the Son of Man cometh. (Joseph Smith 1:29-31, 33-34, 40-46.)

Brothers and sisters, this is the day the Lord is speaking of. You see the signs are here. Be ye therefore ready.

Let us not turn a deaf ear now, but listen to the Brethren as the words that have come from the Lord, inspired of Him, and we will be safe on Zion's hill, until all that the Lord has for His children shall have been accomplished.

I am grateful for strong men like President Tanner and President Romney and the Twelve and all the General Authorities, who are united more so than I have ever experienced before during my lifetime. The General Authorities are united and working together and are speaking with one voice to the world.

Follow the Brethren; listen to the Brethren. I bear you my witness as one whom the Lord has brought to this place. I thank the Lord that I may have passed some of the tests, but maybe there will have to be more before I shall have been polished to do all that the Lord would have me do.

Sometimes when the veil has been very thin, I have thought that if the struggle had been still greater, maybe then there would have been no veil. I stand by, not asking for anything more than the Lord wants to give me, but I know that He is up there and He is guiding and directing.

I extend my blessings to you wonderful Saints. Go back to your homes and take the love of the General

Authorities to your people. We extend to those who are not members of the Church the hand of fellowship. May we reach out to those who have lost their sense of direction and, before it is too late, try to win them back into the fold; because they are all God's children, and He wants us to save all of them.

Peace be with you, not the peace that comes from the legislation in the halls of congress, but the peace that comes in the way that the Master said, by overcoming all the things of the world. That God may help us so to understand and may you know that I know with a certainty that defies all doubt that this is His work, that He is guiding us and directing us today, has done in every dispensation of the gospel, I say with all the humility of my soul, in the name of the Lord, Jesus Christ. Amen.

APPENDIX

Sources of the selected sermons and writings of President Harold B. Lee in this volume are as follows:

Chapter	Source
1	Address delivered at the 143rd Semiannual General Conference, October 5, 1973; in *Ensign*, January 1974, pp. 2-8.
2	Address delivered at the 138th Semiannual General Conference, October 1968; in *Improvement Era*, December 1968, pp. 70-73.
3	Lesson from M Man and Gleaner Manual, Summer 1950, Section IV, pp. 11-18.
4	*Church News*, December 29, 1956, pp. 2, 10.
5	"Church of the Air" Broadcast, CBS Radio Network, April 3, 1955.
6	Address delivered to seminary and institute teachers, Brigham Young University, June 26, 1962.
7	Lesson from M Man and Gleaner Manual, Summer 1950, Section IV, pp. 3-11.
8	Address delivered at the 141st Semiannual General Conference, October 1971; in *Ensign*, December 1971, pp. 28-32.
9	*New Era*, February 1971, pp. 2-4.
10	Address delivered at the 116th Semiannual General Conference, October 1946; in *Improvement Era*, November 1946, pp. 702, 759-60.
11	*Improvement Era*, November 1965, pp. 964-65.
12	Address to Brigham Young University student body, October 2, 1956.
13	Address delivered at the 123rd Annual General Conference, April 1953; in *Improvement Era*, May 1953, pp. 407-408.
14	Address delivered to the Brigham Young University student body, October 15, 1952.
15	Address delivered to seminary and institute teachers, Brigham Young University, July 8, 1964.

16 Address delivered at the Solemn Assembly at the 142nd Semiannual General Conference, October 6, 1972; in *Ensign*, January 1973, pp. 23-25.

17 Address delivered at funeral services for President David O. McKay in the Salt Lake Tabernacle, January 22, 1970; in *Improvement Era*, February 1970, pp. 93-95.

18 Address delivered at the 143rd Annual General Conference, April 1973; in *Ensign,* July 1973, p. 2.

19 *Instructor*, August 1959, pp. 250-51.

20 Address delivered at the 132nd Annual General Conference, April 1962; in *Improvement Era*, June 1962, pp. 418-21.

21 *Instructor*, June 1963, pp. 220-24.

22 *Ensign*, July 1971, pp. 2-3.

23 *Relief Society Magazine*, February 1943, pp. 84-87.

24 Address delivered at the 140th Semiannual General Conference, October 1970; in *Improvement Era*, December 1970, pp. 28-30.

25 Address delivered at MIA June Conference, June 17, 1966; in *Improvement Era*, October 1966, pp. 862ff.

26 Address delivered at the Mexico City Area General Conference, Melchizedek Priesthood session, August 26, 1972.

27 Address delivered at a mission presidents' seminar, Sunday, July 2, 1961.

28 Address delivered at the 123rd Semiannual General Conference, October 1953; in *Improvement Era*, December 1953, pp. 937-38.

29 Address delivered at the 121st Semiannual General Conference, October 1941; in *Liahona*, January 13, 1942, pp. 1ff.

30 Address delivered at the 134th Annual General Conference, April 4, 1964; in *Improvement Era*, June 1964, pp. 469-71.

31 Address delivered at the general priesthood meeting of the 137th Semiannual General Conference, September 30, 1967; in *Improvement Era*, January 1968, pp. 26-31.

32 Churchwide youth fireside talk, Sunday, January 8, 1961; in *Church News*, January 14, 1961, pp. 14, 16.

33 *Instructor,* June 1955.

34 Lesson in the Junior M Man and Junior Gleaner Manual, 1950, pp. 3-28.

35 Lesson in the M Man and Gleaner Manual, Summer 1950, Section IV, pp. 18-25.

36 Address delivered at the 141st Annual General Conference, April 1971; in *Ensign*, June 1971, pp. 5-10.

37 Address delivered at the 126th Annual General Conference, April 1956; in *Improvement Era*, May 1956, pp. 431-33.

38 *Church News*, November 6, 1943, p. 4.

39 Address delivered at the 124th Annual General Conference, April 1954; in *Improvement Era*, June 1954, pp. 408-10.

40 Address delivered at the closing session of the 143rd Semi-annual General Conference, October 1973; in *Ensign*, January 1974, pp. 125-29.

INDEX

Aaron, 7, 155
Aaronic Priesthood (see Priesthood)
Abraham, 7, 9, 17, 175, 269
Abundant life, 96-103, 278
Action, faith in, 37
Adam, 50, 53, 54, 126, 270; and Eve, 50, 69, 363
Administration to sick man, 292-93
Adultery, 332
Advancement in Church, 5
Agrippa, King, 30-31, 290-91
Alberta Temple, young people at, 94-95
Alcohol, educator's report on evils of, 108
Alcoholics Anonymous, 262, 368
Alma, 55, 58-59, 62, 184, 194, 202
Alma the younger, 21
American way of life, 97
Ammon, 174
Amos, prophet, 109, 158, 160
Amulek, 364
Ananias, 100, 209
Antioch, 30, 36
Apollo 13, 230, 233
Apostasy, 125, 272
Apostate group, woman who belonged to, 127-28
Apostles, 41, 42, 46, 64-65; at time of Christ, 213
"Aquarius," 230-31, 237, 238
Arch-deceivers, 86
Area general conference, Manchester, England, 84, 88; Mexico City, 166
Arrogance, 209
Articles of Faith, 160, 173, 320-23, 373
Ascension of Christ, 30
Assistant to the Council of the Twelve, 296, 300, 305
Astronomy, 74
Astronauts, flight of, 230-31, 237
Atheistic teacher, story about, 45
Atonement of Christ, 88, 211, 235, 342
Australia, 201, 203
Authority in the Church, 81, 156, 315, 316-17
Auxiliary workers, responsibilities of, 189, 294
Awareness of needs, 208

Bailey, Temple, 367
Ballard, Melvin J., 53, 280
Banker in New York, 150
Baptism, 41-42, 49-50, 51, 52, 53-54, 60, 116, 128, 184, 200-201, 210, 221, 236, 270, 311, 316-17
Barker, James L., 322-23
Battle of life, 327-29
Beatitudes, 343-47
Belief, 192-93
Benjamin, King, 55, 62, 185, 200, 341
Birth into church, 48 (see also Baptism)
Bishop, talk of, 291
Blessings, 23, 113-14, 117, 241-47
Book of Mormon, 50-51, 72, 381
Born again, meaning of, 54, 116
Breastplate of armor, 330, 332-33
Brigham Young University, 133, 274-75
Brotherhood, 17-18, 223-29
Brotherhoods (organizations), 224, 267
Buoys in sea, story about, 44, 309
Burdens of life, 184
Business ventures of priesthood quorums, 263-64

Cain, 363
Calling and election made sure, 177
Callis, Charles A., 361
Carthage Jail, 153
Catholic exhibit at World's Fair, 149-50; priest, conversion of, 92-93
Celestial glory, 52; marriage, 52, 332, 371, 374-75
Central America, 166
Character, 3
Charity, 224, 228
Charm, indefinable quality of, 6
Charted course, 44, 309
Chastity, 3, 219, 331-32, 376-77
Children, be like, 340-41; of Israel, 310; of the covenant, 336; teach correct principles to, 108-109; woman who can't be bothered with, 218
Christ (see Jesus Christ)
Christian, meaning of, 35-38
Christlike living, 207, 224, 372-78
Christian Century article, 287
Church, at time of Savior, 40, 320-23; founded on revelation, 129-30; growth of early, 43; name of, 314; need for, 81, 83; of the Firstborn, 344; on earth before birth of Savior, 268-69; purpose of, 227; signs of true, 311-19
City of Holiness (City of Enoch), 23
Clark, J. Reuben, Jr., 133-34, 138, 160-61, 216, 253
Cleanliness, moral, 376
Coat of armor, 324-39
Commandments of God, 8, 10, 24, 121, 207, 215-16, 218, 225, 242, 246, 290, 377, 380

Conference talks, importance of, 183, 381-82
Conferences, quarterly, 302, 307-308
Confirmation, 56 (see also Holy Ghost, gift of)
Conscience, peace of, 211
Consecration, 279
Conversion to the gospel, 50, 61-62, 90-95, 276, 311-12, 340-41, 354-55, 375
Coolidge, Calvin, 362
Cornelius, 49
Correct principles, teaching, 85, 108-109
Correlation program, 294-310
Council of gods, 234-35
Counsel of brethren, following, 379-86
Covenant, everlasting, 233
Covenants, 55, 199-200
Coveting, 113, 335-36
Cowdery, Oliver, 48-49, 138, 201
Cowley, Matthew, 262
Crucifixion of Savior, 140
Cyprian, 57, 109, 354

Damascus, 30, 100, 135
Daniel, 138
David, 373
Death, 8-9, 13, 14, 15, 33, 128, 293
Debt, 284
Decalogue (see Ten Commandments)
Decency, standards of, 3, 12
Decisions, making, 102-103
Democracy, Church is not, 151-52
Depew, Chauncey, 198
Desire to learn truth, 75
Devil (see Satan)
Diligence, in searching to know doctrines, 198
Discipleship, 36
Disobedience of children, 5-6; to God's commandments, 235
Disorder, 5
Dispensation of fulness of times, 273, 322
Divine authority, 81
Divine Church, The, 322
Divinity of Jesus Christ, 27, 40
Divorce, couple who sought, 112-13
Duties, instruction in, 201

Earthquake in Peru, 87
Ecclesiastical History by Mosheim, 43, 287-88
Economic philosophy of abundant life, 96
Education, 73, 77, 216
Educational ideas, false, 18
Educational System, Church, 83
Eisenhower, Dwight D., 357
Elijah, 161
Eloheim, 234
Emerson, Ralph Waldo, 156
Emmaus, Christ appears to men at, 29
End of world, signs of, 85, 383-85
Enemies from within, 21
Enoch, 22, 161, 271
Enos, 62, 139, 199, 209, 245-46
Ephesian saints, 40-41
Ephraim, record of, 71-72
Eternal life, 14, 70, 235, 242, 313, 366; marriage, 332; plan of God, 13, 233-36; truth, conversion to, 92
Ether, 118
Evil forces, 19, 20, 328-29
Exaltation, 378
Excommunication, 119-20, 135-37
Experimentation, 76
Ezekiel, 71

Faith, 3, 32, 33, 37, 44, 54, 55, 75, 188, 192-93, 194, 211, 245, 315-16, 337-38, 358
Fall of man, 365
False Christs and prophets, 86, 313; teachings, 355; values, 18
Family, rebellion in, 5
Family home evening, 84, 85, 177, 298-99
Fasting, 23-24
Father dying of incurable disease, 239
Father of spirits, 7
Father's blessing, 117
Fayette, New York, 166
Fear, 333
Feet shod as armor, 330, 331
Fellowshiping, 228
First Council of the Seventy, 296
First Presidency, requisites for establishment of, 165; organization of, 166
Foreordination, 9, 11, 175
Forgiveness, 211
Fornication, 332
Fort Lewis, Washington, 372
Fraternal lodges, 267
Free agency, 9, 11, 219-20, 235
Freedoms, 107
Fruits of self-respect, 5; of gospel, 286-93
Fulness of gospel, 50-51

Galilee, Sea of, 30
Garden of Eden, 50, 151

INDEX

Gates of hell, 127, 131
Gathering of Zion, 278
Genealogy, 296
Gifts (fruits) of gospel, 289
Girdle about your loins, 330-31
Girl who succumbed to temptations, 112
Glory promised for keeping commandments, 8, 237, 269
God, loss of contact with, 5; reverence for, 27; getting to know, 26-34 (see also Jesus Christ)
Gold plates, 31
Gospel, fulness of, 50-51
Gospel plan, 269-70 (see also Salvation, plan of)
Government of God, 151-52, 165, 271-72 (see also Priesthood)
Grace of God, 213, 236
Grant, Heber J., 62-63, 153, 168, 267
Great Britain, 84, 88
Growth of Church, 85, 287, 303-305
Guideposts in water in Sweden, 44, 309

Happiness, 38
Hate, 113
Healings, 314
"Hear, O Men, the Proclamation," 24
Hearing word of the Lord, 134
Heart, understanding with, 92, 93
Helam, baptism of, 55
Helaman, 118
Helmet of armor, 330
Herlzterg, Rabbi Arthur, 349
Herod, 30
Herschel, John Frederick William, 4
Hewett, Ernest, 84
High Priesthood, heads of, 272 (see also Priesthood)
High priests, ordination of, 259
Highway sign of shortest highway, 360-61
Hill Cumorah, 195
Holy Ghost, gift of, 12, 32, 41-42, 43, 48, 51, 56, 57, 94-95, 110-11, 116, 118, 141, 193, 216, 317 (see also Spirit)
Holy places, disciples stand in, 22, 24-25, 87-88
Holy Spirit of Promise, 52
Home industry, 285
Home Primaries, study courses, 83
Home teaching, 296, 297-98
Honesty, 3, 106-107, 113, 199, 369-71
"Hosanna shout," 39, 46
Humility, 32-33, 63, 344
Hunger and thirst after righteousness, 344-45
Huntsville, Utah, 176
Hyde, Orson, 169
Hypocrites, 36

"I Am a Child of God," 14
Idaho Falls Temple, 376
Ignorance of saving principles, 76, 198
Images, worshiping, 10
Immaculate conception, 35
Immodesty, 332
Immorality, 331-32
India, prince of, 26
Inge, Dean, 342
Inspiration, how to receive, 203 (see also Holy Ghost)
Inspired translation of Matthew 24, 190
Institutes and seminaries, 83
Intellect, 334-35
Intellectualism, 353-54
Interpretation of tongues, 314
Iron rod, 349-59
Isaiah, 4, 23
Israel (Jacob), 11
Ivins, Anthony W., 284

Jacob, 355; lineage of, 10-11
Jacobsen, Theodore M., 150
James, apostle, 17
Jared, brother of, 31, 118, 242-44
Jeremiah, 9, 139, 175
Jerusalem, 22, 30, 44, 45
Jesus Christ, getting to know, 17-25; what he would have us do, 26-34; man in image of, 28; descriptions of, 28-29; appears to disciples after crucifixion, 29-30; ascension of, 30; appears to Joseph Smith, 31; followers of are Christians, 36-38; greeted by hosannas, 39-40, 46; ministry of, 40; chooses apostles, 41; ordains disciples, 42; builds church on rock of revelation, 45; triumphs over world, 45-46; replies to Nicodemus's query, 47; reveals birth of Spirit, 48-49; tried before Pilate, 69; defines truth, 70; Church of, teaches truth, 72; crucifixion of, 87; is Son of God, 90-91; purpose of life of, 98; light of, 93, 106, 116; explains rock of revelation, 125-26; sacrifice of, 126; appears to ancient and present-day prophets, 138; teaches about Holy Ghost, 140; the living, 150; is spirit of prophecy,

154; is leading Church today, 190; describes how to receive Spirit of truth, 194-95; farewell sermon of to Nephites, 212; gives parable of good Samaritan, 226; describes last days, 232, 383-85; premortal role of defined, 234-35; atonement of, 235-36; taught plan of salvation to Nephites, 236-37; is chief cornerstone of Church, 238-39; organizes Church on earth, 268-76; describes true conversion, 354-55; describes how to be saved, 366-67
Job, 6, 179
John the apostle, 93, 254
John the Baptist, 41, 138
John the Beloved, 28, 186
John the Revelator, 161, 235
Johnston's Army, 110
Joseph, stick or record of, 71-72
"Joseph Smith's First Prayer," 275
Joshua, 190
Joy, 100, 342
Judah, record of, 71-72
Judas, 21, 64, 379
Justice, 224
Justify, definition of, 51
Juvenile delinquency, 177

Keys of kingdom of God, 171-72, 174, 273-74, 301, 315; of priesthood, 128
Keystone of religion, Book of Mormon is, 381
Kimball, Heber C., 20
Kindergarten teacher, 206
King Agrippa, 30-31, 290-91
King Benjamin, 55, 62, 185, 200, 341
Kingdom of God, membership in, 37; definition of, 161
Knowledge, 76, 195

Lamanite Saints in Mexico, 166
Lame man healed by Peter and James, 254
Laws, obedience to, 241-42
Leadership, need for, 82; training, 85; people in positions of, 102; mustn't be wavering, 105; qualities of, 111; spiritual power needed in, 201; training of by Regional Representatives, 306-307; those who accept positions of, 356
Learning, 210, 357-58
Lee, Freda Joan, 187
Lehi's vision, 290, 350-51
Leicester Stake, 84
Letter from excommunicated man, 120-21
Liberals in Church, 353
Liberty, 235
Liberty Jail, 310
Lift others up, 186
Light, for Jaredites' ship, 243-44; of Christ, 93, 106, 115 (see also Holy Ghost); of gospel, 20; of truth, 362
Lincoln, Abraham, 353
Lion House, 271, 374
Listening to word of God, 135
Live as we preach, 202
Living prophets, 149-64
Lodges, fraternal, 267
Los Angeles Temple, 189
Love, of self, 5; sacred, 113; of God, 189; in teaching, 206-207; greatest commandment is, 225
Lowell, James Russell, 329, 364
Lucifer (see Satan)
Lust, antithetical to love, 113
Lyman, Amasa, 301

MacDougall, psychologist, 6, 12
Maeser, Karl G., 117, 216
Magnetic action, 135
Malachi, 23
Manchester, England, 84
Marriage, 52, 331-32, 371, 374-75
Martha, Savior's words to, 15-16
Martyrdom of Joseph Smith, 153
Martyrs, 43, 347
Mary, mother of Jesus, 35
Mary Magdalene, 29
Mason, and priesthood, 266-67
Material wealth, 97
Matthew 24, inspired translation of, 190, 383
McAllister, G. Stanley, 149-50
McKay, David O., 153, 168, 189, 204, 256, 259, 262, 293, 297, 299; tribute to, 173-82
McKay, Emma Ray, 178
Meads, Frank S., 287
Meekness, 346
Melchizedek Priesthood (see Priesthood)
Membership of Church, 303-305
Mercy, 346
Messianic power, 39
Methodist minister, experience with, 64-65
Mexico, area general conference in, 166; experience with pottery makers in, 114

Micah, 22
Military life, 105-106
Millennial Star, 151
Millikan, Dr. Robert A., 75
Mission Control in Houston, 230
Mission Representatives, 183, 189
Missions, number of, 305
Missionary work, 79-80, 87, 127-28, 198, 203, 214-15, 296, 300, 311-12
Modesty, 332
Monument to pioneers, 27
Moore, George, 356, 357
Moral teachings, 215
Morality, 3, 6, 177, 332, 336, 376-77
Mormon, 106, 118, 361-62
Moroni, 49, 106, 115
Morris, George Q., 262
Mortality, 8
Moses, 7, 9, 10, 12, 63, 138,155, 161, 270, 310, 334
Mosheim, Dr. J. L. von, 43, 277-78
Mosiah, on seer and revelator, 155
Mosiah, sons of, 21, 202
Mother's warning to son, 375-76
Mount of Transfiguration, 340
Mount Olivet, 29-30
Mount Vernon, 356
Mount Zion, 22
Mourn, meaning of, 344
Mutual Improvement Association, 376

Name of Church, 314
Napoleon I, 268
Natural man, 73, 77-78
Nauvoo, Illinois, 153
Nazarene, 39
Negro, policy on, 159
Neighbor, who is, 226
Nephi, 118, 139-40
Nephites, three, 162
New York World's Fair, 149-50
Newton, Sir Isaac, 74
Niagara Falls, rapids of, 237-38
Nicodemus, 47, 98, 210, 236, 271, 351, 372
Nielsen, Dr. Howard, 304
No Man Knows My History, 164
North Star, 251

Obedience, 10, 24, 227, 235, 236, 241, 338-39
Obscenity, 332
Officers of church, 130
Opposition in all things, need for, 364, 370
Ordination to act in God's name, 42, 202
Ordinances, gospel, 271
Organization of the Church, 268-76
Organized religion, 80

Pain and suffering, 239, 291-92
Parables, 91, 98
Parents, disobedience to, 5
Partridge, Edward, 117, 358
Passion Week, 134
Patmos, isle of, 235
Patriarch, letter from, 202
Patriarchal blessing, 116-17, 201-202, 377
Paul, Apostle, 7, 10, 11, 19, 30-31, 40, 44, 46, 54, 58, 65, 83, 98, 100-101, 104-105, 135, 193, 208-209, 270, 290, 312, 329-30, 373
Payroll, men who falsified, 106-107
Peace of conscience, 211
Penitentiary, road to, 360-61
Pentecost, day of, 43, 288, 373
Perfection, 210
Permissiveness, 3
Persecution of Church, 197, 315; for righteousness' sake, 347
Peru, earthquake in, 87
Peter, 29, 30, 40, 45, 90-91, 99, 125, 129, 149, 186, 194, 254
Petersen, Elmer G., 104
Pharisee, 35, 47
Philosophies of world, 377
Philosophy, 82, 198
Physical senses, 73
Pieta, 150
Pikes Peak, 74
Pilate, 69, 70
Pioneer Stake, 137
Pioneers, 27
Plane, ulcer attack on, 187
Political campaign slogans, 96-97
Poor in spirit, 343-44
Pottery making, story about, 114
Pratt, Parley P., 142, 151-52
Prayer, 33, 75, 137, 198, 215, 246, 334; of English weaver, 6
Premortal world, 7, 11, 175, 234-35
Preparation for last days, 79-89
Preparedness, 333
"Present Crisis, The," 329, 364
Presidency, First, requisites in establishment of, 165; organization of, 166
President of Church, can teach new doctrine, 109-110; descriptions of, 167-79
Pride, 82
Priesthood, oath and covenant of, 52;

watchmen, 88; keys of, 128-29, 252; offices of, 130, 252, 323; is authority of God, 251-52, 315; line of authority of, 252; quorums of, 252-53, 259, 260, 261; exercised on principles of righteousness, 253-55; how to magnify, 255-56; promises of Lord to, 256; ordination to, 258-61; reactivation of members of, 262; quorums not to go into business ventures, 263-64; to help in welfare program, 264-66, 281-82; new converts in, 266; order of, 271; instructions to regarding Church correlation program, 297-98; home teachers, 298; executive committees, 298
Priesthood Committee, 294, 295
Primary Association, 14, 15, 83, 192
Primitive church, 320-23
Prince of India, 26
Prince of this world (Satan), 19
Private ownership, 279
"Proclamation" of Parley P. Pratt, 151-52
Promised land, 10
Promises of Lord, 199
"Pronouncement by Catholic Bishops on Church and Social Welfare," 224
Prophecies of last days, 21, 231-33
Prophecy, sure word of, 32; spirit of, 154-55; believe in, 314
Prophet, seer, and revelator, definitions of, 155, 174
Prophets of God, 22, 43, 109-110, 154, 169, 204
Prosperity, 82
Pure in heart, 23, 345
Purity, moral, 376-77

Quarterly conferences, stake, 302, 307-308
Quorum of the Twelve, 165
Quorums, organizations, 259-61 (see also Priesthood)

Rachel, 228
Radio, analogy with revelation, 137
Radio City Music Hall, plaque at, 239-40
Rebellion, 5
Record in heaven, 53
Regional Representatives of the Twelve, 183, 189, 306-307, 308
Relevance, 80
Relief Society, 292
Religion, search for, 349-50
Religious education, 83
Repentance, 51, 54, 55, 109, 118, 122, 139, 184-85, 210, 212, 220-21, 236, 316, 333
Responsibilities of Church membership, 77
Resurrection, 13, 29, 30
Revelation, rock of, 45, 125-31; through Holy Ghost, 56, 64; Peter's, 90-91; men who wanted to do away with, 132; continuous in our day, 133, 144; story about J. Reuben Clark, Jr., and, 133-34; analogy of radio to, 137; was Welfare Program?, 138; received by power of Holy Ghost, 140; Joseph F. Smith on, 141, 143; Parley P. Pratt on, 142, 143; testimony of, 144; need for, described by Ralph Waldo Emerson, 156-57; is foundation of our religion, 157; question about Negro and, 159; found in general conference talks, 159-60, 183; about end of world, 160; Brigham Young statement on, 163; Article of Faith on, 173; by Holy Ghost for testimony, 194-95; sign of true church, 314; for our time found in talks of Brethren, 381-83
Revelator, 153, 155
Reverence for God, 27
Richards, Franklin D., 292
Riches, 344
Rigdon, Sidney, 117, 258, 285, 301
Righteousness, 219, 318, 332-33, 347
Roberts, B. H., 357
Rocky Mountains, 20
Rod of iron, example of, 135
Romans, Paul's writings to, 83
Romney, Marion G., 170, 184, 188, 211, 385
Rony, George, 83
Roses need cultivating, 111
Royal Household, member of, 256

Sabbath Day, 23, 215, 217, 334, 345
Sacrament meeting attendance, 305-306
Sacrifice, 77, 101, 218
Sadducee, 35
Saints, disciples of Christ called, 341
Saipan, marine on, 344
Salt Lake Temple, spires on, 251
Salvation, plan of, 13, 18, 50, 53, 54, 56, 76, 99, 126, 208-216, 233-40, 334, 357-58

Samaritan, parable of, 226
Sarnoff, David, 21
Satan, 8, 12, 19, 20, 64, 70-71, 138, 161, 185, 218, 328-29, 363, 379
Saul of Tarsus, 30, 100, 135, 208, 373 (see also Paul, Apostle)
Schiller, Johanne von, 5
Scholastic studies, 73
Science, 74, 353-54
Scriptures, 71, 315, 370, 381
Sea of Tiberias, 29
Seer, 153, 155, 174
Second coming of Jesus, 71-72, 85-86, 190
Second estate, 269
Self-mastery, 346
Self-respect, 1-16
Seminaries and institutes, 83
Sermon on the Mount, 13, 83, 210, 334, 342
Service to others, 101, 218; in kingdom of God, 202
Servicemen, 344, 371, 372, 374-75
Seventies ordained high priests, 152; duties of, 299
Shaw, George Bernard, 15
Shiblon, 209
Shield of faith, 336-37
Ships constructed by brother of Jared, 242-44
Signs of our times, 382
Signs of true church, 311-19
Sin, overcoming, 112, 185, 236; evils of, 119-20, 121, 217-22, 361-68
"Sinners Anonymous," 212
Sjodahl, Dr. J. M., 365
Slogans, political campaign, 96-97
Smiles, Samuel, 5
Smith, George Albert, 153, 164, 168
Smith, Joseph, on foreordination, 7; on reality of God, 28; sees Father and Son, 31; describes mission of Church, 37; explains baptism of and gift of Spirit to Cornelius, 49-50; on revelation and salvation, 56; describes gifts and effects of Holy Ghost, 57, 58, 60-61; describes spirit of revelation, 58, on salvation, 99; on refining process, 115, 170; on plan of salvation, 126; on baptism of little children, 128; receives revelation on importance of revelation, 129; comforted by the Lord, 130-31; sees Father and Son, 138; on Holy Ghost as revelator, 140, 141, 154; on theocracy, 151; martyrdom of, 153; defines kingdom of God, 161; on when prophet is a prophet, 162, 175; name of shall never die, 164; tribute paid to, 167; on power for those close to the Lord, 171; on building testimony, 195; on priesthood, 272; on dispensation of fulness of times, 273; defines kingdom of God, 274, 321; on responsibilities of Twelve, 301; on doing duty, 310; cries out to Lord in suffering, 367-68; says Book of Mormon is most correct book, 381
Smith, Joseph F., 56, 57, 141, 143, 153, 167, 168, 192, 260, 295-96, 353
Smith, Joseph Fielding, 161, 166-67, 168-69, 266, 303
Snow, Lorenzo, 60, 153, 167-68, 283
Social security, 278
Society, evils in, 231
Solemn assembly, 166
South Dakota, 311
Souvestre, Emil, 374
Spirit, father of, 7; in premortal world, 7-8; definition of, 8; created in premortality, 9-10; born of, 47-65; loss of, 63, 64; of Lord, live to receive, 110-11; when withdrawn from men, 118; personal, 141-43; teach by, 202; converts, 216
Spirit world, 28, 143
Spiritual things, 74-75; truth, 75; knowledge, 75-76; guidance, need for, 80
Spiritually needy, 210
Stake conferences, 311
Stakes, at time of John Taylor, 302; projected number by 1985, 304-305
Stand in holy places, 87-88, 183-91, 233
Standard church works, 109-110, 162, 202
Standards, be true to, 227
Stephen, stoning of, 100
Stewardship, 279
Stick of Judah and Joseph, 71-72
Stockholm, Sweden, 44, 309
Strang, James J., 285
Strengthen thy brethren, 93, 95
Student organizations, 84
Student whose teacher was atheist, story about, 45
Succession in the Presidency, 153
Suicide among students, 12
Sunday Schools, 85
Supernatural, belief in, 77
Sure word of prophecy, 32

Tanner, N. Eldon, 170, 188, 385
Taverns, evils of, 365
Taylor, John, 153, 157, 158, 159, 160, 167, 300, 302
Teach by the Spirit, 202, 216
Teacher, atheistic, story about, 45
Teaching, 82, 186-87, 192, 206-207
Temple building, 176; ordinances, 117, 128
Temptation, overcoming, 112, 121, 122, 219, 365, 376
Ten Commandments, 107, 207, 338, 369-70
Testimony, 17, 32-34, 46, 56, 62-63, 76, 91-93, 101, 109, 139, 144, 187, 192-96, 317-18
Theocracy, Church is, 151-52
Theophany, definition of, 138, 139
"This Is Our Place," 84
Thomas, 29, 32
Three Degrees of Glory, 53
Three Nephites, 162
Three witnesses to Book of Mormon, 48
Tiberius, Sea of, 29
Tithing, 23, 215
Tobacco problem, people with, 213-14
Tomb of Jesus Christ, 29
Tongues, speaking in, 61; gift of, 313
Transfiguration, 138
Transgression, 122
Translated being, 161
Tree of life, 351; of knowledge of good and evil, 364
Trials of life, 114
Trumpet calls, 105-106
Truth, 69-78, 106, 192-93, 214, 331
Twelve apostles, instruction to, 299

Uncleanliness incompatible with Spirit, 214
Underprivileged people, helping, 85
United Order, 279, 280-81
Universal brotherhood, 225
"Universal Church," 311
University professor, conversion of, 92
Utah State Agricultural College, 104
Utah State Highway Department, 360
Utah State Penitentiary, 360-61

Vermont, 37
Virtue, 3, 215, 219
Vision at time of Los Angeles dedication, 189
Visions, 314
Voices of warning, 139

Walk uprightly, 199
Wall Street Journal, 349
War in heaven, 8, 328-29
Washington, George, 356, 357
Washington Post, 356
Weaver, prayer of, 6
Welfare plan, Church, 83, 104, 138, 262-65, 277-85, 296
Well of living water, 351
"Who's on the Lord's Side?" 20
Wickedness, 4, 18, 217-22, 352
Widtsoe, John A., 104, 132-33, 135, 260, 353
Wilkinson, Ernest L., 274
Will of God, 103
Wisdom, 199
Witness of the Spirit, 16, 17, 203
Woodruff, Wilford, 153, 160, 167, 212, 283
Word of God, 19
Word of Wisdom, 24, 215
World, wickedness in, 18, 21
World's Fair, New York, 149-50
Worldly philosophies, 18-19, 73, 217; possessions, 208; conditions, 352

Young, Brigham, 110, 143, 153, 163, 167, 203-204, 244-45, 285, 298, 300, 301, 362
Young Women's Mutual Improvement Association, 374
Youth, testimony of, 33-34

Zacchaeus, 356
Zarahemla, 341
Zion, 22-23, 279
Zoramites, 209